Socialism:
The Real History from Plato to the Present

D1300241

How the Deep State Capitalizes on Crises to Consolidate Control

William J. Federer

SOCIALISM: The Real History from Plato to the Present
—How the Deep State Capitalizes on Crises
to Consolidate Control
by
William J. Federer

Library of Congress
WORLD HISTORY / UNITED STATES HISTORY
ISBN-13: 978-0-9896491-8-6

Sincere appreciation for valuable editorial insight is given to my wife, Susie Federer.

Cover design by Dustin Myers longitudebranding.com

For a limited time, as owner of this book, you may receive it as an **ebook.** Email wjfederer@gmail.com with subject line "Socialism." A pdf file will be sent by reply email.

Amerisearch, Inc.
1-888-USA-WORD, 314-502-8924
wjfederer@gmail.com
www.AmericanMinute.com

*Many people living in the West
are dissatisfied with their own society.
They despise it or accuse it
of no longer being up to
the level of maturity by mankind ...*

*This causes many to sway toward socialism,
which is a false and dangerous current.*

– Alexander Solzhenitsyn,
who spent 11 years in Soviet gulags.

ৰ৹

*A government big enough
to give us everything we want
is a government big enough
to take from us everything we have.*
– Gerald Ford

*The history of liberty is a history
of the limitation of governmental power,
not the increase of it.*
– Woodrow Wilson

*The condition
upon which God hath given liberty
to man is eternal vigilance.*
– John Philpot Curran

CONTENTS

✍

CHAPTER 1
THE DREAM

Socialism will solve the world's problems.

There will be free healthcare, free education, free food, free housing, free public transportation, free childcare, guaranteed jobs, paid vacations, and free welfare for all the poor.

It all sounds so wonderful.

It would be a perfect society.

"From each according to his ability, to each according to his needs," wrote Karl Marx in his *Critique of the Gotha Program*, 1875.

Who would not be in favor of this?

There is one big question. Will it deliver on its promises? Will this idyllic dream be different from its "woke" reality?

This book will consider the origins of socialism and how the concept developed over the centuries.

Did you know the Greek philosopher Plato was one of the first to suggest it?

Are you aware the word "utopia" came from Sir Thomas More's 16th century book *The New Island of Utopia*?

Learn how the modern idea of socialism evolved:

   • from 17th century Pilgrim colony following ancient Israel's covenant with God;

   • to early 18th century Age of Enlightenment's social contract with a distant God;

   • to late 18th century French Revolution's social contract with no God;

   • to 19th century Marxism and 20th century socialism, where the state becomes god?

What did Lenin say was the goal of socialism?

What was the experience of socialism in countries such as Germany, Russia, China, Cuba, Romania, Hungary, Czechoslovakia, Yugoslavia, and Cambodia?

Is the problem between capitalism or socialism, or is the real problem the selfishness in the human heart, which is tempted to abuse any system?

How are crises, whether planned or coincidental, used to implement socialism?

Is it possible to be a Christian and a socialist? What does the Bible say about private property and charity?

Just because something needs to be done, is it always the government's job to do it?

To answer these questions, one must first uncover the origin of the dream of socialism.

❧

CHAPTER 2
PLATO'S ATLANTIS

The Greek philosopher Plato, living in the 4th century BC, wrote in his works *Timaeus* and *Critias* (c.360 BC) about a civilization on a legendary island called Atlantis. It supposedly was a highly structured society, renowned for being advanced and powerful.

Plato described it:

> For many generations, as long as the divine nature lasted in them, they were obedient to the laws ...

> They despised everything but virtue ... thinking lightly of the possession of gold and other property, which seemed only a burden to them ...

> When the divine portion began to fade away, and became diluted too often and too much with the mortal admixture, and the human nature got the upper hand, they then ... behaved unseemly, and ... visibly debased ... they were full of avarice and unrighteous power.

According to Plato, Atlantis fell out of favor with the Greek gods and was submerged into the sea.

Atlantis is thought to be the model of the perfectly structured society that Plato described in his book *Republic,* 380 BC.

∽

CHAPTER 3
A STRUCTURED SOCIETY

First there would be a democracy — "demos" means "people," and "cracy" means "to rule." Plato wrote:

> The manner of life in such a state is that of democrats; there is freedom and plainness of speech, and every man does what is right in his own eyes and has his own way of life ...

> ... Is not the city full of freedom ... a man may say and do what he likes? ...

> ... The great charm is, that you may do as you like; you may govern if you like, let it alone if you like; go to war and make peace if you feel disposed, and all quite irrespective of anybody else.

> When you condemn men to death, they remain alive all the same; a gentleman is desired to go into exile, and he stalks about the streets like a hero; and nobody sees him or cares for him.

Nobel Prize winning author Alexander Solzhenitsyn made a similar remark of the left-leaning legal system:

> And what shall we say about the dark realms of overt criminality? Legal limits ... encourage ... misuse of such freedom. The culprit can go unpunished or obtain undeserved leniency ...

> When a government earnestly undertakes to root out terrorism, public opinion immediately accuses it of violating the terrorist's civil rights.

∽

CHAPTER 4
DEMOCRACY LOVES TOLERANCE

Plato explained in a democracy everything is tolerated:

> The state is ... like a bazaar at which you can

buy anything ... (it) is like a piece of embroidery of which the colors and figures are the manners of men ...

... There will be the greatest variety of human natures ... being an embroidered robe which is spangled with every sort of flower ...

... Such is democracy; —a pleasing, lawless, various sort of government, distributing equality to equals and unequals alike ...

... Democracy ... is a charming form of government, full of variety and disorder, and dispensing a sort of equality to equals and unequals alike ...

... Freedom ... as they tell you in a democracy, is the glory of the state.

Plato warned that freedom, unrestrained by private moral virtue, would eventually lead to licentiousness and sexual promiscuity:

And so the young man passes ... into the freedom and libertinism of useless and unnecessary pleasures ...

... In all of us, even in good men, there is a lawless wild-beast nature ... Unnecessary pleasures and appetites I conceive to be unlawful ...

... Everyone appears to have them, but in some persons they are controlled ... while in ... others they are stronger ... and there is no conceivable folly or crime —not excepting incest or any other unnatural union ... which ... when he has parted company with all shame and sense, a man may not be ready to commit.

Plato described the attitude of youth:

He was supposed from his youth upwards to have been trained under a miserly parent, who encouraged the saving appetites in him ... and then he got into the company of a ... licentious sort of people, and taking to all their wanton ways rushed into the opposite extreme from an abhorrence of his father's meanness ...

... Neither does he receive ... advice; if anyone says to him that some pleasures are ... of evil desires ... he shakes his head ...

... He lives from day to day indulging the appetite of the hour ...

... His life has neither law nor order ... he is all liberty and equality.

In *The Lessons of History* (NY: Simon & Schuster, 1968, p. 74) historians Will and Ariel Durant included an excerpt from Plato's *Republic:*

The father gets accustomed to descend to the level of his son and to fear them, and the son to be on a level with his father, having no shame or fear of his parents ... The teacher fears and flatters his students, and the students despise their masters and tutors ... The old do not like to be thought morose and authoritative, and therefore they imitate the young ...

... Observe, too, how grandly democracy sets her foot upon all our fine theories of education, —how little she cares for the training of her statesmen!

Aristotle, who was a student of Plato, observed:

Tolerance is the last virtue of a dying society.

Samuel Johnson, the renown British compiler of *A Dictionary of the English Language,* 1755, wrote:

Temptation succeeds temptation ... We, in time, lose the happiness of innocence ... with sensual gratifications ... We entangle ourselves in business, immerse ourselves in luxury ...

We then look back upon our lives with horror, with sorrow, and with repentance; and wish, but too often vainly wish, that we had not forsaken the paths of virtue.

❧

CHAPTER 5
DEMOCRACY TO DISSOLUTION

Plato warned further:

Can liberty have any limit? Certainly not ...
By degrees the anarchy finds a way into private
houses ... The son is on a level with his father, he
having no respect or reverence for either of his
parents; and this is his freedom ... They will have
no one over them.

Citizens then yield to selfish human inclinations,
avarice, and vote to spread the city's wealth around,
draining the treasury. Harry Truman stated April 3, 1951:

Selfishness and greed can tear this Nation apart
... When organized crime and vice run loose and are
accepted and patronized by the people, they threaten
our free institutions and debase our national life.

When they run out of money, Plato explains, they
vote to take money from the rich:

Their leaders deprive the rich of their estates
and distribute them among the people; at the
same time taking care to reserve the larger part
for themselves ...

And the persons whose property is taken from
them are compelled to defend themselves before
the people as they best can ...

... Democracy ... of which the insatiable desire
brings her to dissolution.

∾

CHAPTER 6

PROMISCUITY AND DECADENCE

In 1934, Oxford anthropologist J.D. Unwin
published his book *Sex and Culture,* which confirmed
the trend described by Plato.

After studying 86 different tribes and civilizations
over 5,000 years, including Sumerians, Babylonians,
Greeks, Romans, Teutons, and Anglo–Saxons, Unwin
found that sexual promiscuity always preceded the
decline of a civilization.

In contrast, his research also showed a 100 percent
correlation between monogamous heterosexual

marriage and cultural advancement.

Unwin concluded that cultures go through four stages: Pain, Productive, Prosperous, Promiscuous.

At first, people go through a painful time of struggle, famine, or war. They then exhibit self-discipline and become productive, protective, innovative, pioneering and expansionistic.

Eventually, they become prosperous and enjoy their abundance. They soon become lax, cast off discipline, lose courage and self-restraint. They indulge in self-gratification, decadence, the pursuit of pleasure and sexual promiscuity.

The culture weakens and degenerates into lawlessness and insecurity. Solzhenitsyn stated at Harvard, June 8, 1978:

> When the modern Western states were being formed, it was proclaimed ... that man lives in order to be free and pursue happiness. Now at last ... progress has permitted the realization of such aspirations ... Every citizen has been granted the desired freedom and material goods ...
>
> Constant desire to have still more things ... does not in the least open a way to free spiritual development ... Young people *seek* ... happiness ... possession of material goods, money, and leisure, toward an almost unlimited freedom in the choice of pleasures ...
>
> Even biology tells us that a high degree of habitual well-being is not advantageous to a living organism ...
>
> Voluntary self-restraint is almost unheard of ... Destructive and irresponsible freedom ... has turned out to have scarce defense against the abyss of human decadence, for example against the misuse of liberty for ... motion pictures full of pornography, crime, and horror.

CHAPTER 7
LOSS OF MORALS AND COURAGE

Domestic insecurity and upheaval signal weakness to surrounding nations. Unrestrained immigration is followed by outright invasion.

Solzhenitsyn explained that when a society is consumed with selfishness, citizens lack the self-sacrificing willingness to defend it:

> A decline in courage may be the most striking feature that an outside observer notices in the West today. Political functionaries exhibit ... self-serving rationales ... and the decline in courage, at times attaining what could be termed a lack of manhood ...

> They get ... paralyzed when they deal with ... threatening forces, with aggressors and international terrorists. Must one point out that from ancient times a decline in courage has been considered the first symptom of the end?

In ancient times, this happened to Israel. They came out of the painful time of Egyptian bondage and 40 years wandering the desert. Then they became productive, and eventually, very prosperous, culminating with the pinnacle of wealth with Solomon's gold.

Then Solomon became sexually promiscuous with a thousand wives and immediately after his death, Israel was weakened by internal division. This signaled weakness to surrounding nations. Soon there were attacks by Egyptians, Philistines, Arabians, Ethiopians, Assyrians, Syrians, and eventually, the remaining inhabitants of Judah were carried away into Babylon.

Unwin noticed that once a nation begins to go down the path of self-indulgence and promiscuity, it never recovers. Selfish human nature loosed from moral restraints gains cumulative momentum, like a snowball rolling down a hill. Only in rare cases has this fate been delayed.

Aldous Huxley, of *Brave New World,* 1932, wrote:

Unwin's conclusions ... are based upon an enormous wealth of carefully sifted evidence ... The cultural condition of a society rises in exact proportion as it imposes pre-nuptial and post-nuptial restraints upon sexual opportunity.

Author Alex McFarland summarized it this way:

Fire inside the fireplace is productive, providing heat for cooking and warmth for the home; but fire outside the fireplace is destructive, burning the house down.

John Hancock stated on the fourth anniversary of the Boston Massacre, 1774:

Suffer not yourselves to be betrayed, by the soft arts of luxury and effeminacy, into the pit digged for your destruction.

John Adams wrote in *A Dissertation on the Canon and Feudal Law,* 1765:

Let us not suppose that all are become luxurious, effeminate, and unreasonable, on the other side of the water, as many designing persons would insinuate.

John Adams asked Jefferson in 1818:

Have you ever found in history one single example of a nation thoroughly corrupted that was afterwards restored to virtue? ... And without virtue, there can be no political liberty ... Will you tell me how to prevent luxury from producing effeminacy, intoxication, extravagance, vice and folly? ... No effort in favor of virtue is lost.

General Douglas MacArthur warned in a speech to the Salvation Army, December 12, 1951:

History fails to record a single precedent in which nations subject to moral decay have not passed into political and economic decline.

There has been either a spiritual awakening to overcome the moral lapse, or a progressive deterioration leading to ultimate national disaster.

✄

CHAPTER 8
WHO CAN FIX THIS MESS?

Plato described how once citizens give up virtue, yield to passion, and become financially irresponsible, the resulting chaos, anarchy, and insecurity causes them to look for someone to come along and fix the mess:

> Insatiable desire ... and ... neglect ... introduces the change in democracy, which occasions a demand for tyranny.

In describing democracy, Will and Ariel Durant again quote Plato (*The Lessons of History,* NY: Simon & Schuster, 1968, p. 74):

> The democrats contemptuously rejected temperance ... Citizens chafe impatiently at the least touch of authority, and at length ... they cease to care even for the laws, written or unwritten ...
>
> And this is the fair and glorious beginning out of which springs dictatorship (*tyrannis*) ...
>
> The excessive increase of anything causes a reaction in the opposite direction ... And so dictatorship naturally arises out of democracy, and the most aggravated form of tyranny and slavery out of the most extreme form of liberty.

Rep. Fisher Ames, who proposed the wording of the First Amendment, explained:

> Democracy could not last ... When the tyranny of the majority leads to chaos, society will submit to rule by the sword.

British Statesman Edmund Burke told the National Assembly, 1791:

> What is liberty without virtue? It is the greatest of all possible evils ... madness without restraint. Men are qualified for civil liberty in exact proportion to their disposition to put moral chains upon their own appetites ... Society cannot exist, unless a controlling power upon will and appetite be placed somewhere;

and the less of it there is within, the more there must be without.

French political philosopher Montesquieu wrote:

> In a popular state, one spring more is necessary, namely, virtue ... The politic Greeks, who lived under a popular government, knew no other support than virtue.

Montesquieu explained that once citizens abandon virtue, a republic will become lawless, causing individuals to seek someone who can restore order. The power of governing will then gravitate from the many to the few.

Popular government will be usurped by a despotic mayor or governor who will control his subjects through their desire for reward or their fear of punishment, through honor or shame, through pain or pleasure.

Jeremy Bentham wrote in *The Principles of Morals and Legislation* (1789):

> Nature has placed mankind under the governance of two sovereign masters, pain and pleasure.

Montesquieu wrote:

> When virtue is banished, ambition invades the minds of those who are disposed to receive it, and avarice (greed) possesses the whole community ...

> When, in a popular government, there is a suspension of the laws, as this can proceed only from the corruption of the republic, the state is certainly undone.

James Monroe warned in his Inaugural Address, 1817:

> It is only when the people become ignorant and corrupt, when they degenerate into a populace (mob), that they are incapable of exercising the sovereignty.

> Usurpation is then an easy attainment, and a usurper soon found. The people themselves become the willing instruments of their own debasement and ruin.

President Harry S Truman stated April 3, 1951:

> Without a firm moral foundation, freedom degenerates quickly into selfishness and license. Unless men exercise their freedom in a just and honest way, within moral restraints, a free society can degenerate into anarchy.
>
> Then there will be freedom only for the rapacious and those who are stronger and more unscrupulous than the rank and file of the people.

Plato added:

> Such ... is the fair and glorious beginning out of which springs tyranny ... Liberty overmasters democracy ... The excess of liberty, whether in states or individuals, seems only to pass into excess of slavery...
>
> ... The parent will discover what a monster he has been fostering in his bosom; and, when he wants to drive him out, he will find that he is weak and his son strong ... What! Beat his father if he opposes him? Yes, he will, having first disarmed him ... a cruel guardian of an aged parent.

Plato predicted that democracy is destined to devolve into anarchy out of which a tyrant would arise.

∽

CHAPTER 9

PEOPLE CRY FOR A PROTECTOR

At first, a mayor or a governor would appear as a "protector" promising to restore order, but soon they consolidate power and rules as a tyrant. Plato wrote:

> Last of all comes ... the tyrant ... In the early days of his power, he is full of smiles, and he salutes every one whom he meets ... making promises in public and also in private, liberating debtors, and distributing land to the people and his followers, and wanting to be so kind and good to every one ...
>
> This ... is the root from which a tyrant springs; when he first appears above ground, he is a protector ...

Hinting at the abolition of debts and partition of lands ... he ... begins to make a party against the rich ... (to make them) ... impoverished by payment of taxes, and thus compelled to devote themselves to their daily wants and therefore less likely to conspire against him? ...

... When a man who is wealthy ... is ... accused of being an enemy of the people ... he flees.

Plato explained that "the protector" uses his newly acquired power to target his political opponents:

And the protector of the people ... having a mob entirely at his disposal, he is not restrained from shedding the blood of kinsmen; by the favorite method of false accusation he brings (his opponents) into court and murders them, making the life of man to disappear ...

... And if any of them are suspected by him of having notions of ... resistance to his authority, he will have a good pretext for destroying them ...

Plato continued:

How then does a protector begin to change into a tyrant? ... He begins to grow unpopular ...

... The protector ... is ... the overthrower of many, standing up in the chariot of state with the reins in his hand, no longer protector, but tyrant absolute ...

... Tyranny is the wretchedest form of government.

Aristotle stated "A man rules in his own interest, and becomes a tyrant." A tyrant takes money away from his political opponents and funnels it as benefits to his political supporters. Plato described:

(The tyrant) ... will ... attract mobs, and hire voices fair and loud and persuasive, and draw the cities over to tyrannies ...

... Moreover, they are paid for this and receive honor — the greatest honor, as might be expected, from tyrants ...

... Poets ... are the eulogists of tyranny ... praising tyranny as godlike.

☙

CHAPTER 10
RISE OF THE TYRANT

President William Henry Harrison warned:

> The tendencies of all such governments in their decline is to monarchy ... The spirit of faction ... in times of great excitement imposes itself upon the people as the genuine spirit of freedom, and, like the false christs whose coming was foretold by the Savior, seeks to, and were it possible would, impose upon the true and most faithful disciples of liberty.

It is like a one–way ratcheting wrench, where with each click the ratchet tightens – there is no going back.

A rare leader may stall this trend, but like gravity, the next ratchets it again. Pompey wanted to preserve the Roman Republic, but he was followed by Julius Caesar, who slyly claimed to support the poor against the rich, only to usurp power and make himself Emperor.

Bertrand Russell, who won the Nobel Prize in Literature, stated December 11, 1950:

> Power, like vanity, is insatiable. Nothing short of omnipotence could satisfy it completely ... It is, indeed, by far the strongest motive in the lives of important men ...

> Love of power is greatly increased by the experience of power, and this applies to petty power as well as to that of potentates.

William Harrison stated, March 4, 1841:

> The love of power is a dominant passion of the human bosom ... When this corrupting passion once takes possession of the human mind, like the love of gold it becomes insatiable. It is the never-dying worm in his bosom, grows with his growth and strengthens with the declining years of its victim.

Bertrand Russell added:

> In any autocratic regime, the holders of power become increasingly tyrannical with experience of the delights that power can afford.
>
> Since power over human beings is shown in making them do what they would rather not do, the man who is actuated by love of power is more apt to inflict pain than to permit pleasure.

Senator Daniel Webster stated May 27, 1834:

> The contest, for ages, has been to rescue liberty from the grasp of executive power.

Truman recorded in a memorandum, April 16, 1950:

> There is a lure in power. It can get into a man's blood just as gambling and lust for money have been known to do.
>
> This is a Republic. The greatest in the history of the world. I want this country to continue as a Republic ...
>
> When we forget the examples of such men as Washington, Jefferson, and Andrew Jackson, all of whom could have had a continuation in the office, then will we start down the road to dictatorship and ruin.

Henry Adams, the great-grandson of John Adams, wrote: "Power is poison."

Ben Franklin warned, June 2, 1787:

> There is scarce a king in a hundred who would not, if he could, follow the example of Pharaoh — get first all the people's money, then all their lands, and then make them and their children servants forever ... There is a natural inclination in mankind to kingly government.

William Harrison stated:

> The tendency of power to increase itself, particularly when exercised by a single individual ... would terminate in virtual monarchy.

Governor Patrick Henry warned at Virginia's

Convention to ratify the U.S. Constitution, June 5, 1788:

Examples are to be found in ancient Greece and ancient Rome ... of the people losing their liberty by their carelessness and the ambition of a few ...

We are told that we need not fear; because those in power, being our Representatives, will not abuse the power we put in their hands ...

My great objection to this (Federal) Government is, that it does not leave us the means of ... waging war against tyrants ... Did you ever read of any ... punishment of those in power, inflicted by those who had no power? ...

Can the annals of mankind exhibit one single example, where rulers overcharged with power willingly let go ...

A willing relinquishment of power is one of those things which human nature never was, nor ever will be capable of.

President Harry S Truman wrote in his *Memoirs— Volume Two: Years of Trial and Hope*:

The men who wrote the Constitution ... were all well informed on the history of government from Babylon to Britain ...

They knew that arbitrary and even tyrannical government had come about where the powers of government were united in the hands of one man.

The system they set up was designed to prevent a demagogue or "a man on horseback" from taking over the powers of government ...

The most important thought expressed in our Constitution is that the power of government shall always remain limited, through the separation of powers.

Washington warned in his Farewell Address, 1796:

Disorders and miseries ... gradually incline the minds of men to seek security and repose in the absolute power of an Individual ... [who] turns this disposition to the purposes of his own elevation, on the ruins of public liberty.

John Milton wrote in *Paradise Lost,* 1674:

> And with necessity, The tyrant's plea, excus'd his devilish deeds.

Prime Minister William Pitt stated November 18, 1783:

> Necessity is the plea for every infringement of human freedom. It is the argument of tyrants, it is the creed of slaves.

Patrick Henry continued:

> When the American spirit was in its youth ... liberty, Sir, was then the primary object ... We drew the spirit of liberty from our British ancestors; by that spirit we have triumphed over every difficulty:

> But now ... assisted by the ropes and chains of consolidation ... there will be no checks, no real balances ... Suppose it should prove oppressive, how can it be altered?

On June 21, 1776, John Adams, who called the study of political theory a "divine science," wrote:

> The only foundation of a free Constitution is pure virtue, and if this cannot be inspired into our people in a greater measure, than they have it now, they may change their rulers and the forms of government, but they will not obtain a lasting liberty.

❧

CHAPTER 11
POLITICS

"Politics" is derived from the Greek word "polis," which means "city." Politics is the business of the city.

Where kings have "subjects" who are subjected to their will, democracies and republics have "citizens."

"Citizen" is a Greek word which means "co-ruler."

Democracies and republics are "popular governments" where the "population" of citizens co-rule themselves.

Democracies and republics are different in that a "democracy" is a "popular government" where "citizens" rule themselves "directly" by being personally present at every city meeting.

A "republic" is a "popular government" where citizens rule "indirectly" through "representatives." This way citizens can take care of their farms and businesses and send representatives to attend the government meetings in their place. A republic can function over a larger geographic area than a democracy.

As a form of government, a democracy only successfully worked on a small, city-wide basis, where every citizen was physically present at every meeting.

During the era of the Cold War, the word "democracy" came to have a second, more generalized meaning of simply "popular government."

In Montesquieu's definition of a "popular government," each citizen acts as a co-king, being conscious of the fact that each will be held individually accountable to God, who wants them to be fair. The result is citizens exhibit moral and virtuous behavior.

A "monarchy," as described by Montesquieu is where a king rules, but he has strings attached, being limited by a class of powerful noblemen, laws, traditions, and Judeo–Christian beliefs which remind him that he will be held accountable to the King of Kings in the next life.

A "despot," as defined by Montesquieu, is a king with no strings attached. Exemplified by a Sultan, Shah, or godless dictator, he rules through fear, according to his whims and caprices, exercising absolute and arbitrary power:

> • absolute, meaning the moment he says something it is law; and

> • arbitrary, meaning no one can predict what he will say next.

Collins English Dictionary defines "despotism":

> ... the rule of a despot; arbitrary, absolute, or tyrannical government.

SparkNotes on John Locke's *Second Treatise* states:

> Despotical power is absolute, arbitrary power of one person to take the life and property of another against their will.

John Locke wrote in his *Second Treatise on Civil Government* (Ch. 14–15) that a republic should have:

> No absolute or arbitrary power.

Kentucky and Wyoming have in their State Constitutions the phrase:

> Absolute, arbitrary power over the lives, liberty and property of freemen exists nowhere in a republic.

Montesquieu understood that since man's nature was inherently selfish, if an opportunity presented itself, any person could potentially be tempted with power. Initially wanting to do good, they could eventually become despots.

∽

CHAPTER 12
PHILOSOPHER–KING'S SOCIAL ORDER

Since democracy without virtue ends in chaos, and out of chaos arises a tyrant, Plato counseled that the best people could hope for is a nice tyrant, a benevolent slave-master — a "philosopher–king."

He would set up a perfectly structured society consisting of two classes: the governing and the governed.

The philosopher–king is in charge of the governing class. He is the head of gold. His political administrators and military enforcers are the arms and chest of silver.

The governing class rules over the lives of the governed class — the worker class, who are the abdomen of iron and brass.

Plato explained that the philosopher–king would

look to get into wars, as people always want a strong leader in time of war.

A point worth noting is, that even if a philosopher–king was genuinely a good leader, he must eventually leave his power and fortune to another, who may be tempted to use it to stay in power, becoming oppressive.

Oklahoma State University Professor Farida Jalalzai and Purdue University Northwest Professor Meg Rincker wrote in the article "Dynasties Still Run the World" (*The Conversation,* May 7, 2020):

> Power is by nature inherited in monarchies.

In ancient Egypt, Joseph helped concentrate power in the hands of Pharaoh, who used it for good, taking care of the children of Israel, giving them food, the best land of Goshen, and even jobs taking care of his cattle.

But then there was a new Pharaoh who did not know Joseph. He used his inherited power to oppress the Children of Israel, even to the extent of ordering them to throw their male infants in the Nile River.

Economist Milton Friedman stated:

> Concentrated power is not rendered harmless
> by the good intentions of those who create it.

⤚⟋

CHAPTER 13
CHILDREN BELONG TO THE STATE

In Plato's structured socialist state, the family would be abolished, there would be segregation of the sexes, with wives and children held in common by the governing class.

There would be birth-control, with only the governing class having the privilege of selective breeding in state–arranged cohabitation.

From birth, children would be property of the state, not even knowing who their parents were.

Plato wrote:

> When the true philosopher kings are born in a state ... they will set in order their own city ...
>
> They will ... take possession of the children, who will be unaffected by the habits of their parents; these they will train in their own habits and laws.

Children would be raised in government nurseries and schools where they would be indoctrinated with "noble lies," a type of "common core" curriculum designed to perpetuate the socialist society.

Plato wrote: "We want one single, grand lie which will be believed by everybody."

Lord Acton wrote:

> Official truth is not actual truth.

Sydney Schanberg, Pulitzer Prize winning *New York Times* reporter, wrote:

> We Americans are the ultimate innocents. We are forever desperate to believe that this time the government is telling us the truth.

The "noble lie" was described in a review of James Glazov's book, *United in Hate: The Left's Romance with Tyranny and Terror* (Midstream, winter, 2011):

> Plato expressed an idea that is related to thought control: he called for the "Noble Lie," a contradiction in terms if ever there was one.
>
> In particular, he said that the people should be taught that rulers were made with gold, auxiliaries with silver, and craftsmen with iron and brass.

Deceiving people in order to gain power was written about by Machiavelli in *The Prince,* 1513:

> The promise given was a necessity of the past: the word broken is a necessity of the present ...
>
> A prince never lacks legitimate reasons to break his promise ...
>
> A wise ruler ought never to keep faith when by doing so it would be against his interests.

This is similar to Islamic "taqiiya" deception: if strong, attack; and if weak, make "hudna" treaties until strong enough to attack. British philosopher Thomas Hobbes wrote in *Leviathan* (1651, pt. 1, Ch. 13):

> Force, and fraud, are in war the two cardinal virtues.

George Orwell wrote in *Prevention of Literature*, 1946:

> A society becomes totalitarian when its structure becomes flagrantly artificial: that is, when its ruling class has lost its function but succeeds in clinging to power by force or fraud.

On fraud and lies in political speeches, he stated:

> Political language ... is designed to make lies sound truthful and murder respectable, and to give an appearance of solidity to pure wind.

He wrote in a preface to *Animal Farm* (1945), (*The Times Literary Supplement,* Sept. 15, 1972):

> All tyrannies rule through fraud and force, but once the fraud is exposed they must rely exclusively on force.

He added:

> In a time of universal deceit, telling the truth is a revolutionary act.

∾

CHAPTER 14
A DESPOT USES FEAR

In Plato's socialist system, all means of production are owned by the state, and since no one can own private property, workers are rewarded for loyal service to the philosopher–king with honor in front of their peers.

Montesquieu wrote in *The Spirit of the Laws,* 1748:

> As virtue is necessary in a republic ... so fear is necessary in a despotic government: with regard to virtue, there is no occasion for it ...

> Fear must therefore depress their spirits, and extinguish even the least sense of ambition ... Of

a despotic government, that a single person ... rule according to his own will and caprice ...

He who commands the execution of the laws generally thinks himself above them, there is less need of virtue than in a popular government ...

Montesquieu added:

Such are the principles of government ... In a particular republic they actually are virtuous ... In a particular despotic government by fear.

Machiavelli's advice to political leaders was:

It is much more secure to be feared than to be loved ... Men shrink less from offending one who inspires love than one who inspires fear.

Henry Louis Mencken wrote in 1918:

The whole aim of practical politics is to keep the populace alarmed (and hence clamorous to be led to safety) by menacing it with an endless series of hobgoblins, all of them imaginary.

Calvin Coolidge stated at the unveiling of Equestrian Statue of Bishop Francis Asbury, October 15, 1924:

There are only two main theories of government in the world. One rests on righteousness, the other rests on force. One appeals to reason, the other appeals to the sword. One is exemplified in a republic, the other is represented by a despotism.

Coolidge continued:

The history of government on this earth has been almost entirely a history of the rule of force held in the hands of a few. Under our Constitution, America committed itself to ... the power in the hands of the people.

✥

CHAPTER 15
AUTHORITARIAN RULERS

Plato's Republic and the mythical Island of Atlantis were the first seeds of a structured socialist state, influencing all future socialist thinkers.

Attorney General William Barr said February 26, 2020:

> Totalitarian(ism) is almost always secular and materialistic, and its adherents tend to treat politics as a substitute for religion. Their sacred mission is to use the coercive power of the state to remake man and society according to an abstract ideal of perfection.
>
> The virtue of any individual is defined by whether they are aligned with the program. Whatever means used are justified because, by definition, they will quicken the pace of mankind's progress toward perfection ...
>
> All is subsumed within a single project to use the power of the state to perfect mankind rather than limit the state to protecting our freedom to find our own ends. It is increasingly, as Mussolini memorably said, "All within the state, nothing outside the state, nothing against the state."

The World Future Fund Research Project wrote in its article "Totalitarianism, Past Present & Future Policy Case Statement":

> The term totalitarianism was invented by Mussolini but the philosophy it represents is actually thousands of years old.
>
> The centralization of political power and control of citizens by an authoritarian state are political trends that date back to the dawn of history.
>
> In the ancient world, in both the east and the west, totalitarianism evolved into highly elaborate systems of philosophy,
>
> – from Plato's views in the *Republic;*
>
> – to the ideas of Lord Shang in ancient China (who centralized power in the Warring States period, 3rd century BC, to unify China for the first time ever under the Qin Dynasty);
>
> – to the very detailed plans for totalitarian rule described by Kautilya in ancient India (who

centralized rule of the subcontinent, 4th century BC, under Emperor Chandragupta's Mauryan Empire) ...

For almost 5,000 years authoritarian rule has been the norm of the human condition ... Authoritarian rule represents the overwhelming majority of world history.

President Calvin Coolidge warned May 15, 1926:

No plan of centralization has ever been adopted which did not result in bureaucracy, tyranny, inflexibility, reaction, and decline. Of all forms of government, those administered by bureaus are about the least satisfactory to an enlightened and progressive people. Being irresponsible they become autocratic ...

Unless bureaucracy is constantly resisted it breaks down representative government and overwhelms democracy. It ... sets up the pretense of having authority over everybody and being responsible to nobody ...

The national administration is not and cannot be adjusted to the needs of local government.

Jefferson wrote to Joseph C. Cabell, 1816:

What has destroyed the liberty and the rights of man in every government that has ever existed under the sun?

The generalizing and concentrating of all cares and powers into one body, no matter whether of the autocrats of Russia or France, or of the aristocrats of a Venetian Senate.

_❧

CHAPTER 16
SIR THOMAS MORE'S UTOPIA

In the study of socialism, a word always appears – "utopia." Where did that word come from?

After Columbus discovered the New World, there was a fascination among Europeans scholars of setting up ideal societies. One such scholar was Sir Thomas More.

He wrote a book in 1516 describing a fictional *Island of Utopia,* placed off the coast of South America. His book was intended to be a political satire, as the word "utopia" in Greek means "nowhere."

It was written in Plato's style of a dialogue, with a person questioning a traveler, Raphael Hythlodaeus, whose name in Greek means "peddler of nonsense."

Utopia is similar to Plato's perfect society, with an upper-class and commoners. It is a welfare state with free healthcare and free identical clothing.

It has a perfectly organized communistic lifestyle, with shared identical public housing, no locks on any doors, and common meals in community dining halls reminiscent of monastic life. There is no private property and all goods are stored in a communal warehouse.

There are no taverns, no alehouses, and no places for private gatherings. Privacy does not exist.

There are no families, giving rise to concepts like "it takes a village to raise a child." Marriage and childbearing are highly regulated by the government, similar to China's one-child–policy or Planned Parenthood's Margaret Sanger, who charged:

> No woman shall have the legal right to bear a child ... without a permit.

Interestingly, radical environmentalist David Brower, first director of the Sierra Club, held such views:

> Childbearing should be a punishable crime against society, unless the parents hold a government license. All potential parents should be required to use contraceptive chemicals, the government issuing antidotes to citizens chosen for childbearing.

In Utopia, adultery committed by commoners is punished by a lifetime of slavery, and premarital sex is punished by a lifetime celibacy.

Internal passports are required to track everyone's

movements and travel. If a commoner is caught without their passport, they are punished by a lifetime of slavery.

In a reference to Plato's Atlantis, where citizens thought "lightly of the possession of gold ... which seemed only a burden to them," More's Utopia required that those condemned to slavery be weighed down with gold chains.

Utopia has mandatory government assigned jobs, similar to the Soviet Constitution of 1936, Article 12:

> Labor in USSR is a duty and honorable obligation of each able citizen according to the principle: "Those who don't work—don't eat."

Michael Shermer, publisher of *Skeptic Magazine,* wrote in "Utopia Is a Dangerous Ideal" (Aeon, April 2020):

> "Utopia" ... The word means "no place" because when imperfect humans attempt perfectibility – personal, political, economic and social – they fail ...

> The belief that humans are perfectible leads, inevitably, to mistakes when "a perfect society" is designed for an imperfect species.

> There is no best way to live because there is so much variation in how people want to live. Therefore, there is no best society, only multiple variations on a handful of themes as dictated by our nature ...

> Natural differences in ability, interests and preferences within any group of people leads to inequalities of outcomes and imperfect living and working conditions that utopias committed to equality of outcome cannot tolerate.

∞

CHAPTER 17
CAMPANELLA'S CITY OF THE SUN

An Italian scholar fascinated with creating a perfect society was Tommaso Campanella. In 1602, he wrote *The City of the Sun,* describing an imaginary utopian socialist structured society.

It would be ruled by a governing class of men enlightened by reason.

There would be no poverty, no private property, no undue wealth, and no man would be allowed to have more than he needed. Also, only the upper class could breed, while inferior lower classes could not.

Campanella was arrested and spent years in prison.

CHAPTER 18
SIR FRANCIS BACON'S NEW ATLANTIS

In 1626, Sir Francis Bacon wrote *New Atlantis,* harkening back to the original Atlantis described by Plato.

Bacon's book was published at the time English settlers were setting up colonies in Virginia, Massachusetts, and Newfoundland.

Similar to Sir Thomas More's *Utopia,* Bacon's mythical *New Atlantis* was an island discovered by a lost ship in the Pacific Ocean west of Peru.

There, society is governed by a benevolent wise ruler whose structured socialist society was "the chastest nation under heaven," with men and women's behavior being highly regulated.

There is an emphasis on scientific experimentation, observation, inventions, and analysis. Bacon's famous line was "knowledge is power."

A parody of Bacon's *New Atlantis* was written by Jonathan Swift in 1726 titled *Gulliver's Travels.*

Gulliver was shipwrecked on the Island of Lilliput and observed the ridiculousness of their highly structured society of a governing class and a governed class.

It is of note that neither Plato's, nor More's, nor Campanella's, nor Bacon's imagined socialist societies have ever been realized, nevertheless, naive youth are not dissuaded from continually trying.

CHAPTER 19
PILGRIMS & THE "EMPTINESS OF THE THEORY OF PLATO"

Where Plato, More, Campanella, and Bacon were all theoretical, the Pilgrims actually attempted to put the theory into practice, and it failed.

The Pilgrims landed on the shores of Massachusetts in 1620. Their colony by-laws were drawn up by investors in England influenced by Plato, More and Bacon. They attempted to set up a planned "communistic" society.

England had three types of colonies:

1. Royal Crown Colonies run by king appointed governors;

2. Proprietary Colonies given as private property to friends of the king; and

3. Company Colonies run by charters or patents given by the king to investors who drew up company bylaws.

The Pilgrims' "Plymouth Plantation" was a "company" colony, having obtained a land patent from the Virginia Company of London.

The company bylaws were drawn up by investors, called "adventurers," who loaned the money for the Pilgrims' voyage. They expected a financial return on their investment.

The bylaws included elements of Plato's structured socialist–style communal system in which "all profits & benefits" went into "ye common stock" and everyone's livelihood came out of "ye common stock":

> The adventurers & planters do agree that every person that goeth being aged 16 years & upward ... be accounted a single share ...

> The persons transported & ye adventurers shall continue their joint stock & partnership together, ye space of 7 years ... during which time, all profits

& benefits that are got by trade, traffic, trucking, working, fishing, or any other means of any person or persons, remain still in ye common stock ...

That all such persons as are of this colony, are to have their meat, drink, apparel, and all provision out of ye common stock & goods ...

That at ye end of ye 7 years, ye capital & profits, namely, the houses, lands, goods and chattels, be equally divided betwixt ye adventurers, and planters.

After experiencing freezing winters, shortages of food, and deaths, Pilgrim Governor William Bradford complained of "the emptiness of the theory of Plato":

The failure of that experiment of communal service, which was tried for several years, and by good and honest men, proves the emptiness of the theory of Plato and other ancients, applauded by some of later times, — that the taking away of private property, and the possession of it in community, by a commonwealth, would make a state happy and flourishing; as it they were wiser than God ...

For in this instance, community of property was found to breed much confusion and discontent; and retard much employment which would have been to the general benefit ...

For the young men who were most able and fit for service objected to being forced to spend their time and strength in working for other men's wives and children, without any recompense ...

Bradford continued:

The strong man or the resourceful man had no more share of food, clothes, etc., than the weak man who was not able to do a quarter the other could. This was thought injustice.

The aged and graver men, who were ranked and equalized in labor, food, clothes, etc., with the humbler and younger ones, thought it some indignity and disrespect to them.

As for men's wives who were obliged to do service for other men, such as cooking, washing their clothes, etc., they considered it a kind of slavery, and many husbands would not brook (tolerate) it."

Bradford explained how redistribution failed:

If all were to share alike, and all were to do alike, then all were on an equality throughout, and one was as good as another; and so, if it did not actually abolish those very relations which God himself has set among men, it did at least greatly diminish the mutual respect that is so important should be preserved amongst them ...

Let none argue that this is due to human failing, rather than to this communistic plan of life in itself.

Pilgrim Governor William Bradford wrote further:

I answer, seeing that all men have this failing in them, that God in His wisdom saw that another plan of life was fitter for them ... So they began to consider how to raise more corn, and obtain a better crop than they had done, so that they might not continue to endure the misery of want ...

At length after much debate, the Governor, with the advice of the chief among them, allowed each man to plant corn for his own household ... So every family was assigned a parcel of land, according to the proportion of their number ...

This was very successful. It made all hands very industrious, so that much more corn was planted than otherwise would have been by any means the Governor or any other could devise, and saved him a great deal of trouble, and gave far better satisfaction.

The women now went willing into the field and took their little ones with them to plant corn, while before they would allege weakness and inability, and to have compelled them would have been thought great tyranny and oppression.

Though Virginia was the first colony and had a

legislative assembly – the House of Burgesses, it was a royal crown colony under direct control of the King. The Pilgrims are the ones credited with bringing to America the covenant form of government.

Their leaders, notably Pastor John Robinson and elder William Brewster, introduced Biblical concepts:

• that government should be by the consent of the governed;

• that government's purpose is to secure to individuals their God-given rights;

• that all men and women were equal, made in the image of God;

• that there should be no respect of persons in judgment;

• that each should "do to others as you would have them do to you." (Matthew 7:12)

༺

CHAPTER 20
COVENANT TO SOCIAL CONTRACT TO SOCIALISM

After the Pilgrims rejected the "communistic plan," they went on to pioneer a Biblical covenant model of government, drawn from Ancient Israel.

It is important to understand how the Biblical covenant transitioned step-by-step into socialism.

Preceding the Pilgrims, there were Reformation and Puritan scholars. They looked back to the Old Testament and Israel's "covenant" and back to the New Testament's "ekklesia"– the body of Christ, to form the concept of a "congregation" or "assembly" of believers.

The Pilgrims and other colonial New England founders implemented this covenant model, where people were in agreement with each other, having rights from God and being personally accountable to God to care for one another.

A century later, during the Age of Enlightenment,

covenant transitioned into "social contract," with people in agreement with each other, with or without God. If God existed, He was distant, removed, and impersonal — a concept birthed out the Scientific Revolution.

A century after that, the French Revolution transitioned social contract with "a distant God" into social contract with "absolutely no God."

In the final step, Marxism, socialism, and communism made the state god.

Each of these steps will be examined in detail.

∾

CHAPTER 21
PILGRIM COVENANT CONGREGATION

The Pilgrims not only rejected the "communistic plan" designed by their investors, they implemented something new — a government based on "covenant."

In 1534, England had officially established the Church of England. A revival movement began in the church of people wanting to "purify" it from the inside. They were nicknamed "Puritans."

Another group thought the Church of England was beyond hope of "purifying," so they separated themselves, meeting in secret. They called themselves "Separatists" or "Pilgrims."

Like the illegal Chinese house churches, Pilgrim separatists met in secret, often at the large home of William Brewster in Scrooby, England.

This was the beginning of them forming a "covenant" congregation. Governor Bradford wrote:

> Mr. Brewster ... lived in the country ... Tyranny ... against godly preachers ... in silencing ... and persecuting ... caused him ... to feel the burden of ... many anti-Christian corruptions ... They had joined themselves together in communion ...
>
> Brewster was a special help and support to them. On the Lord's day they generally met at his

house, which was a manor ... He entertained them with great kindness when they came, providing for them at heavy expense.

Pilgrim leaders were arrested, jailed and even executed by Britain's oppressive government which denied liberty of conscience and prohibited unauthorized church meetings. Bradford wrote:

Brewster was the leader of those who were captured at ... Lincolnshire, suffering the greatest loss, and was one of the seven who were kept longest in prison and afterwards bound over to the assizes (courts).

In 1607, the Pilgrims fled from King James I, crossed the English Channel and settled in Amsterdam, Holland, further strengthening their tight-knit covenant community, as Bradford wrote of Brewster:

After (Brewster) came to Holland he suffered much hardship, having spent most of his means.

In 1609, the Pilgrims moved to Leiden, Holland, where they would have become acquainted with Jews who had been expelled from Spain.

Spain had been occupied by Islamic conquerors for seven centuries, with episodes of forced conversions, massacres, and slavery. King Ferdinand successfully drove them out in 1492.

Under the pretense that some Muslims might be disguising themselves as Jews to plot assassinations or rebellions and thus regain areas of Spain, Ferdinand decided to force Jews to convert or leave.

Some Jews fled to the Netherlands, Europe's center of religious toleration, and settled in the country's largest city, Amsterdam, which went on to become the wealthiest city in the world in the 1600s.

Other Jews settled in the Dutch city of Leiden. From 1575, the University of Leiden was known as a center of the study of Hebrew, Aramaic and Syriac. There was even a Jewish rabbi as a professor.

After the Pilgrims came to Leiden, William Brewster began teaching. Bradford wrote:

> Towards the latter part of those twelve years spent in Holland, William Brewster's circumstances improved ... for through his knowledge of Latin he was able to teach many foreign students English ...

> Both Danes and Germans came to him, some of them being sons of distinguished men.

In Leiden, Pilgrims would have become familiar with Jewish feasts, including the Feast of Tabernacles at the end of the harvest season, which may have inspired their day of thanksgiving.

Pilgrims identified with Jews, whose ancestors covenanted together with God, fled from Pharaoh's persecution, crossed the waters of the Red Sea, and entered their Promised Land.

Pilgrims, too, had made a covenant with God, fled from the King of England, crossed the waters, and hoped to enter their Promised Land.

Jews may have influenced the Pilgrims in their adaptation of ancient Israel's covenant form of government — a people in covenant with each other, getting their rights from God and being personally accountable to God.

On December 15, 1617, elder William Brewster and Pastor John Robinson wrote a letter from Leiden, Holland, to London financier Sir Edwin Sandys, explaining how the Pilgrims were:

> Knit together as a body in ... covenant of the Lord ... we so hold ourselves ... tied to all care of each other's good.

Pilgrim Pastor John Robinson is considered one of the founders of the "Congregational" Church. The words "congregational" refers to a group of people in "communion" or "covenant" with each other.

After 12 years in Holland, Spain threatened to invade again, so the Pilgrims sailed to America. This account is described in detail in the book *The Treacherous World of the 16th Century & How the Pilgrims Escaped It* (Amerisearch, Inc., 2017).

Commemorating their departure is the painting "Embarkation of the Pilgrims," which hangs in the U.S. Capitol Rotunda. In the painting, William Brewster is holding an open Bible and Pastor John Robinson is kneeling with his hands extended in prayer.

The Pilgrims intended to sail to the Virginia Colony, where the Jamestown settlement had been founded 14 years earlier. High winds and storms on the Atlantic blew their *Mayflower* ship hundreds of miles north.

The captain of the *Mayflower* attempted to sail south from Massachusetts to Virginia, but the ship almost sank on a sand bar in the stormy winds and dangerous currents.

This was providential, for had they landed in Virginia, they may not have set up their system of self-government, plus they may have suffered in Virginia's many droughts, famines, starvation, diseases, and Indian attacks.

Jamestown's mortality rate was so high, that at times the dead were buried in mass graves. Between 1608 and 1624, of the 6,000 settlers that came to Jamestown, only 3,400 survived.

Returning to the coast of Massachusetts, the captain of the Mayflower insisted everyone disembark on the barren shores near Plymouth Rock.

As there was no government to submit to, and not wanting to be lawless, the Pilgrims created their own government, the Mayflower Compact. "Compact" was another word for "covenant."

The Mayflower Compact, signed November 11, 1620, was the first "constitution" written in America:

In ye name of God, Amen.

> We whose names are underwritten ... having
> undertaken, for ye glory of God, and advancement
> of ye Christian faith ... a voyage to plant ye first
> colony in ye Northern parts of Virginia ...
>
> ... in ye presence of God, and one of another,
> covenant & combine our selves together into a
> civil body politick ... to enact ... just & equal laws
> ... as shall be thought most meet & convenient
> for ye general good of ye Colony, unto which we
> promise all due submission and obedience.

Simple, yet revolutionary. It was a polarity change in the flow of power. Instead of a top–down government ruled by a king, it was a bottom–up, ruled by the people.

William Brewster, one of the signers, is portrayed giving thanks to God in the "Frieze of American History" which is in the U.S. Capitol rotunda.

In 1629, after the Pilgrims founded a second church in Massachusetts Bay, William Brewster wrote:

> The church that had been brought over the
> ocean now saw another church, the first-born
> in America, holding the same faith in the same
> simplicity of self-government under Christ alone.

The Pilgrims basically took their "congregational church government" based on covenant and adapted it into a "congregational community government."

❧

CHAPTER 22
REFORMATION COVENANT SCHOLARS

Sandwiched between the 15th century Renaissance and the 17th Age of Enlightenment was the 16th century Reformation, where scholars in Europe were not only fascinated with studying scriptures in the original languages, they were also fascinated with studying the Hebrew concept of "covenant."

In the 16th century, Protestant and Catholic covenant scholars were called "Christian Hebraists," as they studied in depth the ancient Hebrew Republic

— that initial 400 year period from when the Israelites departed Egypt, lived in the Promised Land, and eventually demanded their first king, Saul.

Notable Christian Hebraists were:

- Thomas Erastus (1524–1583);
- Bonaventure Vulcanius (1535–1614);
- Joseph Scaliger (1540–1609);
- Johannes van den Driesche (1550–1616);
- Isaac Casaubon (1559–1614);
- Johannes Buxtorf (1564–1629);
- Daniel Heinsius (1580–1655);
- Hugo Grotius (1583–1645);
- John Selden (1584–1654);
- Thomas Hobbes (1588–1679);
- James Harrington (1611–1677) author of *The Commonwealth of Oceana,* 1656;
- Petrus Cunaeus (1586–1638), author of *The Hebrew Republic*, 1617; and
- John Sadler (1615–1674), whose sister, Ann, married John Harvard, namesake of Harvard University.

Christian Hebraists studied:

- the ancient Hebrew Republic;
- Jewish historian Josephus (37–100);
- the Jerusalem Talmud (2nd century AD);
- the Babylonian Talmud (4th century AD);
- Jewish philosopher Maimonides (1135–1204);
- Rabbinic literature.

Interest in Hebrew influenced Reformers, such as:

- Huldrych Zwingli (1484–1531);
- Thomas Cromwell (1485–1540);
- John Calvin (1509–1564);
- John Knox (1514–1572);

• Scottish Covenanters, beginning in 1557; and

• the translators of the Geneva Bible, 1560; and later translations.

The Hebrew language was taught at Oxford and Cambridge in England, and in America at Harvard and Yale, whose coat of arms has Hebrew characters.

In 1685, Harvard's commencement address was delivered in Hebrew.

In 1722, Harvard hired Judah Monis, its first full-time Hebrew instructor, who published *A Grammar of the Hebrew Tongue* (1735) – the first Hebrew textbook published in North America.

Yale (1701), Columbia (1754), Dartmouth (1769), and other universities had requirements for students to study Hebrew.

Yale President Ezra Stiles addressed Connecticut's General Assembly, May 8, 1783:

> A discourse upon the political welfare of God's American Israel ... Our system of dominion and civil polity would be imperfect without the true religion ... From the diffusion of virtue among the people of any community would arise their greatest secular happiness.

When the U.S. Constitution was being ratified, New Hampshire almost rejected it, until Harvard President Rev. Samuel Langdon gave an address at the state's ratifying convention, titled "The Republic of the Israelites an example to the American States," June 5, 1788:

> The Israelites may be considered as a pattern to the world in all ages ...

> Government ... on republican principles, required laws without which it must have degenerated immediately into ... absolute monarchy ...

> How unexampled was this quick progress of the Israelites, from abject slavery, ignorance, and almost total want of order, to a national establishment perfected in all its parts far beyond

all other kingdoms and states!

From a mere mob, to a well-regulated nation, under a government and laws far superior to what any other nation could boast!

After Rev. Langdon's address, New Hampshire's delegates voted to ratify the U.S. Constitution, and being the 9th State to do so, put it into effect, June 21, 1788.

President Lyndon B. Johnson stated in 1968:

America and Israel have a common love of human freedom and a democratic way of life.

Enoch Cobb Wines wrote in *Commentaries on the Laws of the Ancient Hebrews, with an Introductory Essay on Civil Society & Government* (NY: Geo. P. Putnam & Co., 1853):

Another of those great ideas, which constituted the basis of the Hebrew state, was liberty ... The Hebrew people enjoyed as great a degree of personal liberty, as can ever be combined with an efficient and stable government.

Franklin Roosevelt wrote to Samuel Rosenman of the Jewish Education Committee, December 16, 1940:

Our modern democratic way of life has its deepest roots in our great common religious tradition, which for ages past has taught to civilized mankind the dignity of the human being, his equality before God, and his responsibility in the making of a better and fairer world ...

The world (is) ... engaged in a great spiritual struggle to test whether that ancient wisdom is to endure, or whether ... some few men shall dominate multitudes of others and dictate to them their thinking, their religion, their living ...

We need the sustaining, buttressing aid of those great ethical religious teachings which are the heritage of our modern civilization. For "not upon strength nor upon power, but upon the spirit of God" shall our democracy be founded.

Columnist Don Feder gave an address to the F₁ of Israel, titled "America & Israel–Two Nations J...at the Heart" (Grand Rapids, MI, May 15, 2014):

More than Athens ... more than Roman Law, and English Common Law — Israel shaped America.

∽

CHAPTER 23
THE ANCIENT HEBREW REPUBLIC

The exodus of the Children of Israel out of Egypt occurred sometime around 1,400 BC. After entering the Promised Land, for the next 400 years, their form of government was the "Hebrew Republic," where people were in "covenant" with each other and with God.

• ISRAEL was the first well-recorded instance of a nation without a king. People in each village, town and city met in a "synagogue," which means "house of meeting," where, in addition to learning the law, they chose elders to sit in public judgment at the city gate.

• In ISRAEL, at this time, there was no royal family to ingratiate oneself to. Everyone was equal under the Law, which taught "Ye shall not respect persons in judgment; but ye shall hear the small as well as the great." (Deuteronomy 1:17). This was the beginning of the concept of equality.

• In ISRAEL, the Law stated that every person was made in the image of the Creator, "God created man in his own image, in the image of God created he him; male and female created he them" (Genesis 1:27). Each person possessed God-given rights which no one could take away and government was to guarantee.

• ISRAEL treated non-Israelites as equals. "The stranger who resides with you shall be to you as one of your citizens; you shall love him as yourself, for you were strangers in the land of Egypt: I the LORD am your God" (Leviticus 19:34)

• ISRAEL was tolerant. Though convinced they

were worshiping the only true God, they never waged ideological war to force other nations to accept Him, nor did they force non-Israelites "strangers" living within their borders to convert.

Locke noted in *Letter Concerning Toleration,* (1689):

> Foreigners and such as were strangers to the commonwealth of Israel were not compelled by force to observe the rites of the Mosaical law ... We find not one man forced into the Jewish religion and the worship of the true God ...

> If anyone ... desired to be made a denizen [citizen] of their commonwealth ... to embrace their religion ... this he did willingly, on his own accord, not by constraint.

• ISRAEL had a system of honesty, thus providing a basis for commerce. "Just balances, just weights ... shall ye have" (Leviticus 19:36). "A false balance is abomination to the LORD: but a just weight is his delight" (Proverbs 11:1)

• In ISRAEL, land was permanently titled to each family. This contrasted with most of the world, where kings granted land to loyal vassals, or as in Egypt, where the pharaohs owned the land.

Israel called it the Promised "Land" because each family owned title to their land. This prevented a dictator from gathering up the land and putting the people back into slavery.

If a person owned land, they could accumulate possessions. The Bible called this being "blessed"; Karl Marx called it being a "capitalist."

Marx wrote in his *Manifesto:* "The theory of the communists may be summed up in the single sentence: Abolition of private property."

Noah Webster wrote in the preface of his *Dictionary* (republished 1841):

> Let the people have property and they will have

power — a power that will forever be exerted to prevent a restriction of the press, and abolition of trial by jury, or the abridgment of any other privilege.

• ISRAEL had a bureaucracy–free welfare system. When someone harvested their field, they left the corners and gleanings for the poor, like in the story of Ruth. This way, the poor were taken care of, while maintaining their dignity by doing something, without a political leader collecting everything and doling it back out as favors to those who would keep him in power.

• ISRAEL had relatively few laws, as citizens were accountable to God to treat each other fairly. "You shall not take vengeance or bear a grudge against your kinsfolk. Love your neighbor as yourself" (Leviticus 19:18).

• ISRAEL had no police. Everyone was taught the Law, and everyone was personally accountable to enforce it. It was as if everyone in the nation was "deputized."

• ISRAEL had no prisons. The Law required swift justice at the "gates of the city" and a "city of refuge" where fugitives could flee to await a trial.

• ISRAEL had no standing army as every man was in the militia with "his sword upon his thigh," "able to bear buckler and sword, and to shoot with bow," ready at a moment's notice to defend his family and community.

• ISRAEL was the first nation where everyone was taught to read. Egypt had 3,000 hieroglyphs and reading them was the scribes' secret knowledge. Only one percent of Egypt could read.

Other nations had languages with hundreds or even thousands of characters

When Moses came down Mount Sinai, he not only had the Ten Commandments, but he had them in a 22 character alphabet (first letter "aleph," second letter "beth"). With so few characters, even children could read.

Levites taught the Law and also taught the people how to read it for themselves. In fact, the people were required to read it, as the law was addressed to each person, who was personally accountable to God obey it.

Thomas Sowell wrote in "Degeneration of Democracy" (June 2010):

> A democracy needs informed citizens if it is to thrive, or ultimately even survive.

In the *Lessons of History* (Simon & Schuster, 1968, p. 77), Will and Ariel Durant wrote:

> Democracy is the most difficult of all forms of government, since it requires the widest spread of intelligence.

James Madison wrote to W.T. Barry, August 4, 1822:

> A people who mean to be their own governors, must arm themselves with the power which knowledge gives ... A popular government without popular information, or the means of acquiring it, is but a prologue to a farce or a tragedy, or perhaps both.

E.C. Wines wrote in *Commentaries on the Laws of the Ancient Hebrews* (NY: Geo. P. Putnam & Co., 1853):

> A fundamental principle of the Hebrew government was ... the education of the whole body of the people; especially, in the knowledge of the constitution, laws and history of their own country.

> An ignorant people cannot be a free people. Intelligence is essential to liberty. No nation is capable of self-government, which is not educated to understand and appreciate its responsibilities ...

> Maimonides, in his treatise on the study of the law, says: "Every Israelite, whether poor or rich, healthy or sick, old or young, is obliged to study the law" ... He asks, "How long ought a man to pursue the study of the law?" and replies, "Till death."

Gouverneur Morris, a Signer of the U.S. Constitution, wrote *Observation on Government Applicable to the Political State of France,* 1792:

> Religion is the only solid basis of good morals;

therefore education should teach the precepts of religion, and the duties of man toward God. These duties are, internally, love and adoration; externally, devotion and obedience; therefore provision should be made for maintaining divine worship as well as education.

• In ISRAEL, people chose their leaders. Honest elections allowed for government by the consent of the governed.

"Moses spoke to the children of Israel ... 'How can I alone bear your problems and your burdens and your complaints? Choose wise, understanding, and knowledgeable men from among your tribes, and I will make them heads over you.'" (Deuteronomy 1:3–13 NKJV);

"Judges and officers shalt thou make thee in all thy gates which the Lord thy God giveth thee throughout thy tribes" (Deuteronomy 16:18–19).

E.C. Wines continued:

Moses ... intended, that all his people should share in the management of the public affairs. He meant each to be a depositary of political power ... as a solemn trust ...

On the subject of education, he appears chiefly anxious to have his people instructed in the knowledge of ... their duties as men and citizens.

He ... (did not) desire to see the mass of the people shut out from all political power ... nor ... to see the power of the masses increased, irrespective of their ability to discharge so important a trust beneficially to the community.

In his educational scheme, power and knowledge went hand in hand. The possession of the latter was regarded as essential to the right use of the former ...

In proportion as this idea enters into the constitution of a state, tyranny will hide its head, practical equality will be established, party strife will abate its ferocity, error, rashness, and folly will disappear, and an enlightened, dignified, and venerable public opinion will bear sway ...

It is political ignorance alone, that can reconcile men to ... surrender of their rights; it is political knowledge alone, that can rear an effectual barrier against the encroachments of arbitrary power and lawless violence.

Rather than a pyramid style, top–down form of government where the king's will is law, the Hebrew Republic was a bottom–up form of government, like a living tree drawing nutrients up from the roots. Every citizens was to be educated, moral, and participate.

In Israel, anyone could be drawn up into leadership, as there was no hereditary monarchy: Jephthah was the son of a prostitute; Gideon was from an obscure family; and Deborah was a just woman who knew the Law.

E.C. Wines wrote in *Commentaries on the Laws of the Ancient Hebrews* (NY: Geo. P. Putnam & Co., 1853):

Moses' ... national unity ... was not that ... in which vast multitudes of human beings are delivered up to the arbitrary will of one man.

It was a unity, effected by the abolition of caste; a unity, founded on the principle of equal rights; a unity, in which the whole people formed the state ... contrary to the celebrated declaration of a French Monarch (Louis XIV), who avowed himself to be the state.

CHAPTER 24
PERSONAL ACCOUNTABILITY TO GOD

Why would the Israelites follow this Law?

Ancient Israel introduced to the world the key incentive, namely, there is a God who:

1) is watching everyone;

2) wants you to be fair;

3) and will hold each person individually

accountable in the future.

If, for example, a person had the opportunity to steal and not get caught, they might consider it until they remembered that God was watching them, that He wanted them to be fair, and that He would hold them accountable in the future.

This would cause that person to hesitate, which is called having a "conscience." If every individual believed this, there could be complete order with no police.

An illustration would be, instead of each person having a cell phone with a GPS app telling them where to turn, they would have "a Law app," learned by heart, and it would guide their actions. The Levites acted as computer techs, helping people to download the app.

Margaret Thatcher stated in 1996:

> Ten Commandments are ... the origin of ... the sanctity of the individual ... It is personal liberty with personal responsibility.

Democrat Presidential Candidate William Jennings Bryan stated in 1908:

> A religion which teaches personal responsibility to God gives strength to morality ... There is a powerful restraining influence in the belief that an All-seeing eye scrutinizes every thought and word and act of the individual.

President Reagan stated in 1984:

> Without God there is no virtue because there is no prompting of the conscience.

William Linn, the first U.S. House Chaplain, stated May 1, 1789:

> Let my neighbor ... persuade himself that there is no God, and he will ... pick my pocket, and break not only my leg but my neck ... If there be no God, there is ... no future account.

William Ellery Channing, whose grandfather signed the Declaration of Independence, was quoted in

McGuffey's 5th Eclectic Reader, 1879, "Religion–The Only Basis of Society":

> How powerless conscience would become without the belief of a God ...

> Erase all thought and fear of God from a community, and selfishness and sensuality would absorb the whole man. Appetite, knowing no restraint ... would trample in scorn on the restraints of human laws ... Man would become ... what the theory of atheism declares him to be – a companion for brutes.

CHAPTER 25
NEW TESTAMENT EKKLESIA

Old Testament "assembly" or "congregation" of Israelites was mirrored in the New Testament Greek word "ekklesia."

Jesus used this word to refer the body of Christ, Matthew 16:18, "... upon this rock I will build My church (ekklesia); and the gates of Hades will not overpower it." In Matthew 18:17, Jesus stated:

> If he refuses to listen to them, tell it to the church (ekklesia); and if he refuses to listen even to the church (ekklesia), let him be to you as a gentile and a tax collector."

"Ekklesia" means: a called-out assembly; a gathering of citizens summoned from their homes to a place of meeting; people congregating in a public place; individuals convened into a council for the purpose of deliberating; the assembly of the Israelites.

The Israelite word for "house of assembly" or "place of meeting" is "synagogue" (beit k'nesset).

A word with similar roots is the Greek word "synod," which means "meeting, assembly, advisory council, or governing body."

The synagogue served as the "town hall" of the Jewish community. It was independent, not answering to a central authority.

Each Jewish community chose their own elders, who were capable of carrying out the duties of the synagogue. They would hire a rabbi and a chazzan (cantor).

The synagogue was financed through membership dues paid annually, through voluntary donations. It was also a place to collect and dispense food, aid or money to the poor within the community.

In Israelite tradition, there needed to be a "minyan," a quorum of 10 present, for certain community prayers to be said.

Early Christians, persecuted by the Roman government, similarly met in small groups based on what Jesus said, "Where two or three are gathered together in my name, there am I in the midst of them" (Matthew 18:20).

When persecution was intense, they even met in underground catacombs.

Much later, particularly in Scotland, these small group meetings were called "coventicles," with those gathering being called "covenanters." Reformation scholars understood "ekkelsia" to have the meaning of a gathering or assembly of believers in covenant.

King James of England did not like the reformers' definition of "ekklesia." He insisted "ekklesia" be translated "church" and not "congregation" or "assembly," as he instructed Bible translators in 1604:

> The old ecclesiastical words are to be kept, as the word church, not to be translated congregation.

Why would King James want this?

The answer is, he wanted to be the head of the Church of England, claiming the divine right to rule both the church and the state.

It would be difficult for him to be the head of something where the entire congregation or assembly participated in ministry and in the unity of the Spirit functioned as a deliberative body.

∽

CHAPTER 26
NEW ENGLAND COVENANT

Many New England colonial leaders were Puritans who embraced "covenant" theology.

Puritans were members of the Church of England who wanted to "purify" it from within. The King did not think his Church needed purifying, so he persecuted them.

Ten years after the Pilgrims arrived in America, Puritans also fled persecutions and began arriving in New England in 1630. So many fled in the next 16 years, estimated at 20,000, that it was called the Puritan Great Migration.

One of the main leaders of the Puritans in Massachusetts was John Winthrop. He authored *A Model of Christian Charity,* June 11, 1630, explaining the nature of colonial constitutional "covenant":

> We are a Company, professing ourselves fellow members of Christ, we ought to account ourselves knit together by this bond of love ...

> It is by a mutual consent ... between God and us: we are entered into covenant with Him for this work ... We must be knit together in this work as one man ...

Winthrop continued:

> We must delight in each other, make one another's condition our own, rejoice together, mourn together, labor and suffer together, always having before our eyes our commission and community in this work, as members of the same body ...

> We shall find that the God of Israel is among us, when ten of us shall be able to resist a thousand of our enemies ...

> He shall make us a praise and glory, that men of succeeding plantations shall say, "The Lord make

it like that of New England." For we must consider that we shall be as a City upon a Hill, the eyes of all people are upon us.

"Covenant" theology was held by many New England colonial leaders.

John D. Eusden wrote in "Natural Law and Covenant Theology in New England, 1620–1670" (Notre Dame Law School, *Natural Law Forum,* 1960, Paper 47):

> The idea of the covenant – that central, permeating idea of Puritanism ... Covenanted men actually constructed political communities – the emerging "American character" in the realm of governmental theory and jurisprudence.

Eusden continued:

> Names dominate the dramatis personae:

• John Cotton, influential minister of the First Church in Boston ...

• John Winthrop, long-time governor of the Massachusetts Bay Colony ...

• Nathaniel Ward, chief framer of the 1641 Body of Liberties for the Bay Colony;

• William Bradford, governor of Plymouth Plantation;

• Thomas Hooker, preacher and potentate of Hartford;

• John Norton, official apologist for New England Congregationalism;

• John Eliot, evangelist and occasional political writer;

• and John Davenport, founder of New Haven ...

Eusden concluded:

> Political and social thought of early American Puritanism was drawn from four sources:

> the Bible, the covenant tradition in Reformation theology, the common law of England, and the long Western tradition of natural law.

In 1642, the Puritans who stayed back in England had a civil war, led by Lord Protector Oliver Cromwell, and won. Afterwards, they established a covenant form of government in 1649, called the "English Commonwealth."

It only lasted a few years, and officially ended when King Charles II was restored to the English throne in 1660. Os Guinness stated in an interview ("Thinking in Public," June 5, 2017):

> The covenantal ideas in England were the lost cause, sadly. They failed. The king came back.

> But the lost cause became the winning cause in New England. And covenant shaped constitutionalism ... The American Constitution is a nationalized, secularized form of covenant ... Covenant lies behind constitution.

Protestant Reformers and scholars of the 16th century called Christian Hebraists, considered the perfect example of a "covenant" form of government the ancient nation of Israel – people in agreement with each other, getting their rights from God and being personally accountable to God.

∽

CHAPTER 27

COVENANT INFLUENCED GOVERNMENT

The British government did not like "the people" meeting. In 1664, it passed the Coventicle Act forbidding five or more non-conformists, or dissenters from the Church of England, from gathering.

In 1714, it passed the Riot Act, which authorized local authorities to break up any meeting of 12 or more, and read out loud that everyone must immediately disperse or they could face the death penalty.

In 1772, as tensions were leading up to the Revolutionary War, the British military governor of Massachusetts, General Thomas Gage, commented that "democracy was too prevalent in America," and proceeded to prohibit town meetings.

New England town meetings had been an outgrowth of congregational church meetings.

Baptist congregational church meetings may have even influenced Jefferson. According to an account published in the Boston newspaper *Christian Watchman,* July 14, 1826, Jefferson dined at Monticello prior to the Revolutionary War with Baptist Pastor Andrew Tribble:

> Andrew Tribble was the Pastor of a small Baptist Church, which held its monthly meetings at a short distance from Mr. Jefferson's house, eight or ten years before the American Revolution.
>
> Mr. Jefferson attended the meetings of the church for several months in succession, and after one of them, asked Elder Tribble to go home and dine with him, with which he complied.
>
> Mr. Tribble asked Mr. Jefferson how he was pleased with their church government?
>
> Mr. Jefferson replied, that it had struck him with great force, and had interested him much; that he considered it the only form of pure democracy that then existed in the world, and had concluded that it would be the best plan of government for the American colonies.

Thomas F. Curtis wrote in *The Progress of Baptist Principles in the Last Hundred Years* (Charleston, S.C.: Southern Baptist Publication Society, 1856):

> A gentleman ... in North Carolina ... knowing that the venerable Mrs. (Dolley) Madison had some recollections on the subject, asked her in regard to them. She expressed a distinct remembrance of Mr. Jefferson speaking on the subject, and always declaring that it was a Baptist church from which these views were gathered.

Calvin Coolidge stated at the 150th anniversary of the Declaration of Independence, July 4, 1926:

> This preaching reached the neighborhood of Thomas Jefferson, who acknowledged that his "best ideas of democracy" had been secured at church meetings.

After the Revolutionary War, delegates met in Philadelphia to write the Constitution. Instead of repeating the European model of a top–down monarchy, America's founders created a bottom–up republic, ruled by the people.

Signer of the Constitution James McHenry noted in his diary (*American Historical Review,* 1906), that after Ben Franklin left the Constitutional Convention, he was asked by Mrs. Elizabeth Powel of Philadelphia:

> "Well, Doctor, what have we got, a republic or a monarchy?" Franklin replied, "A republic, if you can keep it."

⤸

CHAPTER 28
SOCIAL CONTRACT WITH A DISTANT GOD

The Scientific Revolution began during the life of Copernicus, and it reached its peak in the 17th century with scientists Francis Bacon, Galileo, Johannes Kepler, Robert Boyle, and Isaac Newton's *Principia,* 1687.

Scientists discovered laws that governed the universe, such as, laws of motion, laws of gravity, laws of planetary motion, laws of cooling, laws of the speed of sound, and laws of gas pressure and volume.

These discoveries led some to suggest that God created the world, set the laws of nature in motion, and then stepped back to let everything run its course.

According to this view, God existed, but He was removed from His creation, like someone winding up a clock and setting in on a table. This gave birth to the Age of Enlightenment and affected political thought.

"Covenant" turned into "social contract," with one very consequential difference:

• "Covenant" was where people were in agreement with each other getting rights *from God* and personally accountable *to God.*

- "Social contract," on the other hand, was people in agreement with each other, *with or without God.*

If God existed, He was distant and removed, possibly even just an impersonal force. In fact, prayer was considered unnecessary, as God was thought to not "intervene" in His creation.

Woodrow Wilson wrote in *The State*, 1889:

> The defects of the social compact theory are too plain to need more than brief mention ...

> Status was the basis of primitive society: the individual counted for nothing; society – the family, the tribe – counted for everything. Government came before the individual ... Man was merged in society ...

> Authority did not rest upon mutual agreement, but upon mutual subordination.

∽

CHAPTER 29
SOCIAL CONTRACT WITH NO GOD

In the 18th century, "social contract" with a distant God turned into "social contract" intentionally excluding God.

The concept embraced by the French Revolution was, that rights came from the state and individuals were accountable to the state. This culminated in the Reign of Terror, 1789–1794, where tens of thousands were killed.

French promoters of a godless state were called "Jacobins," being members of the radical, left-wing Jacobin Club, named for the Paris street they met on – Rue Saint-Jacques.

Their views were examined by Yale President Timothy Dwight in an address, July 4, 1798:

> About the year 1728, Voltaire, so celebrated for his wit and brilliancy and not less distinguished for his hatred of Christianity and his abandonment

of principle, formed a systematical design to destroy Christianity and to introduce in its stead a general diffusion of irreligion and atheism ...

He associated with himself Frederick the II–King of Prussia, and Mess. D'Alembert and Diderot ... all men of talents, atheists and in the like manner abandoned.

The principle parts of this system were ... with great art and insidiousness the doctrines of ... Christian theology were rendered absurd and ridiculous; and the mind of the reader was insensibly steeled against conviction and duty ...

The overthrow of the religious orders in Catholic countries (was) a step essentially necessary to the destruction of the religion professed in those countries ...

Dwight continued:

The appropriation to themselves, and their disciples, of the places and honors of members of the French Academy, the most respectable literary society in France ... In this way they designed to hold out themselves ... as the only persons of great literary and intellectual distinction in that country, and to dictate all literary opinions to the nation.

The fabrication of books of all kinds against Christianity, especially such as excite doubt and generate contempt ... so printed as to be purchased for little or nothing, and so written as to catch the feelings, and steal upon the approbation, of every class of men ...

The formation of a secret academy ... in which books were formed, altered, forged, imputed as posthumous to deceased writers of reputation, and sent abroad with the weight of their names.

These were printed and circulated at the lowest price through all classes of men in an uninterrupted succession, and through every part of the kingdom.

The being of God was denied and ridiculed

... The possession of property was pronounced robbery. Chastity and natural affection were declared to be nothing more than groundless prejudices.

Adultery, assassination, poisoning, and other crimes of the like infernal nature, were taught as lawful ... provided the end was good ... The good ends proposed ... are the overthrow of religion, government, and human society, civil and domestic.

These they pronounce to be so good that murder, butchery, and war, however extended and dreadful, are declared by them to be completely justifiable.

The means ... were ... the education of youth ... every unprincipled civil officer ... every abandoned clergyman ... books replete with infidelity, irreligion, immorality, and obscenity ...

Dwight concluded:

Where religion prevails ... a nation cannot be made slaves, nor villains, nor atheists, nor beasts. To destroy us therefore ... our enemies must first destroy our Sabbath and seduce us from the house of God ...

Religion and liberty are the meat and the drink of the body politic. Withdraw one of them and it languishes, consumes, and dies. If indifference ... becomes the prevailing character of a people ... vigorous defense is lost, and the hopes of their enemies are proportionally increased ...

Without religion we may possibly retain the freedom of savages, bears, and wolves, but not the freedom of New England.

If our religion were gone, our state of society would perish with it and nothing would be left which would be worth defending.

Adam Weishaupt, a 19th century professor of law at the University of Ingolstadt, Germany, proposed using Jacobin tactics worldwide, secretly inciting anarchist dissension within countries, and between countries, to create wars, after which power could be usurped under the pretense of restoring order, ultimately resulting in a global government.

In 1798, John Robison documented anarchist Jacobin plans in *Proofs of a Conspiracy Against all the Religions and Governments of Europe, carried on in the Secret Meetings* (NY: George Forman, 1798).

Once religion was largely removed from French culture, the naive citizens were slow to connect that a society without moral restraints would end in lawlessness, out of which a dictator would arise.

On the eve of the French Revolution, April 29, 1789, Gouverneur Morris, the first U.S. Minister to France, wrote:

> The materials for a revolution in France are very indifferent ...
>
> Everybody agrees that there is an utter prostration of morals; but this general proposition can never convey to an American mind the degree of depravity.
>
> It is not by any figure of rhetoric, or force of language, that the idea can be communicated. A hundred anecdotes, and a hundred thousand examples, are required to show the extreme rottenness of every member.
>
> There are men and women who are greatly and eminently virtuous. I have the pleasure to number many in my acquaintance; but they stand forward from a background deeply shaded ...
>
> The great masses of the common people have no religion but their priests, no law but their superiors, no morals but their interest.
>
> These are the creatures who, led by drunken curates, are now in the high road a la liberté, and the first use they make of it is to form insurrections everywhere for the want of bread.

Morris wrote to Jefferson, December 3, 1792:

The open contempt of religion, also cannot but be offensive to all sober minded men.

∽

CHAPTER 30
GODLESS FRENCH REVOLUTION

The situation in France came to a head after they helped America win independence from Britain. In return, the only thing France got was enormous debt.

This was followed by a few years of severe famine and the people were starving. The poor blamed the rich royalty.

According to Jean-Jacques Rousseau, when Queen Marie Antoinette was told the people did not have bread, her reply was: "Let them eat cake."

A mob formed in Paris which beheaded King Louis XVI and Queen Marie Antoinette in 1793.

As rights now came solely from the group – "fraternité," those who resisted the group were brutally beheaded in a bloody Reign of Terror, 1789–1794.

Rousseau, considered the Father of the French Revolution, wrote in *The Social Contract* (1762):

> The citizen is no longer the judge ... When the prince says to him: "It is expedient for the state that you should die," he ought to die ... because his life is no longer a mere bounty of nature, but a gift made conditionally by the state.

The idea was for the government to intentionally create panic to terrorize and frighten citizens into submission.

Like cowboys shooting guns in the air to scare cattle into a round up, despots throughout history, such as Attila the Hun, Genghis Khan, Tamerlane, Ivan the Terrible, and Sultan Abdul Hamid, have used terror to frighten people into submitting to their rule.

Sultan Balban of Delhi, India (1266–1286), stated:

> Fear of the governing power ... is the basis of all good government.

Maximilien Robespierre led the "Committee of Public Safety," giving a speech to the National Assembly titled "The Terror Justified," 1794, stating:

> Lead ... the enemies of the people by terror ... The basis of popular government during a revolution is both virtue and terror ... Terror is nothing more than swift, severe and inflexible justice.

Another member of the Committee of Public Safety was Billaud-Varenne, who demanded:

> Indeed ... make us equal to the task of exterminating our enemies ... The time has come to act ... We must place all our enemies under arrest this very day ... Let us crush the enemies of the revolution, and starting today, let the government take action, let the laws be executed.

Robespierre accused, arrested and beheaded:

- first all the royalty;
- then the wealthy;
- then the farmers and businessmen;
- then those hoarding food;
- then the clergy;
- then the former revolutionary radicals, who Robespierre wanted to purge from the party.

During France's Reign of Terror, some 10,000 were arrested and died in prison without a trial; 40,000 were beheaded by the guillotine; and 300,000 were butchered in the region of the Vendée.

Robespierre began an intentional campaign to de-Christianize French society and replace it with a civic religion of state worship.

Not wanting a constitution "Done in the year of the Lord," as the U.S. Constitution was, France retroactively made 1792 the new "Year One."

They did not want a seven–day week with a Sabbath day of rest, as that was derived from the Bible, so they devised a ten day "decade" week, and ten month year.

French Revolutionary Time divided the day into 10 decimal hours, each consisting of 100 decimal minutes, with each minute made up of 100 decimal seconds.

Every measurement was divisible by ten, as ten was considered the "number of man" who had ten fingers and ten toes. This was called "the metric system."

The new secular government proceeded to:

- Forbid crosses as being offensive;
- Christian religious monuments were destroyed;
- Public & private worship & education outlawed;
- Priests & ministers, along with those who harbored them, were executed on sight;
- Christian graves were desecrated, including that of Ste. Genevieve, the patron saint of Paris who called the city to pray when Attila the Hun was attacking in 451 AD;
- Churches were closed or used for "immoral ... lurid ... licentious ... scandalous ... depravities."

The Cathedral of Our Lady of Strasbourg was made into a Temple of Reason.

French privateers ignored treaties and by 1798, seized nearly 300 American ships bound for British ports. Talleyrand, the French Minister of Foreign Affairs, demanded millions of dollars in bribes to leave America's ships alone.

A master of political deception called "obfuscation" – intentionally being obscure, speaking out of both sides of the mouth, Talleyrand stated: "We were given speech to hide our thoughts."

The anti-Christian French government sent its army to a rural, very religious Catholic area of western France called the Vendée. Hundreds of thousands who refused to embrace new socialist secularism were killed in what is considered the first modern genocide.

French General Francois Joseph Westermann wrote to the Committee of Public Safety stating:

> There is no more Vendée ... According to the orders that you gave me, I crushed the children under the feet of the horses, massacred the women who, at least for these, will not give birth to any more brigands. I do not have a prisoner to reproach me. I have exterminated all.

A young French officer named Napoleon pleaded poor health to avoid participating in the slaughter.

Author Don Feder wrote in the article "Observations and Fulminations: The French Revolution and Jacobins in Our Streets" (July 13, 2018):

> The Reign of Terror wasn't an episode of the French Revolution; it was the Revolution.
>
> In *Citizens: A Chronicle of the French Revolution,* historian Simon Schama writes, "The terror ... was not just an unfortunate side effect ... it was the Revolution's source of collective energy ... From the very beginning, violence was the motor of the revolution."

In 1799, Alexander Hamilton condemned the French Revolution's attack on Christianity as:

> ... [depriving] mankind of its best consolations and most animating hopes, and to make a gloomy desert of the universe ... The praise of a civilized world is justly due to Christianity; – war, by the influence of the humane principles of that religion, has been stripped of half its horrors.
>
> The French renounce Christianity, and they relapse into barbarism; – war resumes the same hideous and savage form which it wore in the ages of Gothic and Roman violence.

Upon receiving news of the French Revolution, British statesman Edmund Burke wrote October 10, 1789:

This day I heard ... the portentous state of France — where the elements which compose human society seem all to be dissolved, and a world of monsters to be produced in the place of it.

On November 4, 1789, Burke wrote to Charles-Jean-François Depont in France:

You may have subverted monarchy, but not recovered freedom.

Burke publicly condemned the French Revolution in Parliament, February 9, 1790:

The French had shown themselves the ablest architects of ruin that had hitherto existed in the world. In that very short space of time they had completely pulled down to the ground, their monarchy; their church; their nobility; their law; their revenue; their army; their navy; their commerce; their arts; and their manufactures ...

There was a danger of an imitation of the excesses of an irrational, unprincipled, proscribing, confiscating, plundering, ferocious, bloody and tyrannical democracy ...

In religion, the danger of their example is no longer from intolerance, but from atheism; a foul, unnatural vice, foe to all the dignity and consolation of mankind; which seems in France, for a long time, to have been embodied into a faction.

British Statesman Lord Acton wrote:

What the French took from the Americans was their theory of revolution, not their theory of government – their cutting, not their sewing.

Best-selling author Os Guinness stated in a radio interview (Thinking in Public, 6/5/17):

The culture war now at its deepest roots is actually a clash between 1776, what was the American Revolution, and 1789 and heirs of the French Revolution.

CHAPTER 31
"LIBERTY, EQUALITY, FRATERNITY"

Completely overthrowing the old order, French governing elites set about creating an idealistic society of liberté, égalité, fraternité or "liberty, equality, fraternity" – "fraternity" meaning the brotherhood, the association, the group, the mob, the socialist state.

At issue was the mutually exclusive nature of these words. "Liberty" and "equality" are experienced individually, but "fraternity" is the collective.

Without an individual having Creator–given rights, fraternity demands a complete surrendering of an individual's liberty and equality to the overriding "general will" of the socialist state, with the governing elite class deciding what that "general will" was.

Michael Shermer wrote in his article "Utopia Is a Dangerous Ideal" (Aeon, April 2020):

> Utopias are especially vulnerable when a social theory based on collective ownership, communal work, authoritarian rule and a command–and–control economy collides with our natural–born desire for autonomy, individual freedom and choice.

Reagan stated October 27, 1964:

> Government can't control the economy without controlling people and they know when government sets out to do that, it must use force and conversion to achieve its purpose.

Also at issue was the two different ways to understand "equality." The first understanding is equal standing before the law, equal rights, and equal opportunity. The second way is for everyone to have an equal amount of material possessions.

When the second definition is used, the socialist fraternité forcibly takes possessions from those it thinks have too much, accusing them of selfishness

SOCIALISM: THE TRUE HISTORY

and robbery, and redistributes to those it thinks have too little. Unfortunately, those doing the redistribing become discretionary and act as new corrupt dictators. Tocqueville warned of this:

> Egalité ... means, no one shall be better off than I am; and (if) this is preferred to good government, good government is impossible.

An earlier French socialist proposing equal ownership of property was Étienne-Gabriel Morelly, who wrote *Code of Nature–Sacred and Fundamental Laws,* 1755:

> Now, if you were to take away property, the blind and pitiless self-interest that accompanies it, you would cause all the prejudices in errors that they sustain to collapse ... There would be no more furious passions, ferocious actions, notions or ideas of moral evil ...

> I. Nothing in society will belong to anyone, either as a personal possession or as capital goods, except the things for which the person has immediate use, for either his needs, his pleasures, or his daily work.

> II. Every citizen will be a public man, sustained by, supported by, and occupied at the public expense.

> III. Every citizen will make his particular contribution to the activities of the community according to his capacity, his talent and his age; it is on this basis that his duties will be determined, in conformity with the distributive laws ...

> VIII. All children upon reaching the age of ten, will leave the common paternal residence and go into the workshops, where they will be housed, fed and dressed, and where they will be instructed by the masters and chiefs of the various professions, whom they will obey as they would their own parents. They will all receive common treatment ...

> XI. The chiefs ... will ... see to it that ... education of children are everywhere exactly and uniformly observed, and to see to it above all that those faults of childhood that could tend to develop into the spirit of private ownership are wisely prevented or corrected.

What happens when the government decides to redistribute property?

Inevitably, those carrying out the redistribution are tempted to funnel possessions to their friends and supporters in return for favors and political support.

The person doing the redistributing is thus elevated into a position of influence and power, which ironically undermines the very equality he had professed to establish. As the maxim goes, "he who controls the purse strings has the power."

∽

CHAPTER 32

FRENCH REVOLUTION: A WARNING

Britain's Lord Thomas Macaulay told Democrat New York Secretary of State, Henry Randall, May 23, 1857:

> Institutions purely democratic must, sooner or later, destroy liberty, or civilization, or both ... France is an example ... a pure democracy was established there.

> During a short time there was ... a general spoliation, a national bankruptcy, a new partition of the soil, a maximum of prices, a ruinous load of taxation laid on the rich for the purpose of supporting the poor in idleness ...

> You may think that your country enjoys an exemption from these evils ... I am of a very different opinion. Your fate I believe to be certain, though it is deferred.

Macaulay explained how agitators tempt with breaking commandments "thou shalt not covet" and "thou shalt not steal":

> The time will come when ... distress everywhere makes the laborer mutinous and discontented, and inclines him to listen with eagerness to agitators who tell him that it is a monstrous iniquity that one man should have a million while another cannot get a full meal.

SOCIALISM: THE TRUE HISTORY

In bad years there is plenty of grumbling ... and sometimes a little rioting ... Your government will never be able to restrain a distressed and discontented majority ...

The day will come when, in the State of New York, a multitude of people, none of whom has had more than half a breakfast, or expects to have more than half a dinner, will choose a legislature ...

On one side is a statesman preaching patience, respect for vested rights, strict observance of public faith.

On the other is a demagogue ranting about the tyranny of capitalists and usurers (moneylenders) and asking why anybody should be permitted to drink champagne and to ride in a carriage, while thousands of honest folks are in want of necessaries.

Which of the two candidates is likely to be preferred by a working man who hears his children cry for more bread? ...

Lord Macaulay concluded:

I seriously apprehend that you will, in some such season of adversity ... devour all the seed-corn, and thus make the next year, a year not of scarcity, but of absolute famine ...

When a society has entered on this downward progress, either civilization or liberty must perish. Either some Caesar or Napoleon will seize the reins of government with a strong hand.

Alexander Hamilton warned of French ideas coming to America:

Opinions ... have been gradually gaining ground, which threaten the foundations of religion, morality, and society.

An attack was first made upon the Christian revelation, for which natural religion was offered as the substitute.

The Gospel was to be discarded as a gross

imposture, but the being and attributes of God, the obligations of piety, even the doctrine of a future state of rewards and punishments, were to be retained and cherished.

The French Republic experienced continual instability as citizens looked for someone who could fix the mess and restore order.

∽

CHAPTER 33

EMPEROR NAPOLEON

Out of the French chaos rose their version of a philosopher–king. Don Feder wrote in "Observations and Fulminations: The French Revolution and Jacobins in Our Streets" (July 13, 2018):

> Slaughter in the name of the "people," atheism, thought police, the ruthless suppression of dissent, mass murder for ideological purity, – all started in the orgy of murder and nihilism unleashed by the furies of Jacobinism.

> They started by killing aristocrats and royalists, then moderates (like the Girondists), then dissidents, then any who had doubts, until, finally, an emperor (Napoleon) with a genius for conquest took the place of a relatively benign monarch.

Napoleon usurped power, at first taking the less threatening title of "First Consul," but on December 2, 1804, in Notre Dame Cathedral, he placed the crown on his own head, making himself Emperor of the French.

Napoleon arrested Pope Pius VI, who died in captivity, and waited five months to bury him in order to get political concessions. He arrested the next Pope, Pius VII, and held him in confinement for six years.

Napoleon conquered across Europe and the Middle East, resulting in 6 million deaths as he invaded the countries of Italy, Austria, Poland, German states, Holland, Denmark, Norway, Spain, Egypt, and Russia.

He chose the motto "liberty, public order." He

instituted a top–down structured society called the Napoleonic Code, which had no concept of Creator-given rights.

The Code was simply orders given from whoever was the human authority – the head of gold, administered and carried out with force by the governing class – the arms and chest of silver, upon the governed class – the abdomen of iron and brass.

Noah Webster wrote "Political Fanaticism, No. III" (*The American Minerva,* September 21, 1796):

> The reason why severe laws are necessary in France, is, that the people have not been educated republicans — they do not know how to govern themselves [and so] must be governed by severe laws and penalties, and a most rigid administration.

❧

CHAPTER 34
STATE IS GOD: G.W.F. HEGEL

In the 19th century, social contract without God turned into socialism where the state becomes god.

After Napoleon's lightning fast conquering of Europe, Prussian King Frederick William III wanted to strengthen his German state. This led him to embrace the philosophy of Georg Wilhelm Friedrich Hegel. A professor at the University of Berlin. Hegel taught:

> The state is god walking on earth ... We must worship the state ...

> ... All the worth which the human being possesses ... he possesses only through the state ...

> ... The state ... recognizes no authority but its own ... acknowledges no abstract rules of good and bad ...

> ... The state is ... the ultimate end which has the highest right against the individual, whose highest duty is to be a member of the state ...

... The nation state ... is therefore the absolute power on earth. A single person, it hardly needs saying, is something subordinate ...

... The important aspect lies in self-subordination to the universal cause.

Harry S Truman stated, March 6, 1946:

Dictatorship ... is founded on the doctrine that the individual amounts to nothing ... the state is the only thing that counts, and that men, women and children were put on earth solely for the purpose of serving the state.

Under G.W.F. Hegel's system, the "general will" is determine by the ruler. In *Philosophy of History* (Jacob Loewenberg, ed., *Hegel: Selections,* New York: C. Scribner's Sons, 1929, p. 398), he wrote:

... It is not the isolated will of individuals that prevails; individual pretensions are relinquished, and the general will is the essential bond of political union ...

The origin of a state involves imperious lordship on the one hand, instinctive submission on the other.

Obedience — lordly power, and the fear inspired by a ruler.

Hegel was against citizens ruling themselves. He wanted power to be in the hands of one person. He wrote in *Philosophy of Law* (Section 279):

When it is contrasted with the sovereignty of the monarch, the phrase "sovereignty of the people" turns out to be merely one of those confused notions which arise from the wild idea of the "people." Without its monarch ... the people are just a formless multitude.

Students at the University of Berlin who admired Hegel formed a radical student group called the Young Hegelians, a member of which was Karl Marx.

Kelly O'Connell wrote in "Pagan Government

Theory Insures Tyranny Returns to the West" (*Canada Free Press,* June 18, 2012):

> ... but Marx did get his idea of "government as god" from Hegel.

∽

CHAPTER 35
19TH CENTURY UTOPIAN COMMUNITIES

In the early 19th century, German immigrants attempted many utopian communities in rural America. The more successful ones had Christian beliefs aiding them, i.e., caring for others. Others had pseudo-Christian, non-Christian, or even cult-like beliefs.

Transcendentalists attempted communal living experiments in Massachusetts. Brook Farm was begun in 1840, inspired by socialist Charles Fourier. Each member could chose whatever work they wanted to do. It failed financially in 1847. Fruitlands was founded in 1843 by Amos Bronson Alcott, father of *Little Women* author Louisa May Alcott. It failed in seven months, as she wrote in *Transcendental Wild Oats.*

In 1870, Dr. Cyrus Teed founded Koreshan Unity communal utopia. Communities started in New York, Chicago, San Francisco, and Estero, Florida, which was their New Jerusalem. Koreshans believed the universe existed inside the Earth. They founded the Progressive Liberal Party to influence local politics. Living celibate lives, they attracted few followers and dissolved.

Another socialist utopian experiment was the Oneida Community. It had common ownership of property, free love, polygamy, pederasty, and control over procreation with children raised by "villages."

Psychological cult abuse and rape brought legal action and dissension. Younger members wanted to return to traditional marriages. By 1879, members were leaving, one of whom was Charles Guiteau, who assassinated U.S. President James Garfield, July 2, 1881.

Another socialist utopia was New Harmony, Indiana, begun by German immigrants in 1814. The founder, George Rapp, complained March 20, 1819, that the experiment attracted unproductive people:

> It is astonishing how much trouble the people who have arrived here have made, for they have no morals and do not know what it means to live a moral and well-mannered life, not to speak of true Christianity, of denying the world or yourself.

Social reformer Robert Owen took over New Harmony in 1825, hoping to make it a new moral world of happiness, enlightenment, and prosperity through education, science, technology, and communal living.

They adopted "The New Harmony Community of Equality," February 5, 1826, with equal rights, equality of duties, common property and equal economic benefits. Unfortunately, it attracted "crackpots, free-loaders, and adventurers whose presence in the town made success unlikely." One participant, Josiah Warren of New Harmony, explained in 1856 that the experiment failed due to lack of individual sovereignty and private property:

> It seemed that the difference of opinion, tastes and purposes increased just in proportion to the demand for conformity.

> Two years were worn out in this way; at the end of which, I believe that not more than three persons had the least hope of success.

> Most of the experimenters left in despair of all reforms, and conservatism felt itself confirmed. We had tried every conceivable form of organization and government ...

Josiah Warren continued:

> We had a world in miniature. — we had enacted the French revolution over again with despairing hearts instead of corpses as a result ... It appeared that it was nature's own inherent law of diversity that had conquered us ...

Our "united interests" were directly at war with the individualities of persons and circumstances and the instinct of self-preservation ... and it was evident that just in proportion to the contact of persons or interests, so are concessions and compromises indispensable.

A more recent example of a failed utopia due to the "instinct of self-preservation" was reported by an AP article "400 foreigners stranded in Panama after 'tribal' festival" (ABCNews 3/18/20), and "Dozens of Hippies Stuck at Festival in Panama Due to Coronavirus" (Paul Joseph Watson, *PrisonPlanet.com,* 4/28/20):

Hippies who got stuck at a festival in Panama due to coronavirus realized that the collectivist utopia they sought after is actually "hell" as they bicker over food and territory ...

The Tribal Gathering Festival, billed as "paradise on earth," was supposed to end on March 15, but 40 western hippies remain trapped at the site because Panama announced a national emergency due to COVID-19 and placed them under quarantine.

A subsequent ban on all entry and departure flights now means the hippies are likely to be stuck in "paradise" until the end of May.

A *VICE* documentary short about their plight shows attendees complaining about how they are "stuck in hell" as they struggle with bad weather and major sewage issues at the campsite.

"At first it was like a paradise, but when you are locked in, it's not paradise anymore," one attendee said.

VICE reports that the festival was "designed to be a temporary paradise where people from western cities could learn from indigenous communities about how to rebalance society and live in symbiosis with the earth."

However, any sense of communitarian oneness appears to have been washed away as attendees bicker and fight over food and territory.

"Don't try to steal our food, I'll get really upset with you," one organizer tells the rest of the crowd. "And remember where you are, you're in my !@%#ing manor," he adds.

"I've been camping on a beach for 80 days!" said Doug Francisco, who led Extinction Rebellion climate change activists last year. "While the festival was still going on, the police came in and tried to shut it down."

Food, cleaning products and tobacco is all in short supply, with some hippies having to do manual labor to stay fed.

Attendees decided to visit the festival at the end of February despite serious government warnings against international travel and the expectation, which was obvious by that time, that coronavirus would devastate flight routes.

"While the situation is terrible, of course, it has also become extremely comical," reports the *District Herald.* "The hippies are now being forced to live in their theoretical utopia — and they aren't having the amazing time that they imagined."

The Smithsonian Magazine (Oct. 2019) published "When Socialism Came to Oklahoma." In the early 1900s, southeast Oklahoma's old Indian Territory was controlled by cotton landowners who rented land to tenant farmers from southern states in search of opportunity. Rents and interest became exorbitant, compounded by poor soil and boll weevil pestilence.

In 1907, German-born socialist Oscar Ameringer organized the evangelical Christian tenant farmers by portraying Jesus as a carpenter throwing money-changers out of the temple, that it was easier for a camel to pass through the eye of a needle than for a rich man to go to heaven. Imitating revival meetings, thousands attended his week long camps, hearing him promise a socialist paradise on earth – a Cooperative Commonwealth.

Hiding socialism's goal of eliminating private

property, he attracted 20,000 followers by promising them the land. Some robbed banks, burned barns, dynamited farm equipment, cut telegraph lines, set fire to bridges, and threatened to murder snitches.

In 1917, the same year as Russia's Bolshevik Revolution, the Green Corn Rebellion took place. Armed with Winchesters, shotguns and squirrel-guns, they dodged the World War I draft and hatched a delusional plot to march toward Washington and overthrow the capitalist government.

The sheriff recruited a posse of 1,000 and surrounded them on Spears Mountain, Oklahoma, where they surrendered.

Michael Shermer wrote in his article "Utopia Is a Dangerous Ideal" (*Aeon*, April 2020):

> Most of these 19th–century utopian experiments were relatively harmless because, without large numbers of members, they lacked political and economic power. But add those factors, and utopian dreamers can turn into dystopian murderers.

∽

CHAPTER 36
GERMANY'S KARL MARX

Karl Marx was a member of a radical student group at the University of Berlin, the Young Hegelians. After being refused a university post due to his extreme views, he published a paper in 1842 which was banned in Germany. He fled to Paris, then Brussels, then London, where he founded the International Workingmen's Association and the Social Democrat Labor Party.

In 1848, Marx and Friedrich Engels wrote *The Communist Manifesto,* with the motto "Working Men of All Countries Unite." The plan was for the "forcible overthrow of all existing social conditions" in order set up a socialist system. Marx wrote of eliminating the bourgeois (middle–class small business owners):

In a higher phase of communist society, after the enslaving subordination of the individual to the division of labor ... labor has become not only a means of life but life's prime want ...

Only then can the narrow horizon of bourgeois right be crossed in its entirety and society inscribe on its banners: From each according to his ability, to each according to his needs!

Marx's plan included a progressive income tax with everyone working for the state. Inheritances and private property would be confiscated and there would be centralized control of land, banking, communication and transportation. Education would not only be free, but a mandatory means of indoctrination.

Marx read and reread Charles Darwin's *Origin of Species,* and was so affected that he dedicated a personal copy his book *Das Kapital* to him, inscribing that he was a "sincere admirer" of Darwin. Marx saw "survival of the fittest" as validating the "dialectical conflict," where labor and community organizers attacked capitalist business owners (antithesis) to allow communists to usurp power (synthesis).

He wrote to Lassalle, January 16, 1861:

Darwin's book is very important and serves me as a basis in natural selection for the class struggle in history.

Marx applied Darwin's theory of evolution to politics, believing that socialism was just "a lower stage of communism," and would evolve into communism. Socialism is the road, communism is the destination.

The difference between socialism and communism is simply one of degrees. Ayn Rand wrote in *For the New Intellectual* (1961):

Socialism is the doctrine that man has no right to exist for his own sake, that his life and his work do not belong to him, but belong to society, that the only justification of his existence is his service to society, and that society may dispose of him in any way it pleases for the sake of whatever it deems to be its own tribal, collective good.

Attorney General William P. Barr addressed the National Religious Broadcasters, February 26, 2020:

Political divisions of today result from a conflict between two fundamentally different visions of the individual and his relationship to the state.

One vision ... limits government and gives priority to preserving personal liberty.

The other vision propels a form of totalitarian(ism) ... which seeks to submerge the individual in a collectivist agenda. It subverts individual freedom in favor of elite conceptions about what best serves the collective.

Marx's philosophy influenced:

- Vladimir Lenin's Social–Democrat Party;
- Joseph Stalin's Union of Soviet Socialist Republics;
- Benito Mussolini's Italian Socialist Party;
- Mao Zedong's Socialist Education Movement; and
- Adolph Hitler's National Socialist Workers Party.

∽

CHAPTER 37

NATIONAL SOCIALIST WORKERS PARTY

"Nazi" is the abbreviation of National Socialist Workers Party (national sozialistische arbeiterpartei).

Its leader was Adolph Hitler, who became Chancellor of Germany on January 30, 1933. One month later, there was the crisis. Germany's capitol, the Reichstag, was set on fire under suspicious conditions.

Historians implicate Hitler's supporters as being responsible in what is called a "false flag" event – a crisis perpetrated by an innocent-looking government to create a panic to allow the government to seize control.

On February 28, 1933, immediately after the

Reichstag fire, Hitler declared the "Fire Act," which nullified civil liberties and suspended basic rights. In the confusion, he had his political opponents falsely accused, arrested and shot without a trial.

Hitler had radical homosexual activist Ernst Röhm and his Brownshirts, also called Sturmabteilung (storm troopers), storm into meetings of his political opponents, disrupting and shouting down speakers, as Mussolini's Squadrismo or Blackshirts did in Italy.

Brownshirts organized Antifa-style protests and street riots, smashing windows, blocking traffic, setting fires, vandalizing, and even beating to death innocent bystanders to spread fear and panic. They started boycotts of Jewish businesses, and on Kristallnacht (Night of Broken Glass), November 9, 1938, smashed windows of over 7,500 Jewish stores and 200 synagogues.

When Hitler no longer needed Brownshirt leaders, he had hundreds of them killed by his SS and Gestapo secret police kill in the Night of the Long Knives.

CHAPTER 38

UNIVERSAL HEALTHCARE

Hitler swayed the public with mesmerizing speeches. He began implementing a plan of free healthcare for all with no regard for conscience.

The *New York Times* reported October 10, 1933:

NAZI PLAN TO KILL INCURABLES ... The Ministry of Justice ... explaining the (National Socialist Workers Party) ... intentions to authorize physicians to end the sufferings of the incurable patient ...

The Catholic newspaper *Germania* hastened to observe: "The Catholic faith binds the conscience of its followers not to accept this method" ... In Lutheran circles, too, life is regarded as something that God alone can take ...

Euthanasia ... has become a widely discussed word

in the (Third) Reich ... No life still valuable to the state will be wantonly destroyed.

A healthcare crisis can be an effective opportunity to demand citizens give up their rights, as anyone who resists can be maligned as uncaring. Lenin had stated:

Socialized medicine is a keystone to the establishment of a socialist state.

Saul Alinsky stated:

Control healthcare and you control the people.

In a 1961 recorded message "Reagan Speaks Out Against Socialized Medicine," he stated:

One of the traditional methods of imposing statism or socialism on a people has been by way of medicine. It's very easy to disguise a medical program as a humanitarian project ... We want no further encroachment on these individual liberties and freedoms ... We do not want socialized medicine ...

If you don't (stop) this program I promise you it will pass ... and behind it will come other federal programs that will invade every area of freedom as we have known ... until, one day ... we will awake to find that we have socialism.

When Germany's economy struggled, expenses had to be cut, such as the cost of keeping alive handicapped, chronically ill, insane, those with dementia, and the elderly. They were considered "lebensunwertes leben" – life unworthy of life, and terminated.

Then the criminals, convicts, street bums, beggars and welfare dependents were considered "useless eaters" and "leeches" on society. They were sent to the gas chambers. Incredibly, Germany's utilitarian philosophy was influenced by leftists in America.

Germans looked to Supreme Court Justice Oliver Wendell Holmes, Jr., who decided to "play God" in his 1927 *Buck v. Bell* decision, writing that "for the protection and health of the state," the intellectually disabled should be forcibly sterilized, remarking:

Three generations of imbeciles are enough.

Founder of Planned Parenthood Margaret Sanger, with a grant from the Rockefeller Foundation, organized the World Population Conference in 1927. A featured speaker was Eugen Fischer, who, prior to World War I, ran a concentration camp in German–controlled Namibia where he performed gruesome medical experiments on Africans.

Fischer wrote a pseudo-scientific eugenics work, *Principles of Human Heredity and Race Hygiene,* which was read by Hitler in prison and became a basis for Hitler's racial superiority in *Mein Kampf.*

Eugen Fischer's writings led to the Nazi's Law for the Prevention of Hereditarily Diseased Offspring, 1933, which resulted in hundreds of mixed-race German–Africans and French–Africans being subjected to compulsory sterilization.

An associate of Margaret Sanger was eugenicist Madison Grant, founder of the New York Zoological Society. He put Ota Benga, an African from the Congo Mbuti pygmy tribe, in a cage in the Monkey House of the Bronx Zoo. Madison Grant wrote a Darwinian book, *The Passing of the Great Race* (1916), that was read by Hitler, who sent him a thank you letter.

Margaret Sanger recommended, January 1, 1932:

Apply a stern and rigid policy of sterilization and segregation to that grade of population whose progeny is tainted, or whose inheritance is such that objectionable traits may be transmitted to offspring.

She founded a magazine called *The Birth Control Review.* In April of 1933, her magazine published an article "Eugenic Sterilization" by German eugenicist Ernst Rudin, considered a "father of racial hygiene" for the National Socialist Workers Party.

Rudin insisted that the state prevent defective genes of the "untermensch" (under mankind) from being transmitted to future generations. He considered the

Aryan race as "ubermensch" (super mankind) and "herrenvolk" (master race). The word "Aryan" is derived from the country of Iran, from where Indo–Iranian people purportedly descended.

Nazi state planners enacted unconscionable plans to reduce the population of those they considered inferior races, namely, Jews, Gypsies, Slavs, and Negroes, through sterilization and extermination.

In their mad effort to "purge" the human gene pool, six million Jews, and millions of others, were barbarically killed in gas chambers and ovens.

Nazi anatomists harvested human body parts from prisoners for scientific research and gruesome laboratory experimentation. One cannot help but see similarities in recent headlines:

- "Planned Parenthood, fetal body parts subject of controversial video" (CNN,7/15/15¬

- "Planned Parenthood Harvests Baby Parts" (Plam.org);

- "New Documents Prove Planned Parenthood Illegally Profited from Selling Aborted Baby Parts," (LifeNews.com);

- Cardinal Timothy Dolan described New York Governor's Reproductive Health Act which allows killing of babies as they are being born, as "ghoulish, grisly, gruesome" (Fox and Friends, 1/28/19);

- "Report: China still harvesting organs from prisoners at a massive scale" (CNN, 6/24/16).

U.S. Surgeon General C. Everett Koop stated in 1977:

When the first 273,000 German aged, infirm and retarded were killed in gas chambers there was no outcry from that medical profession ... and it was not far from there to Auschwitz.

British Journalist Malcolm Muggeridge explained:

We have ... for those that have eyes to see, an object lesson in what the quest for "quality of life" without reference to "sanctity of life" can involve ...

The origins of the Holocaust lay, not in Nazi terrorism ... but in ... Germany's acceptance of euthanasia and mercy-killing as humane and estimable.

∽

CHAPTER 39
CHRISTIAN RESISTANCE

The next victims of socialist statism were political and religious prisoners. Religious ministers who resisted the National Socialist Workers Party were imprisoned, such as Rev. Martin Niemöller, a founder of the Confessing Church. Niemöller made a statement, of which several versions exist:

> In Germany they first came for the communists, and I didn't speak up because I wasn't a communist.
>
> Then they came for the Jews, and I didn't speak up because I wasn't a Jew.
>
> Then they came for the trade unionists, and I didn't speak up because I wasn't a trade unionist.
>
> Then they came for the Catholics, and I didn't speak up because I was a Protestant.
>
> Then they came for me and by that time no one was left to speak up.

Another Confessing Church leader who resisted Hitler was Dietrich Bonhoeffer. He studied in New York in 1930, where he met Frank Fisher, an African–American seminarian who introduced him to Harlem's Abyssinian Baptist Church.

Bonhoeffer was inspired by Negro spirituals and the preaching of black pastor Adam Clayton Powell, Sr., who helped him turn his theology "from phraseology to reality," motivating him to stand up against injustice.

Bonhoeffer stated:

> Silence in the face of evil is itself evil: God will not hold us guiltless.

In his book, *The Cost of Discipleship,* Bonhoeffer rebuked nominal Christians:

Cheap grace is the preaching of forgiveness without requiring repentance, baptism without church discipline. Communion without confession. Cheap grace is grace without discipleship, grace without the cross, grace without Jesus Christ.

Bonhoeffer stated in a 1932 sermon:

The blood of martyrs might once again be demanded, but this blood, if we really have the courage and loyalty to shed it, will not be innocent, shining like that of the first witnesses for the faith. On our blood lies heavy guilt, the guilt of the unprofitable servant.

Bonhoeffer warned Germans not to slip into the cult of Führer (leader) worship, as Hitler could turn out to be a Verführer (misleader, seducer).

Jimmy Carter wrote in *Sources of Strength,* 1997:

Rev. Niebuhr urged Dietrich Bonhoeffer to remain in America for his own safety. Bonhoeffer refused. He felt he had to be among the other Christians persecuted in Germany.

So he returned home, and ... in resistance to Hitler ... preached publicly against Nazism, racism, and anti-semitism ... Bonhoeffer was finally arrested and imprisoned.

Of his return to Germany, Bonhoeffer wrote:

Jesus Christ lived in the midst of his enemies. At the end all his disciples deserted him. On the cross he was utterly alone, surrounded by evildoers and mockers. For this cause he had come, to bring peace to the enemies of God. So the Christian, too, belongs not in the seclusion of a cloistered life but in the thick of foes.

Jimmy Carter continued:

Dietrich Bonhoeffer died April 9, 1945, just a few days before the allied armies liberated Germany. He was executed on orders of Heinrich Himmler. He died a disciple and a martyr ...

The same Holy Spirit ... that gave Bonhoeffer

the strength to stand up against Nazi tyranny is available to us today.

Bonhoeffer proclaimed:

To endure the cross is not tragedy; it is the suffering which is the fruit of an exclusive allegiance to Jesus Christ.

On February 16, 2002, Dr. James Dobson told the National Religious Broadcasters:

Those of you who feel that the church has no responsibility in the cultural area ... What if it were 1943 and you were in Nazi Germany and you knew what Hitler was doing to the Jews ... Would you say, "We're not political — that's somebody else's problem?"

I thank God Dietrich Bonhoeffer did not give that answer, and he was arrested by the Nazis and hanged in 1945, naked and alone because he said, "This is not right."

∽

CHAPTER 40

SILENCING THE CHURCH

Martin Luther began the Reformation in 1517, after having an personal revelation of the verse "the just shall live by faith" (Habakkuk 2:4), but when some German kings wanted to break away from Rome, they decided that everyone in their kingdom had to be Lutheran.

To many in these kingdoms, it was not the same personal revelation that Martin Luther had, but just an acknowledgment of state-approved doctrine.

Soon a revival movement began called "pietism."

Pietists believed that being a Christian was more than just acknowledging a new set of doctrines, as scriptural as they may be. A person needed to have a personal experience with Jesus, and when they do, their life should change by the in-dwelling power of the Holy Spirit.

They would no longer do the worldly things they

used to do, such as go to bars, brothels, lewd theaters, or be involved in worldly government.

Wait? What was that last item?

Yes, government! The pietist attitude was, if someone was truly a Christian they would not be involved in government, as it was filled full of worldly people. This was an early version of separation of church and state. Some pietists even refused to vote.

Pietists stressed the positive and vital message of a personal relationship with Christ, but the emphasis was so personal that it abandoned responsibility to fulfill another scriptural command, "a good man leaves an inheritance to his children's children" (Proverbs 13:22).

There were accounts of German princes financially supporting pietists so that they would teach followers to stay out of the prince's business. This separation concept kept German churches silent, allowing ambitious politicians, like Hitler, to seize power.

Rev. Dr. Martin Luther King, Jr., challenged this:

> The church must be reminded that it is ... the conscience of the state.

The National Socialist Workers Party usurped power and killed millions in over 1,200 concentration camps.

It took the sacrifice of millions of courageous Allied lives to stop what German church leaders refused to because they were silent and taught church members it was more spiritual not to be involved in politics.

Like many politicians, Hitler at first pretended to be sympathetic to Christianity to get elected, duping naive ministers with placating rhetoric. Once in power, he dispensed with pretense and revealed his nazified social Darwinism and hostility toward Christianity.

Recent headlines reflect similar hostility:

> • "China Trying to 'Rewrite the Bible,' Force Churches to Sing Communist Anthems" (*The Christian Post*, 9/28/18);

• "In China, they're closing churches, jailing pastors and even rewriting scripture. China's Communist Party is intensifying religious persecution as Christianity's popularity grows. A new state translation of the Bible will establish a 'correct understanding' of the text" (*The Guardian*, 1/13/19).

Other recent examples are:

• Kansas, public health orders allowed people to go to bars and dine in public restaurants but denied any church from gathering 10 or more people, even if they observed social distancing;

• Michigan, Gov. Gretchen Whitmer issued draconian lockdown orders and used state police against peaceful protesters while allowing abortion clinics to stay open;

• Mayor of Greenville, Mississippi, declared it a crime for people to sit alone in their cars in a church parking lot. The Department of Justice said: "The City appears to have thereby singled churches out as the only essential service ... that may not operate despite following ... recommendations regarding social distancing";

• Illinois Governor announced that churches will be limited until a vaccine is developed;

• Mass. Governor Targeted Churches For Shutdown Rules He Didn't Apply To Home Depot.

• New York Mayor broke up a Jewish funeral.

In *The Goebbels Diaries* 1939–1941, Nazi Minister of Propaganda Joseph Goebbels confided:

(Hitler) hates Christianity, because it has crippled all that is noble in humanity.

Franklin D. Roosevelt stated December 15, 1941:

To Hitler, the church ... is a monstrosity to be destroyed by every means.

Hitler attempted to "nazify" German Protestant Churches. He pressured old military generals who might resist him to retire, thus purging his administration of any still retaining a remnant of "archaic" Judeo–Christian values. Roosevelt stated January 6, 1942:

> The world is too small ... for both Hitler and God ... Nazis have now announced their plan for enforcing their ... pagan religion all over the world ... by which the Holy Bible and the Cross of Mercy would be displaced by *Mein Kampf* and the swastika.

Roosevelt stated of Hitler, December 15, 1941:

> Government to him is not the servant ... of the people but their absolute master and the dictator of their every act ... The rights to life, liberty, and the pursuit of happiness which seemed to the Founders of the Republic inalienable, were, to Hitler and his fellows, empty words ...

FDR continued:

> Hitler advanced: That the individual human being has no rights whatsoever in himself ... no right to a soul of his own, or a mind of his own, or a tongue of his own, or a trade of his own; or even to live where he pleases or to marry the woman he loves;
>
> That his only duty is the duty of obedience, not to his God, not to his conscience, but to Adolf Hitler ... His only value is his value, not as a man, but as a unit of the Nazi state.

George Orwell observed that people not only want material things, they want purpose, even if it is a false one. He wrote in his 1940 review of *Mein Kampf*:

> "Progressive" thought has assumed tacitly that human beings desire nothing beyond ease, security and avoidance of pain ... Hitler knows that human beings don't only want comfort, safety, short working–hours, hygiene, birth-control ... they also, at least intermittently, want struggle and self-sacrifice ...
>
> Socialism ... said to people "I offer you a good time," Hitler has said to them "I offer you struggle,

danger, and death," and as a result a whole nation flings itself at his feet ... We ought not to underrate its emotional appeal.

Philosopher Eric Hoffer explained in his 1951 classic, *The True Believer*:

The permanent misfits can find salvation only in a complete separation from the self; and they usually find it by losing themselves in the compact collectivity of a mass movement.

Attorney General Bill Barr noted February 26, 2020:

"Progressives" have become increasingly militant and totalitarian ...They seek power through the democratic process ... Their policy agenda has become more aggressively collectivist, socialist, and explicitly revolutionary.

෴

CHAPTER 41
GUN CONFISCATION

Hitler began to confiscate weapons from law-abiding citizens. A SA Oberführer wrote of an ordinance by the provisional Bavarian Minister of the Interior:

The deadline set ... for the surrender of weapons will expire on March 31, 1933. I therefore request the immediate surrender of all arms ...

Whoever does not belong to one of these named units (SA, SS, and Stahlhelm) and ... keeps his weapon without authorization or even hides it, must be viewed as an enemy of the national government and will be held responsible without hesitation and with the utmost severity.

Foreshadowing present-day political candidates, Heinrich Himmler, head of Nazi S.S. ("Schutzstaffel"– Protection Squadron), announced:

Germans who wish to use firearms should join the S.S. or the S.A. Ordinary citizens don't need guns, as their having guns doesn't serve the state.

Disarming the civilian population was a necessary

step in state control, as Lenin explained: "One man with a gun can control 100 without one. "

George Mason, a Virginia founding father, wrote:

> To disarm the people is the best and most effectual way to enslave them.

Noah Webster wrote:

> Before a standing army can rule, the people must be disarmed.

Machiavelli wrote:

> It is not reasonable to suppose that one who is armed will obey willing one who is unarmed.

Gandhi wrote in *An Autobiography of the Story of My Experiments with the Truth* (trans. M. Desai, 1927):

> Among the many misdeeds of the British rule in India, history will look upon the Act depriving a whole nation of arms as the blackest.

Theoretical arguments for disarming citizens become indefensible when faced with actual situations:

- disarmed North Koreans sentenced to labor camps;
- disarmed Nigerians killed by Islamist Boko Haram;
- disarmed Iranians killed by their fundamentalist state; and
- disarmed Venezuelans killed by military forces of a corrupt dictator.

When a suspected homosexual youth shot Nazi diplomat Ernst vom Rath in Paris, it was used as an excuse to confiscate all firearms from Jews.

This left Jewish neighborhoods defenseless, setting the stage for Jews to be maligned, rounded up, and eventually sent to concentration camps.

German newspapers printed, November 10, 1938:

> Jews Forbidden to Possess Weapons by Order of SS Reichsführer Himmler, Munich ...

> "Persons who, according to the Nürnberg law, are regarded as Jews, are forbidden to possess

any weapon. Violators will be condemned to a concentration camp and imprisoned for a period of up to 20 years."

The *New York Times,* November 9, 1938, reported:

The Berlin Police ... announced that ... the entire Jewish population of Berlin had been "disarmed" with the confiscation of 2,569 hand weapons, 1,702 firearms and 20,000 rounds of ammunition.

Any Jews still found in possession of weapons without valid licenses are threatened with the severest punishment.

In light of Nazi threats, George Orwell wrote in 1941:

A million British working men now have rifles in their bedrooms and don't in the least wish to give them up.

Of the Waffengesetz (Nazi Weapons Law), March 18, 1938, Hitler stated at a dinner, April 11, 1942 (*Hitler's Table Talk 1941–44: His Private Conversations,* 1973, p. 425–6):

The most foolish mistake we could possibly make would be to allow the subject races to possess arms. History shows that all conquerors who have allowed their subject races to carry arms have prepared their own downfall by so doing ...

So let's not have any native militia or native police. German troops alone will bear the sole responsibility for the maintenance of law and order.

∽

CHAPTER 42
HITLER'S AFFINITY FOR ISLAMISTS

Hitler was initially going to allow Jews to be deported to Palestine, but was persuaded against it.

He met with the Grand Mufti of Jerusalem, Mohammad Amin al-Husseini, who also held anti-Jewish views.

Beginning in 1931, al-Husseini attempted to follow

Hitler's example by expelling Jews from Palestine. The Muslim Brotherhood did the same in Egypt.

Mufti al-Husseini recruited 30,000 Bosnian Muslims to join Hitler's Waffen–SS. Hitler gave al-Husseini financial assistance, and then asylum in 1941, with the honorary rank of an SS Major General.

During the final battle in Berlin in April of 1945, the Allies closed in on Hitler's bunker. There they confronted a hundred Muslims of the Mufti's Arab Legion making their last suicidal stand defending him.

Hitler believed that the Nazi's had the right solution but the wrong religion, stating:

> Had Charles Martel not been victorious at Poitiers (732 AD) ... then we should in all probability have been converted to Mohammedanism, that cult which glorifies the heroism and which opens up the seventh Heaven to the bold warrior alone. Then the Germanic races would have conquered the world.

Winston Churchill, in *From War to War* (*Second World War,* Vol. 1) described Hitler's *Mein Kampf* as:

> ... the new Koran of faith and war: turgid, verbose, shapeless, but pregnant with its message.

Hitler stated of the Nazis:

> The peoples of Islam will always be closer to us than, for example, France.

Hitler stated in private, as recorded by Albert Speer, Nazi Minister of Armaments and War Production:

> The Mohammedan religion too would have been much more compatible to us than Christianity ... with its meekness and flabbiness?

CHAPTER 43
NUREMBERG TRIALS

After World War II ended, officials of the National Socialist Workers Party were arrested and put on trial for killing millions of Jews and others in the Holocaust.

At the Nuremberg Trials of 1945–1946, on full display was the socialist idea that of rights come from "the group," and not God. Nazi officials defended their actions by explaining they were only following "laws agreed upon" by the people of the German state.

An insight into the perpetrators mindset was provided by Nazi General Hans Frank, who carried out orders to plunder Poland and commit the mass murder of millions of Poles and Jews in death camps.

After the war, Hans Frank was tried and executed. During his final confinement, he was visited by Fr. O'Conner, who led him to repent, believe in the atonement of Christ for his sins, and become a Catholic.

At his trial, August 31, 1945, Hans Frank was remorseful as he described the false justification for his acts and the slippery slope of socialist thought:

> At the beginning of our way we did not suspect that our turning away from God could have such disastrous deadly consequences and that we would necessarily become more and more deeply involved in guilt.

> At that time we could not have known that so much loyalty and willingness to sacrifice on the part of the German people could have been so badly directed by us. Thus, by turning away from God, we were overthrown and had to perish ...

Hans Frank continued:

> Before all, God pronounced and executed judgment on Hitler and the system which we served with minds far from God. Therefore, may our people, too, be called back from the road on which Hitler – and we with him – have led them.

> I beg of our people NOT to continue in this direction, be it even a single step; because Hitler's road was the way without God, the way of turning from Christ, and, in the last analysis, the way of

political foolishness, the way of disaster, and the way of death ...

His path became more and more that of a frightful adventurer without conscience or honesty, as I know today at the end of this Trial.

We call upon the German people ... to return from this road which, according to the law and justice of God, had to lead us and our system into disaster and which will lead everyone into disaster who tries to walk on it ... everywhere in the whole world.

∽๑

CHAPTER 44
UNITED NATIONS

Nuremberg prosecutors realized there needed to be a law higher than the laws of a country, but they did not want to acknowledge a Creator, so they decided that the "higher law" would be what all the nations of the world collectively agreed upon.

This was the concept behind the "United Nations."

Eleanor Roosevelt proudly helped compose the U.N. Declaration of Human Rights in 1948.

It listed rights all nations agreed upon, such as freedom of religion and that women are equal to men, but nowhere in the document was any reference made to the Creator as being the source of those rights.

This introduced a dilemma, for if the "higher law" was just what nations agree upon, then globalists, communists, or Islamists could simply bribe or threaten smaller nations to agree upon their totalitarian policies.

The naiveté of this effort was revealed when human rights violators were put on the U.N. Council for Human Rights, and when a subgroup of 57 Muslim states formed the Organization of Islamic Cooperation.

On June 30, 2000, the O.I.C. rejected the U.N. Declaration of Human Rights and agreed on their own

Cairo Declaration on Human Rights in Islam, which allowed for beating of women and killing of apostates.

If laws are simply what a group agrees upon, what is wrong with them agreeing upon sharia?

Sharia organizer Anjem Choudary of Islam4UK declared (*London Daily Express*, October 15, 2009):

> We have had enough of democracy and man-made law ... We will call for a complete upheaval of the British ruling system ... and demand full implementation of sharia in Britain.

A sign carried by sharia demonstrator in Dearborn, Michigan, reported by Dr. Irwin Lutzer in *The Cross in the Shadow of the Crescent* (2013), stated:

> We will use the freedoms of the Constitution to destroy the Constitution.

Instead of defeating communism, the United Nations took the attitude of "containment." General MacArthur disagreed with this and Truman made the unpopular decision to remove him. MacArthur stated:

> It is fatal to enter a war without the will to win it ... In war there is no substitute for victory.

President Dwight Eisenhower confided to the National Junior Chamber of Commerce, June 10, 1963:

> The United Nations has seemed to be two distinct things to the two worlds divided by the iron curtain ...

> To the free world it has seemed that it should be a constructive forum ... To the communist world it has been a convenient sounding board for their propaganda, a weapon to be exploited in spreading disunity and confusion.

Five years after the United Nations was established, Herbert Hoover proposed reorganizing it to exclude socialist–communist countries due to their atrocious record of human rights violations, as recorded by the American Newspaper Publishers Association, April 27, 1950:

What the world needs today is a definite, spiritual mobilization of the nations who believe in God against this tide of Red agnosticism.

It needs a moral mobilization against the hideous ideas of the police state and human slavery ... I suggest that the United Nations should be reorganized without the communist nations in it.

If that is impractical, then a definite New United Front should be organized of those peoples who disavow communism, who stand for morals and religion, and who love freedom ...

Hoover continued:

It is a proposal based solely upon moral, spiritual and defense foundations.

It is a proposal to redeem the concept of the United Nations to the high purpose for which it was created. It is a proposal for moral and spiritual cooperation of God-fearing free nations.

And in rejecting an atheistic other world, I am confident that the Almighty God will be with us.

CHAPTER 45
MARSHALL PLAN AFTER WWII

After World War II, General MacArthur warned:

Japan is a spiritual vacuum ... If you do not fill it with Christianity, it will be filled with communism.

He pleaded that Youth for Christ and other ministries send 10,000 missionaries to Japan: "Send missionaries and Bibles."

After the War, Europe was also experiencing crises. The U.S. State Department sent John Foster Dulles to France in 1947, to assess the situation. He observed strikes, strife and sabotage which were making the country vulnerable to a takeover by communists who had the second largest political party in France.

Dulles recommended immediate economic

assistance in the form of $12 billion of aid through the Marshall Plan. Ironically, the Marshall Plan's distribution of aid through government handouts inadvertently set post-war Europe on the path of dependency upon future socialist–style welfare programs. Ayn Rand wrote:

> The difference between a welfare state and a totalitarian state is a matter of time.

◆⑥

CHAPTER 46
THE TERM "SOCIALISM"

The term "socialism" was coined by French political philosopher Henri de Saint-Simon (1760–1825) as the opposite of "individualism."

Use of the term was popularized by mid-to-late 1800s by European theorists, such as Karl Marx, Friedrich Engels, Leon Trotsky, and Antonio Gramsci, where power is concentrated into the hands of the state.

During Russia's Bolshevik Revolution of 1917, "socialism" became identified as a distinct transition phase between capitalism and communism.

The term "communism" comes from the Latin word "communis," meaning everything held in common. There is no private ownership of anything. The government controls both production and consumption.

The term "capitalism" is the private ownership of production by individuals using their own capital, with the goal for their effort being the earning of a profit, which they get to decide how to consume.

Karl Marx wrote in *The Critique of the Gotha Programme,* Part IV:

> Between capitalist and communist society there lies the period of the revolutionary transformation.

Lenin commented in *Report on the Activities of the Council of People's Commissars,* January 24, 1918:

The whole history of socialism, particularly of French socialism ... is ... revolutionary striving.

Lenin considered socialism as a transition phase from capitalism to communism, stating:

The goal of socialism is communism.

Democratic socialism is a step in the wrong direction. Friedrich Engels wrote in *The Principles of Communism*:

Democratic socialists ... favor some of the same measures the communists advocate.

Ayn Rand wrote:

There is no difference between communism and socialism, except in the means of achieving the same ultimate end: communism proposes to enslave men by force; socialism – by vote. It is merely the difference between murder and suicide.

Socialism, in this sense, is simply "communism–lite." Despite the rhetoric, socialism and communism are effectively just varying degrees of repackaged top–down control.

In Europe, socialist–leaning countries function with varying degrees of capitalism, but regulations favor corporate monopolies which in turn support socialist politicians. Socialist government bureaucrats determine a person's educational path, career choices, healthcare and welfare.

Many of these countries maintain a privileged elite-ruling class, often with monarchs and royal families. In the article "Dynasties Still Run the World" (*The Conversation,* May 7, 2020), Oklahoma State University Professor Farida Jalalzai and Purdue University Northwest Professor Meg Rincker wrote:

Want to get into politics? It helps if you come from the right family.

Our study, published in the journal *Historical Social Research* in December 2018, shows that, on average, one in 10 world leaders comes from households with political ties … in sub-Saharan Africa, Asia, Europe, North America and Latin America.

Family political connections mattered … in monarchies and democracies, and in rich countries and poor ones.

∽

CHAPTER 47
EUGENE DEBS

In 1894, socialist Eugene Debs organized the Pullman Railroad Strike. Rioters destroyed $80 million worth of property in 27 states, interrupting freight and passenger trains and killing 30 people. Grover Cleveland, the first Democrat President after the Civil War, sent in the U.S. Army to stop union strikers. He attempted to appease the rioters by declaring an annual "Labor Day."

Debs spent six months in prison and afterwards founded: the Social Democracy of America, 1897; the Social Democratic Party of America, 1898; and the Socialist Party of America, 1901. He was the Socialist candidate for U.S. President five times from 1900 to 1920.

In 1919, the Communist Party USA split off from the Socialist Party of America.

∽

CHAPTER 48
UNION OF SOVIET SOCIALIST REPUBLICS

Riots, pograms and massacres drove over 2 million Jews out of Tsarist Russia between 1880 and 1920, as portrayed in the play *Fiddler on the Roof.*

When World War I started in 1914, Tsar Nicholas II sent 3 million Russian troops to fight in Eastern Europe and Ottoman Turkey. Russian forces were unprepared for Germany's Kaiser Wilhelm II's heavy artillery. At the Battle of Tannenberg, August 26–30, 1914, over 78,000 Russians were killed or wounded and 90,000 captured.

Within a year, over 1.4 million Russian soldiers

were killed and nearly a million captured. Russian General Denikin described:

> The German heavy artillery swept away whole lines of trenches, and their defenders with them. We hardly replied. There was nothing with which we could reply.
>
> Our regiments, although completely exhausted, were beating off one attack after another by bayonet ... Blood flowed unendingly, the ranks became thinner and thinner and thinner. The number of graves multiplied.

Russia's disillusionment with the Tsar grew. This, together with severe cold weather and food shortages, allowed Vladimir Lenin's community organizers to agitate and fan unrest, culminating in the Bolshevik Revolution – Red October of 1917.

Lenin distributed propaganda, incited class warfare, provoked strikes, staged bank robberies, attacked police, and ordered assassinations.

∞

CHAPTER 49
VLADIMIR LENIN

Lenin forced the Tsar from power, who was soon shot with his family. Lenin convinced Russian military leaders that if they did not defend the Tsar, they would be given positions in the new government. When they arrived expecting to receive posts, Lenin had them shot.

Saul Alinsky wrote in *Rules for Radicals,* 1971:

> The essence of Lenin's speeches during this period was 'They have the guns and therefore we are for peace and for reformation through the ballot. When we have the guns then it will be through the bullet.'

Lenin followed the example of France's Reign of Terror by executing thousands in mass killings during the Red Terror of 1918. Leon Trotsky wrote in 1920:

> The severity of the proletarian dictatorship in Russia,

let us point out here, was conditioned by no less difficult circumstances than the French Revolution.

Lenin initially had few followers, but his skillful use of terror as a coercive tactic caused people to panic and unwittingly surrendered their freedoms. He wrote:

It is necessary–secretly and urgently to prepare the terror.

This followed Machiavelli's advice:

No enterprise is more likely to succeed than one concealed from the enemy until it is ripe for execution.

History repeated itself. Just as the French Revolution overthrew King Louis XVI by promising followers equality in a socialist "fraternity," but ended with a dictator Napoleon, so the Russian Revolution overthrew Tsar Nicholas II by promising followers equality in a socialist system, only to end up with a dictator Lenin.

Lenin sent a telegram to his socialist revolutionaries in the city of Nizhny Novgorod with instructions "to introduce mass terror." He instituted a policy of "dekulakization" – the intentional killing off of millions of middle-class "kulak" farmers and small businessmen, as they were the only ones with resources to challenge the power of the new communist ruling class.

Lenin claimed to champion common workers – "the proletariat," by eliminating the middle-class – "the bourgeoisie." He is attributed with saying:

The way to crush the bourgeoisie is to grind them between the millstones of taxation and inflation.

Lenin wrote in *State and Revolution* (1917):

The dictatorship of the proletariat will produce a series of restrictions of liberty in the case of the ... capitalists. We must crush them ... Their resistance must be broken by force ... There must also be violence, and there cannot be liberty or democracy.

He instructed:

Comrades! The kulak uprising in your five districts must be crushed without pity ... You must make example of these people. Hang (I mean hang publicly, so that people see it) at least 100 kulaks, rich bastards, and known bloodsuckers. Publish their names. Seize all their grain.

Single out the hostages per my instructions in yesterday's telegram. Do all this so that for miles around people see it all, understand it, tremble, and tell themselves that we are killing the bloodthirsty kulaks and that we will continue to do so ...

Yours, Lenin. P.S. Find tougher people.

Lenin had not anticipated that the killing off kulak farmers would devastate food production. As a result, it created the horrendous national famine of 1921–1922, in which an estimated 5 million starved to death.

Lenin stated (Maxim Gorky, *V.I. Lenin*, 1924):

I can't listen to music very often, it affects my nerves. I want to say sweet, silly things, and pat the little heads of people ... These days, one can't pat anyone on the head ... they might bite your hand off. Hence, you have to beat people's little heads, beat mercilessly, although ideally we are against doing any violence to people ... Hm–what a devilishly difficult job!

Lenin killed some of his followers, writing in "Party Organization and Party Literature," *Novaya Zhizn,* November 13, 1905:

The party ... would inevitably break up ... if it did not cleanse itself of people advocating anti-party views.

George Orwell explained:

Bolsheviks could not have retained power ... without the most rigorous and truly iron discipline in (their) party.

∽

CHAPTER 50
JOSEPH STALIN

Joseph Stalin was influenced by Darwin, as recounted in the book *Landmarks in the Life of Stalin*:

At a very early age, while still a pupil in the ecclesiastical school, Comrade Stalin developed a critical mind and revolutionary sentiments. He began to read Darwin and became an atheist.

Stalin commented of state-controlled indoctrination:

There are three things that we do to disabuse the minds of our seminary students. We had to teach them the age of the earth, the geologic origin, and Darwin's teachings.

When Lenin fell ill, Stalin seized the authoritarian title of "Secretary–General and Premier." Too sick to stop Stalin, Lenin confided in 1922, two years before his death, that after years of promising his followers that if they violently killed off the old order they would achieve a wonderful classless society, in the end it was all for naught, a failure, as Stalin ruled as a dictator:

Comrade Stalin, having become Secretary–General, has unlimited authority concentrated in his hands.

A theme expounded in Shakespeare's play Macbeth was reflected in a line attributed to Lenin:

Authority poisons everybody who takes authority on himself.

Lenin wrote January 4, 1923:

Stalin is too crude, and ... unacceptable in the position of General Secretary. I therefore propose to comrades that they should devise a means of removing him from this job.

In 1924, after years of tormenting headaches, Lenin died. Though he and Stalin had been political opponents, Stalin doctored a fake photo and circulated it to make it look as if he and Lenin were good friends.

Stalin rewrote history, tearing down statues and renaming streets, museums, and ships, even changing the name of St. Petersburg to Leningrad.

Under Stalin's iron fist Soviet dictatorship:

• privacy was nonexistent; • press was

censored; • free speech disappeared; • healthcare was rationed; • economy was regulated; • private industry was collectivized; • political dissent was punished; • media and entertainment were propagandized; • children's education became indoctrination; • marriage and families were subject to social engineering; • religion was suppressed; and • human life was valued only by its usefulness to the soviet society.

To stay in power, Stalin conducted purges and orchestrated famines, resulting in an estimated 40 million deaths. "Fear and food" were tools of control:

• people were kept in constant fear that the government agencies monitoring them would falsely accuse them and drag them away in the night; and

• people were kept in a continual food shortage, so they could not have the resources to rebel.

Stalin engineered a food shortage that killed millions of anti-Stalinist peasants. Richard Pipes discussed in *Communism–A History* (Random House, 2001):

To break the resistance of the peasants in the Ukraine, the North Caucasus, and the Kazakhstan, Stalin inflicted on these areas in 1932–33 an artificial famine, shipping out all the food from entire districts and deploying the army to prevent the starving peasants from migrating in search of nourishment.

It is estimated that between 6 and 7 million people perished in this man-made catastrophe.

In his Great Purge of 1936–38, Stalin executed an estimated 1.2 million Communist Party members, government officials, military leaders, and peasants who were accused of being disloyal.

Just a rumor of holding politically incorrect views or associating with "enemies of the people," would result in a person losing their job, being arrested and executed, or being one of the 4.5 million people sentenced to "gulag" labor camps.

His notorious 1937 order No. 00447 called for the mass executions and exile of "socially harmful elements" as "enemies of the people."

Total deaths during Stalin's dictatorship range from 8 to 61 million. Roosevelt explained to the American Youth Congress, Washington, D.C., February 10, 1940:

> I disliked the regimentation under communism. I abhorred the indiscriminate killings of thousands of innocent victims. I heartily deprecated the banishment of religion ...

> I, with many of you, hoped that Russia would work out its own problems, and that its government would eventually become a peace-loving, popular government ... That hope is today ... shattered ...

> The Soviet Union, as everybody who has the courage to face the fact knows, is run by a dictatorship as absolute as any other dictatorship in the world.

Orwell wrote in his original preface to *Animal Farm* (*George Orwell: Some Materials for a Bibliography,* 1953):

> It was of the utmost importance ... that people in western Europe should see the Soviet regime for what it really was ... a hierarchical society, in which the rulers have no more reason to give up their power than any other ruling class.

Richard Nixon wrote:

> Russia was ... governed by a tyranny ... The Soviet term is "the cult of personality" ... Stalin and his followers ... became infected with a mistaken view of Stalin's proper role ...

> Stalin ruled without the check of constitutional forms ... In the words of Aristotle, written some 23 centuries ago, "This is why we do not permit a man to rule ... because a man rules in his own interest, and becomes a tyrant."

> It is plain that Stalin ... became a tyrant.

C.S. Lewis warned in *The Abolition of Man,* 1943:

I am very doubtful whether history shows us one example of a man who, having stepped outside traditional morality and attained power, has used that power benevolently.

Judge Learned Hand wrote:

By far the most powerful of all the European nations (Russia) had been a convert to communism for over thirty years; its leaders were the most devoted and potent proponents of the faith; no such movement in Europe of East to West had arisen since Islam.

∞

CHAPTER 51

WESTERN ELITES BACK SOCIALISM

Democrat President Woodrow Wilson had naively supported Lenin, even sending the U.S. Army 339th Infantry Regiment to intervene on Lenin's behalf in North Russia. Wilson told Congress, April 2, 1917:

Does not every American feel ... hope for the future peace of the world by the wonderful and heartening things that have been happening within the last few weeks in Russia?

Beginning in 1920, the Communist Party USA ran candidates for U.S. President every year till World War II when Democrat President Franklin Roosevelt made a treaty with Stalin against Hitler. After that, the Communist Party USA, which received direct funding from the U.S.S.R., supported Democrat Presidential candidates.

Reagan stated October 27, 1964:

In 1936, Mr. Democrat himself, Al Smith, the great American, came before the American people and charged that the leadership of his Party was taking ... (it) down the road under the banners of Marx, Lenin, and Stalin.

And he walked away from his Party, and he never returned ... To this day, the leadership of that Party has been taking (it) ... down the road in the image of the labor Socialist Party.

On January 25, 1936, Alfred E. Smith, the four-term Democrat Governor of New York and the 1928 Democrat Presidential Candidate, opposed Democrat President Franklin Roosevelt's New Deal Program:

> I was born in the Democratic Party and I expect to die in it ... I must make a confession. It is not easy for me to ... talk ... against the Democratic Administration ... but ... I put patriotism above partisanship ...

> Make a test for yourself. Just get the platform of the Democratic Party, and get the platform of the Socialist Party, and lay them down on your dining room table ... Study the record of the present Administration ... and you will put your hand on the Socialist platform ... Men have stolen the livery of the church to do the work of the devil ...

> What is worrying me is where does that leave us millions of Democrats? ... We can either take on the mantle of hypocrisy or we can take a walk ... This is pretty tough on me to have to go at my own party this way, but I submit that there is a limit to blind loyalty ...

> In conclusion let me give this solemn warning. There can be only one Capitol – Washington or Moscow. There can be only one atmosphere of government, the clear, pure, fresh air of free America, or the foul breath of Communistic Russia.

> There can be only one flag, the Stars and Stripes, or the Red Flag of the godless union of the Soviet. There can be only one National Anthem. The Star Spangled Banner or the Internationale (Soviet Anthem).

George Orwell explained the mentality of leftist professors and "champagne socialists," May 18, 1944:

> Intellectuals are more totalitarian in outlook than the common people. On the whole, the English

intelligentsia have opposed Hitler, but only at the price of accepting Stalin.

Most of them are perfectly ready for dictatorial methods, secret police, systematic falsification of history etc. so long as they feel that it is on "our" side.

Solzhenitsyn wrote in *The Gulag Archipelago* (1973):

A state of war only serves as an excuse for domestic tyranny.

Orwell wrote in "Second Thoughts on James Burnham" (*Polemic,* summer 1946):

It was only after the Soviet régime became unmistakably totalitarian that English intellectuals ... began to show an interest in it ...

English ... intelligentsia is really voicing their secret wish ... to destroy the old ... and usher in a hierarchical society where the intellectual can at last get his hands on the whip.

Orwell wrote in his preface to *Animal Farm* (*George Orwell: Some Materials for a Bibliography,* 1953):

Intelligentsia in a country like England cannot understand the U.S.S.R. ... Totalitarianism is completely incomprehensible to them.

∽

CHAPTER 52

ALEXANDER SOLZHENITSYN

One of those arrested under Stalin's regime was Alexander Solzhenitsyn, born December 11, 1918. He was detained for writing a letter criticizing Stalin and spent 11 years in "gulag" labor camps.

He began secretly compiling horror stories of life in the gulags. For several years of his imprisonment, 1947–1952, he was denied pen and paper, so he composed and memorized chapters as poems.

He put these accounts into his book *The First Circle,* 1968, and then *The Gulag Archipelago.*

An "archipelago" is a chain of islands in the ocean.

Solzhenitsyn used this metaphor to describe a chain of FEMA–style citizen detention camps across Russia.

Horrendous camps were also used by:

> Hitler's National Socialist Workers Party; Pol Pot's Communist Khmer Rouge; Communist Chinese; and North Korea.

Alexander Solzhenitsyn's writings were smuggled out of the Soviet Union and translated. They quickly became internationally popular, leading him to receive the Nobel Prize for Literature in 1970, even though he was still in the U.S.S.R.

He wrote in his Nobel Prize acceptance letter:

> During all the years until 1961, not only was I convinced I should never see a single line of mine in print in my lifetime, but, also, I scarcely dared allow any of my close acquaintances to read anything I had written because I feared this would become known.

International pressure led to Solzhenitsyn being expelled from Russia on February 12, 1974.

Warning naive American students of the horrible realities of socialism, Alexander Solzhenitsyn stated in Washington, D.C., June 30, 1975:

> In pre-revolutionary Russia ... there were attempts on the Tsar's life ... During these years about 17 persons a year were executed ...

> The Cheka (Lenin's Communist Secret Police) ... in 1918 and 1919 ... executed, without trial, more than a thousand persons a month! ...

> At the height of Stalin's terror in 1937–38 ... more than 40,000 persons were shot per month!

> Here are the figures: 17 a year ... 1,000 a month, more than 40,000 a month!

Solzhenitsyn addressed Harvard, June 8, 1978:

> (In) Soviet society ... there is a multitude of prisoners in our camps who are termed criminals, but most of them never committed any crime;

they merely tried to defend themselves against a lawless state by resorting to means outside the legal framework.

Solzhenitsyn explained how government–run healthcare provided a cover for Stalin's political opponents to be "diagnosed" with psychiatric problems and given compulsory "treatment."

Solzhenitsyn stated in June 30, 1975:

> It is not detente (a lessening of tension) if we here ... can spend our time agreeably while over there people are groaning and dying and in psychiatric hospitals. Doctors are making their evening rounds ... injecting people with drugs which destroy their brain ...
>
> There are tens of thousands of political prisoners in our country ... under compulsory psychiatric treatment.

Near the end of World War II, in declining health, President Roosevelt attended the Tehran Conference, and the Yalta Conference, where he surrendered half of Europe to the iron-fisted control of the Union of Soviet Socialist Republics, led by Stalin.

Solzhenitsyn stated:

> Roosevelt, in Tehran, during one of his toasts, said ... "I do not doubt that the three of us" (meaning Roosevelt, Churchill and Stalin) "lead our peoples in accordance with their desires" ... We were astonished. We thought, "when we reach Europe, we will meet the Americans, and we will tell them."

He added:

> I was among the troops that were marching towards the Elbe (River) ... A little bit more and I would have ... shaken the hands of your American soldiers.
>
> But just before that ... I was taken off to prison and my meeting did not take place ... After a delay of 30 years, my Elbe is here today. I am here to tell you ... what ... we wanted to tell you then.

✥

CHAPTER 53
MATERIALISTIC HUMANISM

Communists replaced the Christian religion with materialistic atheism. Church property was confiscated or destroyed. Free speech and free press were prohibited. Private property was abolished.

Herbert Hoover warned at a reception on his 80th birthday in West Branch, Iowa, August 10, 1954:

> I have witnessed on the ground in 20 nations the workings of the philosophy of that anti-Christ, Karl Marx. There rises constantly in my mind the forces which make for progress and those which may corrode away the safeguards of freedom in America ...

> I want to say something ... not in the tones of Jeremiah but in the spirit of Saint Paul ... Our Founding Fathers did not invent the priceless boon of individual freedom and respect for the dignity of men. That great gift to mankind sprang from the Creator and not from governments ...

> Today the socialist virus and poison gas generated by Karl Marx and Friedreich Engels have spread into every nation on the earth ... Their dogma is absolute materialism which defies truth and religious faith ...

Hoover continued:

> A nation is strong or weak, it thrives or perishes upon what it believes to be true. If our youth are rightly instructed in the faith of our fathers ... then our power will be stronger ...

> To this whole gamut of socialist infections, I say to you ... God has blessed us with another wonderful word – "heritage."

> The great documents of that heritage are not from Karl Marx. They are from the Bible, the Declaration of Independence and the Constitution

of the United States. Within them alone can the safeguards of freedom survive.

Winston Churchill stated, March 5, 1946:

The power of the state is exercised without restraint, either by dictators or by compact oligarchies operating through a privileged party and a political police ...

We must never cease to proclaim in fearless tones the great principles of freedom and the rights of man which are the joint inheritance of the English-speaking world and which through the Magna Carta, the Bill of Rights, the Habeas Corpus, trial by jury, and the English common law find their most famous expression in the American Declaration of Independence.

Solzhenitsyn explained at Harvard, June 8, 1978, how the Judeo–Christian concept of the individual, minus God, morphed into materialist humanism:

The West kept advancing ... with a dazzling progress. And all of a sudden it found itself in its present state of weakness ...

The mistake must be at ... the very foundation of thought in modern times. I refer to the prevailing Western view of the world which was born in the Renaissance and has found political expression since the Age of Enlightenment – rationalistic humanism ... autonomy of man from any higher force above him.

It could also be called anthropocentricity, with man seen as the center of all ...

The humanistic way of thinking ... did not admit the existence of intrinsic evil in man, nor did it see any task higher than the attainment of happiness on earth. It started modern Western civilization on the dangerous trend of worshiping man and his material needs ...

He continued:

Everything beyond physical well-being and

the accumulation of material goods ... were left outside the area of attention of state and social systems, as if human life did not have any higher meaning.

Thus gaps were left open for evil ... Mere freedom per se does not in the least solve all the problems of human life ...

Solzhenitsyn added:

In early democracies, as in American democracy at the time of its birth, all individual human rights were granted on the ground that man is God's creature.

That is, freedom was given to the individual conditionally, in the assumption of his constant religious responsibility ...

It would have seemed quite impossible, in America, that an individual be granted boundless freedom with no purpose, simply for the satisfaction of his whims.

Subsequently, however, all such limitations were eroded everywhere in the West; a total emancipation occurred from the moral heritage of Christian centuries with their great reserves of mercy and sacrifice.

State systems were becoming ever more materialistic. The West has finally achieved the rights of man, and even excess, but man's sense of responsibility to God and society has grown dimmer and dimmer ...

The world has found itself in a harsh spiritual crisis ...

As humanism in its development was becoming more and more materialistic, it also increasingly allowed concepts to be used first by socialism and then by communism, so that Karl Marx was able to say, in 1844, that "communism is naturalized humanism ..."

He continued:

Socialism: boundless materialism; freedom

from religion and religious responsibility (which under communist regimes attain the stage of anti-religious dictatorship) ...

All of communism's rhetorical vows revolve around Man ... and his earthly happiness ... Materialism ... is farthest to the left ... always proves to be ... more attractive ...

Confucianism or Islam did not give birth to humanism, but rather it evolved out of the Biblical concept of the individual. Humanism then deleted the idea of mankind being made in the Divine image, and replaced it with mankind being divine.

Solzhenitsyn explained:

Humanism ... lost its Christian heritage ... Liberalism was inevitably pushed aside by radicalism; radicalism had to surrender to socialism; and socialism could not stand up to communism.

Solzhenitsyn was struck by seeing individuals who have lived under communism rejecting it, yet liberal Western professors keep promoting it:

In our Eastern countries, communism has suffered a complete ideological defeat ... yet Western intellectuals still look at it with considerable interest and empathy ...

It has made man the measure of all things on earth — imperfect man, who is never free of pride, self-interest, envy, vanity, and dozens of other defects ...

On the way from the Renaissance to our days we have enriched our experience, but we have lost the concept of a Supreme Complete Entity which used to restrain our passions and our irresponsibility.

We have placed too much hope in politics and social reforms, only to find out that we were being deprived of our most precious possession: our spiritual life ...

If, as claimed by humanism, man was born

only to be happy, he would not be born to die.

Since his body is doomed to death, his task on earth evidently must be more spiritual: not a total engrossment in everyday life, not the search for the best ways to obtain material goods and then their carefree consumption.

It has to be the fulfillment of a permanent, earnest duty so that one's life journey may become above all an experience of moral growth: to leave life a better human being than one started it ...

Only by the voluntary nurturing in ourselves of freely accepted and serene self-restraint can mankind rise above the world stream of materialism ...

Solzhenitsyn added:

Today it would be retrogressive to hold on to the ossified (obsolete) formulas of the Enlightenment. Social dogmatism leaves us helpless before the trials of our times ...

Is it true that man is above everything? Is there no Superior Spirit above him? Is it right that man's life and society's activities should be ruled by material expansion above all?...

He concluded:

If the world has not approached its end, it has reached a major watershed in history, equal in importance to the turn from the Middle Ages to the Renaissance.

It will demand from us a spiritual blaze; we shall have to rise to a new height of vision, to a new level of life, where our physical nature will not be cursed, as in the Middle Ages, but even more importantly, our spiritual being will not be trampled upon, as in the Modern Era ... No one on earth has any other way left but — upward!

President Ronald Reagan began his address at Berlin's Brandenburg Gate, June 12, 1987:

Twenty-four years ago, President John F.

Kennedy visited Berlin, speaking to the people of this city and the world ...

Behind me stands a wall that encircles the free sectors of this city, part of a vast system of barriers that divides the entire continent of Europe. From the Baltic, south, those barriers cut across Germany in a gash ...

There remain armed guards and checkpoints all the same – still a restriction on the right to travel, still an instrument to impose upon ordinary men and women the will of a totalitarian state ...

The most fundamental distinction of all between East and West ... the totalitarian world produces backwardness because it does such violence to the spirit, thwarting the human impulse to create, to enjoy, to worship.

The totalitarian world finds even symbols of love and of worship an affront.

Reagan added:

Just as truth can flourish only when the journalist is given freedom of speech, so prosperity can come about only when the farmer and businessman enjoy economic freedom ...

There stands before the entire world one great and inescapable conclusion: Freedom leads to prosperity ...

General Secretary Gorbachev, if you seek peace, if you seek prosperity for the Soviet Union and Eastern Europe, if you seek liberalization: Come here to this gate! Mr. Gorbachev, open this gate! Mr. Gorbachev, tear down this wall!

CHAPTER 54

CLARENCE MANION

Clarence Manion, Dean of Notre Dame Law School, was chosen by President Dwight D. Eisenhower to chair a commission to return to the states powers that had been usurped by the Federal government during

Roosevelt's New Deal Era.

Eisenhower declined Manion's recommendations in favor of a Republican big government. Manion was released from the administration but continued his cause, writing "The Constitution of the United States versus Communism," November 19, 1962:

> Never before in the history of the human race has atheism – naked, materialistic, power-hungry, activated atheism – ever mounted its horse and started to ride across the world and do it so successfully. Communism is this activation of atheism. This is the personalization of anti-God. This is Armageddon.

> And anybody in this room who has a shred of belief in God or immortality or in his or her personal responsibility ... must recognize that the understanding and the defeat of communism is the first order of business on the part of everybody who has a shred of interest in the perpetuation of Christian civilization. This thing must be destroyed.

Manion pioneered conservative talk radio with *The Manion Forum* during the 1950s–60s, influencing leaders such as California Governor Ronald Reagan. His radio guests included Jesse Helms, Strom Thurmond, Harry Byrd Sr., Barry Goldwater, Henry Regnery, Stan Evans, and Phyllis Schlafly. He was on the board of the Committee to Proclaim Liberty with Conrad Hilton, Cecile B. DeMille, Douglas MacArthur, Herbert Hoover, and Eddie Rickenbacker.

∽

CHAPTER 55

FIFTH COLUMN

Whereas Hitler's National Socialist Workers Party was nationalistic, espousing racial superiority of the Aryan race, Stalin's socialism was an international movement, infiltrating and mobilizing any race through a psychological weapon called the "fifth column."

The term "fifth column" referred to ancient warfare, where two columns of soldiers were in the middle of the battlefield, with two flanks on either side. The fifth column consisted of spies who had infiltrated the enemy camp to demoralize and confuse them.

This practice was used by Philip II of Macedon, the father of Alexander the Great, who took gold from the mines near the Greek city of Amphipolis and used it to bribe citizens of Athens to sow division in the city.

The paid betrayers and bribed politicians organized around themselves naive people who believed their propaganda, later referred to as "useful idiots."

A classic example of naive people incited for political gain was Mark Anthony's speech at Julius Caesar's funeral in 44 BC. Shakespeare's play *Julius Caesar,* 1599, portrayed Mark Anthony beginning with a calming tone: "Friends, Romans, countrymen, lend me your ears."

Then, he used charged rhetoric to stoke mob emotions with hatred, revenge and violence. Lighting a proverbial fire, he said "Now let it work. Mischief, thou art afoot. Take thou what course thou wilt."

Cicero addressed the Roman Senate, c.42 BC:

> A nation can survive its fools and even the ambitious. But it cannot survive treason from within. An enemy at the gates is less formidable, for he is known and he carries his banners openly against the city.

> But the traitor moves among those within the gates freely, his sly whispers rustling through all alleys, heard in the very halls of government itself ...

> He works secretly and unknown in the night to undermine the pillars of a city; he infects the body politic so that it can no longer resist. A murderer is less to be feared.

In 1936, during the Spanish Civil War, the Nationalist General Emilio Mola marched toward Madrid with four columns of soldiers, having supporters inside the city as a "fifth column" to undermine the Republican government from within.

While in Madrid, Ernest Hemingway wrote a play which he included in his 1938 book *The Fifth Column*.

Psychological warfare tactics were further developed during World War II. Roosevelt stated May 16, 1940:

> We have seen the treacherous use of the "fifth column" by which persons supposed to be peaceful visitors were actually a part of an enemy unit of occupation.
>
> Lightning (fast) attacks, capable of destroying airplane factories and munition works hundreds of miles behind the lines, are a part of the new technique of modern war ...
>
> We must be strong in heart and mind; strong in our faith ... This nation requires also a toughness of moral and physical fiber ... characteristics of a free people ... a people willing to defend a way of life that is precious to them all, a people who put their faith in God.

Roosevelt stated December 29, 1940:

> Their secret emissaries are active in our own and in neighboring countries. They seek to stir up ... dissension to cause internal strife. They try to turn capital against labor, and vice versa.
>
> They try to reawaken long slumbering racial and religious enmities which should have no place in this country ... These trouble-breeders have but one purpose. It is to divide our people into hostile groups and to destroy our unity and shatter our will to defend ourselves ...
>
> There are also American citizens, many of them in high places, who, unwittingly in most cases, are aiding and abetting the work of these agents.
>
> I do not charge these American citizens with being foreign agents. But I do charge them with doing exactly the kind of work that the dictators

want done in the United States.

Following World War II, Britain, France, Germany and other colonial powers gave independence to their former colonies. This left a power vacuum which the Soviet Union sought to fill by gaining control over these newly independent nations.

Winston Churchill mentioned Soviet use of "fifth columns" in his famous "Iron Curtain" speech at Westminster College, Fulton, Missouri, March 5, 1946:

> In a great number of countries, far from the Russian frontiers and throughout the world, communist "fifth columns" are established and work in complete unity and absolute obedience to the directions they receive from the communist center.

> Except in the British Commonwealth and in the United States where communism is in its infancy, the communist parties or "fifth columns" constitute a growing challenge and peril to Christian civilization ...

> Last time I saw it all coming and cried aloud to my own fellow-countrymen and to the world, but no one paid any attention.

Fifth column methods included: espionage, propaganda, infiltration of college campuses, getting Marxist professors hired, establishing student groups to recruit revolutionaries, infiltrate music and movie industries to produce entertainment eroding moral fiber, malign patriotism, gain control of the leadership of all political parties, place moles in government bureaucracies and courts, and finally, sway churches to de-emphasize salvation through the Gospel of Jesus Christ and replace it with social justice issues.

Like a software virus infecting computers, fifth column tactics infected Western Civilization with socialist ideology. Reagan stated in 1961:

> Now back in 1927 an American socialist, Norman Thomas, six times candidate for president on the Socialist Party ticket, said the American people would never vote for socialism. But he said

under the name of liberalism the American people will adopt every fragment of the socialist program.

Upton Sinclair, best known for his 1906 novel *The Jungle*, formed a socialist utopian community in Englewood, New Jersey, the Helicon Home Colony, which burned down within a year. He then ran for U.S. Congress as a Socialist Party candidate, but lost.

Upton Sinclair wrote to Norman Thomas in 1951:

> The American People will take Socialism, but they won't take the label. I certainly proved it ... Running on the Socialist ticket I got 60,000 votes, and running on the slogan to 'End Poverty in California' I got 879,000. I think we simply have to recognize the fact ... There is no use attacking it by a front attack, it is much better to out-flank them.

Former Democrat New York Governor and Presidential Candidate Alfred Smith opposed Democrat Roosevelt's New Deal Program, January 25, 1936:

> What are these dangers that I see? The first is the arraignment of class against class. It has been freely predicted that if we were ever to have civil strife again in this country, it would come from the appeal to passion and prejudices that comes from the demagogues that would incite one class of our people against the other ...
>
> The next thing that I view as being dangerous ... is government by bureaucracy instead of ... government by law.
>
> Let me quote something from the President (Roosevelt) ... "In thirty-four months we have built up new instruments of public power" ... Now, I interpret that to mean: If you are going to have an autocrat, take me, but be very careful about the other fellow ...
>
> We don't want autocrats ... we wouldn't even take a good one ...
>
> The next danger ... is the vast building up of new

bureaus of government, draining the resources of our people into a common pool and redistributing them ... by the whim of a bureaucratic autocracy ... The alphabet was exhausted in the creation of new departments ...

How can you balance a budget if you insist upon spending more money than you take in? ...

This country was organized on the principles of representative democracy, and you can't mix Socialism or Communism with that. They are like oil and water; they refuse to mix ...

How do you suppose all this happened? Here is the way it happened: The young Brain Trusters (Columbia and Harvard professors advising Roosevelt) caught the Socialists in swimming and they ran away with their clothes ... They want to disguise themselves as Norman Thomas or Karl Marx, or Lenin, or any of the rest of that bunch ...

This is the first time that I have known a party, upon such a huge scale, not only not to carry out the planks, but to do the directly opposite thing to what they promised ...

Stop attempting to alter the form and structure of our Government ... I suggest that they read their Oath of Office to support the Constitution of the United States. And I ask them to remember that they took that oath with their hands on the Holy Bible, thereby calling upon God Almighty Himself to witness their solemn promise.

Soviet leader Nikita Khrushschev reportedly told Ezra Taft Benson, Eisenhower's Secretary of Agriculture, in 1959:

Your children's children will live under communism. You Americans are so gullible.

No, you won't accept communism outright, but we'll keep feeding you small doses of socialism until you will finally wake up and find that you already have communism.

We won't have to fight you; We'll so weaken

your economy, until you fall like overripe fruit into our hands.

General Douglas MacArthur warned the Michigan legislature in Lansing, Michigan, May 15, 1952:

Talk of imminent threat to our national security through ... external force is pure nonsense.

It is not of any external threat that I concern myself but rather of insidious forces working from within which have already so drastically altered the character of our free institutions – those institutions we proudly called the American way of life.

Eisenhower addressed Congress, February 2, 1953:

No single country, even one so powerful as ours, can alone defend the liberty of all nations threatened by communist aggression from without and subversion within.

FBI Director J. Edgar Hoover stated:

The communist threat from without must not blind us to the communist threat from within.

The latter is reaching into the very heart of America through its espionage agents and a cunning, defiant, and lawless communist party, which is fanatically dedicated to the Marxist cause of world enslavement and destruction of the foundations of our republic.

✺

CHAPTER 56
THE COLD WAR

The Cold War was at its height from 1947 to 1991, with nuclear attacks prevented by mutually assured destruction (MAD) and proxy wars fought between the U.S. and the U.S.S.R. and China.

Countries experienced their political parties infiltrated, Communist Parties being established, coup d'etat plots to removed leaders, and military conquests.

During this time, 45 countries became communist

satellites, often with brutal purges which killed millions. Countries included:

Afghanistan, Albania, Angola, Armenia, Azerbaijan, Belarus, Benin, Bosnia, Bulgaria, Cambodia, China, Congo, Cuba, Croatia, Czech Republic, East Germany, Egypt, Eritrea, Estonia, Ethiopia, Georgia, Herzegovina, Indonesia, Hungary, Kazakhstan, Kyrgyzstan, Laos, Latvia, Lebanon, Lithuania, Macedonia, Moldova, Mongolia, Montenegro, Mozambique, Nicaragua, North Korea, Poland, Romania, Russia, Serbia, Slovakia, Slovenia, Somalia, South Yemen, Syria, Tajikistan, Tibet, Turkmenistan, Ukraine, Uzbekistan, Vietnam, Yemen, and Yugoslavia.

The main takeover tactic was to:

- Find groups within a country with grievances;
- Organize these groups to protest and riot;
- Escalate riots to violence and bloodshed;
- Bribe, threaten, and co-opt media to control the narrative of blaming the existing leadership;
- In the midst of the national confusion, carry out a coup or a rigged election overthrowing the country's representative government and replacing it with a totalitarian dictatorship;
- Citizens are initially relieved that order is restored but when the dust settles, they will have a rude awakening to find their freedoms gone.

The U.S.S.R.'s Committee for State Security (Komitet Gosudarstvennoy Bezopasnosti – KGB) organized clandestine opposition groups to destabilize pro-western countries.

The KGB, with the help of Fidel Castro, created the National Liberation Army of Columbia (FARC) in 1964; and with the help of Ernesto "Che" Guevara, created the National Liberation Army of Bolivia (ELN).

In 1964, the KGB, with the help of Yasir Arafat, the Egyptian-born nephew of Mufti Amin al-Husseini, created the Palestine Liberation Organization (PLO).

In 1968, the KGB created "liberation theology" to promote a progressive Marxist "social justice" agenda of class-warfare to destabilize western democracies.

In response, the U.S. sought to keep countries free, with the CIA mimicking KGB tactics.

In the 1952, U.S. Secretary of State Dean Acheson, CIA Director Allen Dulles, and CIA Operative Kermit "Kim" Roosevelt, Jr., grandson of Theodore Roosevelt, participated in Project FF with elements of Egypt's military to replace Egypt's King Farouk and replace him with Gamal Nassar.

In 1953, Iran's Prime Minister Mohammad Mossadegh aligned with the U.S.S.R. He nationalized the country's oil industry, taking control away from Britain's Anglo-Iranian Oil Company (BP).

Britain appealed to the U.S. for help, but Truman refused. The next President, Dwight Eisenhower, approved the CIA's first operation to overthrow a foreign government – Operation Ajax. Though controversial, had Eisenhower not responded, much of the world may have fallen to communist KGB tactics.

Orchestrated by Kermit Roosevelt Jr., Operation Ajax involved identifying groups with grievances and organizing them to protest. The news media was bribed and threatened to control the narrative of blaming Mossadegh. Radical imams were recruited, along with the most feared mobsters in Tehran, and agitators were paid to stage violent riots and attack mosques.

Relationships were cultivated within the Iranian military. When public opinion turned against Mossadegh and the country was sufficiently destabilized, the coup was carried out with Mossadegh being placed under house arrest till he died. He was replaced with the pro-West Shah Resa Pahlavi.

KGB and Communist China continued overthrowing

countries, being countered by similar CIA operations in: Guatemala, 1954; Congo, 1960; Dominican Republic, 1961; South Vietnam, 1963; Brazil, 1964; Chile, 1973; and other countries, to varying degrees with Britain's MI6, being the material for innumerable spy novels.

Secretary of State John Dulles stated April 11, 1955:

> Men face the great dilemma of whether to use force to resist aggression which imposes conditions which violate the moral law and the concept that man has his origins and his destiny in God.

At the 1954 Geneva Conference, Dulles reportedly refused to shake hands with the first Premier of the People's Republic of China, Zhou Enlai, as he orchestrated the persecutions committed by Mao Zedong's Communist Party killing an estimated 20 million.

Zhou Enlai stated:

> One of the delightful things about Americans is that they have absolutely no historical memory.

During the Cold War, Dulles described communism as "godless terrorism," stating April 11, 1955:

> Man, we read in the Holy Scriptures, was made a little lower than the angels. Should man now be made little higher than domesticated animals which serve the purpose of their human masters?

Solzhenitsyn warned at Harvard, June 8, 1978:

> Many people living in the West are dissatisfied with their own society. They despise it or accuse it of no longer being up to the level of maturity by mankind. And this causes many to sway toward socialism, which is a false and dangerous current.

Churchill noted regarding youth who felt that since ten percent of citizens were not experiencing prosperity that they should consider socialism, June 13, 1948:

> I do not at all wonder that British youth is in revolt against the morbid doctrine that nothing matters but the equal sharing of miseries, that what used to be called the "submerged tenth" can

only be rescued by bringing the other nine-tenths down to their level.

David Horowitz, a conservative author who had previously been a 1960s radical Marxist, wrote in the *Jewish World Review*, September 6, 2001:

> The social justice organizations ... protesters are the "fifth column" vanguards envisaged by Weatherman, declaring war on the Empire and plotting to tear down its walls from within.

Solzhenitsyn warned June 30, 1975:

> I ... call upon America to be more careful with its trust ... Prevent those ... from falsely using the struggle for peace and for social justice to lead you down a false road.

Friedrich Hayek wrote:

> I am certain that nothing has done so much to destroy the judicial safeguards of individual freedom as the striving after this mirage of social justice.

On February 7, 2020, MSNBC commentator Chris Matthews addressed a panel following the Democrat Presidential debate, where some of the candidates espoused socialism. Chris Matthews had stated:

> The issue of this campaign, it is that word "socialism" ... Younger people like it.

> Those of us like me, who grew up in the Cold War and saw some aspects of it if you're visiting places like Vietnam like I have, and seen countries like Cuba, being there. I've seen what socialism is like, and I don't like it. OK? It's not only not free, it doesn't frickin' work.

> My own views of the word socialist ... go back to the early nineteen fifties ... I remember the Cold War ...

> I believe that if Castro and the Reds had won the Cold War, there would have been executions in Central Park, and I might have been one of the ones being executed! And certain other people would have been there, cheering, OK?"

Two week after Matthews made those comments, MSNBC found an excuse to end his 23 year employment.

Churchill stated October 22, 1945:

> The inherent vice of capitalism is the unequal sharing of blessings. The inherent virtue of socialism is the equal sharing of miseries.

Ayn Rand wrote:

> If a businessman makes a mistake, he suffers the consequences. If a bureaucrat makes a mistake you suffer the consequences.

Churchill stated in Perth, Scotland, May 28, 1948 (*Churchill, Europe Unite: Speeches 1947 & 1948*, London: Cassell, 1950, 347):

> Socialism is the philosophy of failure, the creed of ignorance and the gospel of envy.

> Unless we free our country while time remains from the perverse doctrines of socialism, there can be no hope for recovery ... Our place in the world will be lost forever, and not only our individual self-respect but our national independence will be gone.

❧

CHAPTER 57
YURI BEZMENOV – KGB DEFECTOR

Yuri Bezmenov was a KGB agent stationed in India, who defected in 1970 to the U.S. Embassy in Greece and was given asylum in Canada. In 1984, he gave an interview to G. Edward Griffin revealing Soviet fifth column subversion methods:

> The main emphasis of the KGB ... is a slow process which we call either ideological subversion, or active measures – "activitia perionachia" in the language of the KGB, or psychological warfare ...

> It basically means is to change the perception of reality of every American to such an extent that despite the abundance of information no one is able to come to sensible conclusions in the interests

of defending themselves, their families, their community, and their country. (ie. "Gaslighting")

It is a great brainwashing process which goes very slow and is divided into four basic stages.

The first one being "demoralization." It takes from 15 to 20 years to demoralize a nation. Why that many years? Because this is the minimum number of years which requires to educate one generation of students ...

Marxist-Leninism ideology is being pumped into ... students without being challenged or counter-balanced by the basic values of Americanism ...

Even if you start right now ... educating a new generation of Americans, it will still take 15 or 20 years to turn the tide of ideological perception ...

Most of the people who graduated in the 1960s ... are now occupying the positions of power in the government, civil service, business, mass media, educational system ... They are programmed ... You cannot change their mind even if you expose them to authentic information.

Even if you prove that white is white and black is black. You cannot change the basic perception and illogical behavior ...

The demoralization process in the United States is basically completed ... Actually, it is over-fulfilled ... Not even Comrade Andropov (1911-1984) and all his experts would even dream of such a tremendous success.

Most of it is done by Americans to Americans, thanks to lack of moral standards.

As I mentioned before, exposure to true information does not matter anymore. A person who is demoralized is unable to assess true information ...

Even if I take him, by force, to the Soviet Union and show him concentration camps, he will refuse to believe it until he is going to receive a kick ... when the military boot crashes ... then he will understand, but not before that. That is the tragedy of this situation of demoralization ...

TIME Magazine described in "The Secret History of the Shadow Campaign That Saved the 2020 Election" (2/421):

> There was a conspiracy unfolding behind the scenes ... an informal alliance between left-wing activists and business titans ... a sort of implicit bargain–inspired by the summer's massive, sometimes destructive racial-justice protests – in which the forces of labor came together with the forces of capital ... much of this activity took place on the left ...

> Their work touched every aspect of the election. They got states to change voting systems and laws and helped secure hundreds of millions in public and private funding. They ... recruited armies of poll workers and got millions of people to vote by mail for the first time ... pressured social media companies ... and used data-driven strategies to fight viral smears ... executed national public-awareness campaigns ...

> This is the inside story of the conspiracy ... based on access to the group's inner workings, never-before-seen documents and interviews with dozens of those involved from across the political spectrum ... Ian Bassin, co-founder of Protect Democracy ... "But it's massively important for the country to understand that it didn't happen accidentally" ...

> The secret history of the 2020 election ... a well-funded cabal of powerful people, ranging across industries and ideologies, working together behind the scenes to influence perceptions, change rules and laws, steer media coverage and control the flow of information."

Noam Chomsky and Edward Herman wrote in *Manufacturing Consent: The Political Economy of the Mass Media* (1988):

> The media ... propagandize on behalf of the powerful societal interests that control and finance them ... accomplished ... by the editors' and working journalists' internalization of

priorities and definitions of newsworthiness that conform to the institution's policy ... The mass media of the United States are effective and powerful ideological institutions that carry out a system-supportive propaganda function.

Yuri Bezmenov continued his 1984 interview:

The next stage is "destabilization" ... This only takes from 2 to 5 years to destabilize a nation.

What matters is essentials: economy, foreign relations, defense systems ... I could never have believed 14 years ago when I landed in this part of the world that the process would go that fast ...

The next stage is "crisis." It may take only 6 weeks to bring a country to the verge of crisis. You see it in Central America now.

And after crisis, with a violent change in power, structure, and economy, you have the period of so-called "normalization" will last indefinitely.

"Normalization" is a cynical expression borrowed from Soviet propaganda. When the Soviet tanks moved into Czechoslovakia in 1968, Brezhnev said, "now brother Czechoslovakia is normalized."

This is what will happen in the United States if you allow them to destabilize your economy, to eliminate the principle of free market competition, and to put a big brother government in Washington, D.C.

The United States is in a state of war against the basic principles and the foundations of this world communist system ... If you are not scared by now, nothing can scare you ... You have literally several years to live on unless the United States wake up. The time bomb is ticking. Every second the disaster is coming closer and closer. Unlike myself, you will have nowhere to defect to ... This is the last country of freedom.

Who did the KGB recruit? Bezmenov explained:

Most of the activity of the Department was to compile ... information on individuals who were instrumental in creating public opinion: publishers, editors, journalists, actors, educationalists, professors of political science, members of Parliament, representatives of business circles ... conservative media.

Reach the filthy rich movie makers, intellectuals, so-called academic circles, cynical, ego-centric people who can look into your eyes with an angelic expression and tell you a lie.

These are the most recruit-able people. People who lack moral principles who are either too greedy or suffer from self-importance, they feel that they matter a lot. These are the people who KGB wanted very much to recruit.

What will happen to leftists? Bezmenov concluded:

Your leftists in the United States, all these professors and all these beautiful civil rights defenders, they are instrumental in the process of subversion, only to destabilize the nation. When the job is completed .. they are not needed any more. They know too much.

Some of them, when they see the Marxist-Leninists come to power, obviously, they get offended. They think that they will come to power. That will never happen, of course. They will be lined up against the wall and shot ...

They may turn into the most bitter enemies of Marxist-Leninism ... And that is what happened in Nicaragua. You remember, most of the former Marxist-Leninist either were put to prison. And one of them split and now he is working against the Sandinistas.

It happened in Grenada, when Maurice Bishop, he was already a Marxist. He was executed by a new Marxist who was more Marxist than this Marxist.

The same happened in Afghanistan. First there was Taraki. He was killed by Amin and Amin was killed by Brabak Karbakil with the help of the KGB. The same happened in Bangladesh when Mungi Burackman, the very pro-Soviet leftist, was assassinated by his own Marxist-Leninist military comrades.

It's the same pattern everywhere. The moment they serve their purpose, all these useful idiots are either executed entirely, or exiled, or put in prison. Many former Marxists in Cuba are in prison ...

Because they know too much ... the useful idiots, the leftists who are idealistically believing in the beauty of Soviet socialist system, when they get disillusioned, they become the worst enemies ... Because of the psychological shock when they will see the future ... they will revolt. They will be very unhappy, frustrated people.

A Marxist-Leninist regime does not tolerate these people. They obviously will join the leagues of dissenters, dissidents.

Unlike in present United States, there will be no place for dissent in future Marxist-Leninist America. Here ... you can get popular ... like Jane Fonda, for being dissident, for criticizing your Pentagon. In future these people will simply be squashed.

Manning Johnson similarly stated:

The white socio-liberal, philanthropic, humanitarian supporter ... while communists unite with and support them today, it is necessary to keep in mind that 'it may be necessary to denounce them tomorrow and the day after tomorrow hang them.'

CHAPTER 58
MANNING JOHNSON: RACIAL CONFLICT

Manning Johnson (1908-1959) was a black man who lost faith in America and joined the communist movement for ten years. He was the Communist Party USA's candidate for the U.S. Congress, New York's 22nd District, in 1935.

He finally came to realize that communists cared little for the plight of the black community but were simply using them to bring political division. He wrote:

> Ten years later, thoroughly disillusioned, I abandoned communism. The experiences of those years in 'outer darkness' are like a horrible nightmare.

In 1947, he testified before Congress on the subversive plots deep-state communist operatives.

In 1958, Manning Johnson wrote an exposé titled *Color, Communism and Common Sense*, with the Foreword written by Lt. Col. Archibald B. Roosevelt, son of President Theodore Roosevelt.

In 1959, less than a year after publishing his tell-all book, Johnson was killed in a suspicious automobile accident – "a veil of mystery obscures the true circumstances of Manning Johnson's death."

Johnson had written of his life's journey:

> To me, the end of capitalism would mark the beginning of an interminable period of plenty, peace, prosperity and universal comradeship. All racial and class differences and conflicts would end forever after the liquidation of the capitalists, their government and their supporters ...

> Being an idealist, I was sold this 'bill of goods' ... Like other Negroes, I experienced and saw many injustices and inequities around me based upon color, not ability.

> I was told that 'the decadent capitalist system is responsible,' that 'mass pressure' could force concessions but 'that just prolongs the life of capitalism'; that I must unite and work with all those who ... agree that capitalism must go.

> Little did I realize until I was deeply enmeshed in the red conspiracy, that ... grievances are exploited to transform idealism into a cold and ruthless weapon against the capitalist system — that this is the end toward which all the communist efforts among Negroes are directed ...

I saw communism in all its naked cruelty, ruthlessness and utter contempt of Christian attributes and passions. And, too, I saw the low value placed upon human life, the total lack of respect for the dignity of man.

Johnson continued:

After two years of practical training in organizing street demonstrations, inciting mob violence, how to fight the police and how to politically 'throw a brick and hide' ... I was given an ... intensive course in the theory and practice of red political warfare ... that changed me from a novice into a dedicated red — a professional revolutionist.

He explained further:

I began to realize the full implications of how the Negro is used as a political dupe by the Kremlin hierarchy ...

White leftists descended on Negro communities like locusts, posing as 'friends' come to help 'liberate' their black brothers ... Everything was inter-racial, an inter-racialism artificially created, cleverly devised as a camouflage of the red plot to use the Negro.

Malcolm X gave a similar statement in 1963:

The liberal is more deceitful, more hypocritical than the conservative ...

The white liberal is the one who has perfected the art of posing as the Negro's friend and benefactor, and by winning the friendship and support of the Negro, the white liberal is able to use the Negro as a pawn or a weapon in this political football game that is constantly raging between the white liberal and the white conservative ... and the white liberals control this ball through tricks or tokenism, false promises of integration and civil rights ...

The white liberals have complete cooperation of the Negro civil rights leaders who sell our people out for a few crumbs of token recognition, token gains, token progress.

Retired NBA player Charles Barkley stated on a CBS panel, April 3, 2021:

Man, I think most white people and black people are great people ... but I think our system is set up where our politicians, whether they're Republicans or Democrats, are designed to make us not like each other so they can keep their grasp of money and power. They divide and conquer.

Johnson explained how communists manipulated liberal churches to deemphasize forgiveness of sins through faith in Christ and replace it with a "social justice" message with Jesus as a Palestinian activist:

A large number of Negro ministers are all for the communists ... They in common believe that beating the racial drums is a short cut to prominence, money and the realization of personal ambitions even if the Negro masses are left prostrate and bleeding — expendables in the mad scramble for power ...

White ministers acting as missionaries, using the race angle as bait, aided in the cultivation of Negro ministers for work in the red solar system ...

The new line went like this: Jesus, the carpenter, was a worker like the communists. He was against the 'money changers,' the 'capitalists,' the 'exploiters' of that day. That is why he drove them from the temple. The communists are the modern day fighters against the capitalists or money changers. If Jesus were living today, he would be persecuted like the communists who seek to do good for the common people ...

Of all their methods used, it was generally agreed that the Church is the 'best cover for illegal work.' Where possible we should build units in the church youth organizations ... under the illegal conditions, as it will be easier to work in the church organizations.

In 1963, Rep. Albert Herlong listed communist goals in the *Congressional Record,* which included:

Discredit the Bible ... Infiltrate the churches and replace revealed religion with 'social' religion.

The Apostle Paul gave a rebuke:

For if someone comes and proclaims a Jesus other than the One we proclaimed ... or a different gospel than the one you accepted, you put up with it way too easily (2 Corinthians 11);

I am amazed how quickly you ... are turning to a different gospel — which is not even a gospel (Galatians 1).

Manning Johnson explained socialist tactics:

Setting up situations that bring about racial bitterness, violence and conflict; putting forth demands so unrealistic that race relations are worsened; attacking everybody in disagreement as reactionaries, fascists, Ku Kluxers among whites; and Uncle Toms among Negroes, constitute the red's pattern of operation ...

Stirring up race and class conflict is the basis of all discussion of the communist party's work ...

The evil genius, Stalin, and the other megalomaniacal leaders in Moscow ordered the use of all racial, economic and social differences, no matter how small or insignificant, to start local fires of discontent, conflict and revolt ...

Black rebellion was what Moscow wanted. Bloody racial conflict would split America. During the confusion, demoralization and panic would set in. Then finally, the reds say:

'Workers stop work, many of them seize arms ... Street fights become frequent ... Seize the principal government offices, invade the residences of the President and his Cabinet members, arrest them, declare the old regime abolished, establish their own power ...'

What if one or five million Negroes die ... is not

the advance of the cause worth it? A communist is not a sentimentalist. He does not grieve over the loss of life in the advancement of communism.

This plot to use the Negroes as the spearhead, or as expendables, was concocted by Stalin in 1928, nearly ten years after the formation of the world organization of communism ...

From the bloody gun battles at Camp Hill, Alabama (1931), to the present ... the heavy hand of communism has moved, stirring up racial strife, creating confusion, hate and bitterness so essential to the advancement of the red cause.

Manning Johnson continued:

The reds and so-called progressives never spend money on projects to 'help' the Negroes unless these projects pay off in race conflict and animosity ... resentment that can be exploited ...

Some people describe New York City as a 'melting pot' ... German sections, Italian sections, Irish sections, Jewish sections, Puerto Rican sections, Chinese sections, Negro sections, etc ... like five fingers on the hand, yet they are one solid fist as Americans.

The communists try to exploit these national, racial and religious differences in order to weaken, undermine and subjugate America to Moscow.

Like a serpent, they use guile to seduce each group. The communists, through propaganda, have sold a number of Negro intellectuals the idea that the Negro section is a ghetto; that white Americans created it, set its geographical boundaries; that it is the product of race hate and the inhumanity of white Americans.

Therefore, it is a struggle of Negro against 'white oppressors' for emancipation ... Obviously, this line, deliberately spread by the communists, leads to the worst kind of mischief. It strengthens and creates racial prejudices and lays the basis for sharp racial conflicts ...

Johnson explained:

Blaming others may be the easy way, but it is only a short cut to communist slavery ...

Reds called those persons 'Uncle Toms' who sought solution of the race problem through the medium of education, patience, understanding and discussion which would lead to mutual agreement.

Since any program leading to a peaceful solution of the race problem automatically excludes and dooms red efforts among Negroes, it goes without saying that the reds are going to oppose it ... They must 'be discredited and isolated from the masses.'

So, in addition to the tags of 'enemy of the race,' 'tool of the white ruling class,' 'traitor to the race,' the reds have added the opprobrium of 'Uncle Tom.'

In their usual diabolically clever way, the reds took the name of a fine, sincere and beloved character made famous in the greatest indictment of chattel slavery and transformed him into a dirty, low, sneaky, treacherous, groveling, snivering coward.' This the reds did in order to make the name 'Uncle Tom' the symbol of social, economic and political leprosy.

Today, the name 'Uncle Tom' among Negroes ranks with the term 'McCarthyism' generally, turning many ministers into moral cowards, many politicians into scared jackrabbits ... No man dare stand up and proclaim convictions counter to red agitation without running the certain risk of being pilloried ...

Johnson continued:

The top white communist leaders know that ... differences can be used to play race against race, nationality against nationality, class against class, etc., to advance the cause of communism ...

Under the guise of a campaign for Negro rights, set race against race in the cold-blooded struggle for power.

Franklin Roosevelt told Congress, January 3, 1940:

Doctrines that set group against group, faith against faith, race against race, class against class, fanning the fires of hatred in men too despondent, too desperate to think for themselves, were used as rabble-rousing slogans on which dictators could ride to power. And once in power they could saddle their tyrannies on whole nations.

Manning continued:

Social equality for the Negro is a major slogan of the communists. They use it on the one hand to mislead the Negro American, and on the other hand to create anxieties and fears among white Americans to better exploit both racial groups ...

The red propagandists distort the facts concerning racial differences for ulterior motives ... Moscow's Negro tools in the incitement of racial warfare place all the ills of the Negro at the door of the white leaders of America ...

This tends to make the Negro:

(a) feel sorry for himself;

(b) blame others for his failures;

(c) ignore the countless opportunities around him;

(d) jealous of the progress of other racial groups;

(e) expect the white man to do everything for him;

(f) look for easy and quick solutions as a substitute for the harsh realities of competitive struggle to get ahead.

The result is a persecution complex — a warped belief that the white man's prejudices, the white man's system, the white man's government is responsible for everything.

Such a belief is the way the reds plan it, for the next logical step is hate that can be used by the reds to accomplish their ends ...

Johnson stated:

The media of public information is far from

free of communists ... who operate under the guise of liberalism. They are ready at all times to do an effective smear job.

Among these red tools may be found editorial writers, columnists, news commentators and analysts, in the press, radio and television.

They go overboard in giving top news coverage to racial incidents, fomented by the leftists, and also those incidents that are interpreted so as to show 'biased' attitudes of whites against Negroes.

This is a propaganda hoax aimed, not at helping the Negro, but at casting America in a bad light in order to destroy it ... widespread racial hate which the leftists are creating.

The energizing of race hate is an asset to the red cause ... Thus all racial progress based upon understanding, goodwill, friendship and mutual cooperation, built up painfully over the years, is wiped out ...

Too few Americans in our day have the courage ... in the face of leftist opposition ... The words God, country and posterity have lost much of their substance and are becoming only a shadow in the hearts and minds of many Americans.

Johnson concluded with some words of hope:

Great Negro Americans such as Booker T. Washington and George Washington Carver should serve both as an inspiration and a reminder to the present and successive generations of Negro Americans that they too

'can make their lives sublime,

and in departing leave behind them

footprints in the sands of time.' (Longfellow)

The great surge of progress of the Negro since slavery can be largely traced to the work and efforts of these two men, their supporters, their emulators and their followers.

Theirs was a deep and abiding pride of race, a

firm belief in the ability of their benighted people to rise above their past and eventually stand on an equal plane with all other races.

Moreover, equality was to them, not just a catchword — the prattle of fools — but a living thing to be achieved only by demonstrated ability ...

We must try to bring America back to sanity. And let us pray and work, that the misunderstanding, the bitterness, the hate, and the frustration and the tension that exists may disappear and that the Spirit of God, the Spirit of Truth, the Spirit of Charity may prevail again amongst our people.

Manning Johnson's testimony was corroborated by Julia Clarice Brown in her 1966 book *I testify: My years As An F.B.I. Undercover Agent.*

As a black woman, Julia Clarice Brown unknowingly became involved in the communist party. When she realized their agenda, she quit, but was later persuaded by the FBI to rejoin in order to serve as an undercover agent for 9 years. Julia identified over 150 top officials in the U.S. Government working for the communists.

∽

CHAPTER 59
PSYCHOLOGICAL PROJECTION

Fifth column infiltration subversion tactics include "blame–shifting," where the attacker blames the victim.

Sigmund Freud wrote in *Case Histories II* (PFL 9, p. 132) about "psychological projection," where humans resort to the defensive mechanism of denying in themselves the existence of unpleasant behavior while attributing that exact behavior to others, ie., a rude person accusing others of being rude.

When Adam sinned, he projected blame on God, "the woman you gave me" (Gen. 3:12). Children do this, saying "I didn't start the fight – you did." A cheating spouse will accuse their mate of unfaithfulness. Wife-beaters blame their wife for provoking them. Sharia men blame the women they rape for tempting them.

Marx is attributed with saying "Accuse the victim of what you do." Guilty candidates accuse their opponents of the very unethical acts they are committing.

The New York Times (4/23/15) reported "Cash Flowed to Clinton Foundation Amid Russian Uranium Deal," yet she paid for a Steele dossier to accuse her opponent of colluding with Russia. Democrat Political advisor David Axelrod explained this tactic (NPR 4/19/10):

> In Chicago, there was an old tradition of throwing a brick through your own campaign office window, and then calling a press conference to say that you've been attacked.

The innocent candidate is put on the defensive as the media repeats the accusation, implanting negative word associations in voters' minds – no one gets a second chance to make a first impression. If the first candidate's guilt is discovered, by that time the water is muddied, the public is confused, and the crime goes unpunished.

In Acts 24, those who stirred up a riot accused the Apostle Paul of being responsible for it:

> Tertullus began to accuse him, saying ... We have found this man a pestilent fellow, and a mover of sedition among all the Jews ... and a ringleader of the sect of the Nazarenes: Who also hath gone about to profane the temple ...

> Then Paul ... answered ... they neither found me in the temple disputing with any man, neither raising up the people, neither in the synagogues, nor in the city: Neither can they prove the things whereof they now accuse me.

A companion tactic of psychological projection is called "seizing the moral high ground" or "virtue-signaling," where those pushing an unjust cause want to appear before the public as more virtuous, while portraying those opposing them as uncaring.

A classic use of this is when a casino wants to move into an area. Opponents may cite an increase in crime, drugs, prostitution, bankruptcies and broken homes. But if the casino gives some money to schools, they can claim that they are morally superior, because they want to "help the children," while condemning those who are opposing casinos as hating children.

Woe unto them that call evil good, and good evil. (Isaiah 5:20)

❧

CHAPTER 60
FALSE FLAGS

A common pirate tactic was to fly a flag of surrender or truce, or the flag of a friendly country, as a disguise to lure an unsuspecting ship to draw near. Once the targeted ship was close enough to discover the deception, it was too late for them to escape.

This tactic was called flying a "false flag." It has since become a political term to describe incidents orchestrated by deep state government operatives for the purpose of inciting panic so people quickly surrender their freedoms in exchange for order being restored.

Perpetrators of "false flags" often blame the incidents on their innocent political opponents using "psychological projection."

In 1788, Sweden's King Gustave III had some of his soldiers dress in Russian uniforms and attack a Swedish outpost in order to convince his parliament to invade Russia. In 1939, Operation Himmler, Gleiwitz Incident, had Nazi soldiers dress in Polish uniforms and attack a German town to provide an excuse to invade Poland.

On January 6, 2021, ANTIFA-type individuals infiltrated the Trump rally and attacked the Capitol, a tactic described by Sanford D. Horwitt in *Let Them Call Me Rebel: Saul Alinsky: His Life & Legacy* (1992):

In 1972 ... students asked Alinsky to help plan a protest of a scheduled speech by George H.W. Bush, then a U.S. representative to the United Nations ... He told them ... to go ... dressed as members of the Klu Klux Klan, and whenever Bush said something in defense of the Vietnam War, they should cheer and wave placards reading "The KKK Supports Bush." And that is what the students did, with very successful results.

Joseph P. Kennedy stated (*New York Times*, 1/8/61):

There are no accidents in politics.

∽

CHAPTER 61

SOCIALISM: A MONARCHY MAKEOVER

To the annoyance of liberal academia praising the ideals of a classless society, communist countries inevitably end up having a hierarchy of classes.

Though they call their countries "republics," they are ruled by dictators who punish those who threaten their power, such as:

Stalin, Mao Zedong, Pol Pot, Castro, Ho Chi Min, Kim Jong–Il, Ceausescu, Tito, Xi Jinping, Ali Khamenei, Daniel Ortega, Nicolás Maduro, Recep Erdoğan, Kim Jong–un, and others.

These leaders may have friendly–sounding titles, such as president, chairman, prime minister, comrade, or head of state, but they effectively function as monarchs. No one dare cross them or their families.

They are the ones who decide what are the "party views," and demand enforcement with iron discipline. There may be elections for the sake of show, but the opposition is suppressed, the media is manipulated, and outcomes are predetermined.

Those who are members of the "communist Party" act as "the new royalty." They are the upper-class, deep-state ruling elites. They lived in special neighborhoods with special shops and getting special treatment before the law.

They exist as long as they are faithful to the party and its leader. If they are suspected of opposing the party or leader, they become social pariahs and are ostracized. Some suspiciously disappear or are "suicided."

Reagan stated October 27, 1964:

> This is the issue ... whether we believe in our capacity for self-government or whether we abandon the American revolution and confess that a little intellectual elite in a far-distant capitol can plan our lives for us better than we can plan them ourselves.

"Citizens" in socialist or communist countries never have any real elective control of the government. They are the equivalent to "subjects of the crown," serfs, and peasants, with their fate dictated by a totalitarian dictator and his enforcer-class.

Patrick Henry warned, June 5, 1788:

> If you make the citizens of this country agree to become the subjects of one great consolidated empire ... there will be no checks, no real balances, in this government ...

> My great objection (is) ... that the preservation of our liberty depends on the single chance of men being virtuous enough to make laws to punish themselves.

Eisenhower called it "totalitarian imperialism" in a letter to the Senate, February 20, 1953:

> The Soviet Communist Party who now control Russia ... subjected whole nations to the domination of a totalitarian imperialism.

He told Congress, May 5, 1953:

> In Greece, the onrush of communist imperialism has been halted ... We are proposing to make substantial additional resources available to assist the French ... in their military efforts to defeat the Communist Viet Minh aggression.

CHAPTER 62
CHINA

In 1912, the last Chinese Emperor abdicated, ending 2,000 years of Imperial rule. China then experienced decades of unrest with warlord factionalism and invasion from Imperial Japan.

Franklin D. Roosevelt recited on January 6, 1942, the reason the U.S. States entered into World War II:

> Japan's ... conquest goes back half a century ... War against China in 1894 ... Occupation of Korea (1910) ... War against Russia in 1904 ... Fortification of the mandated Pacific islands following 1920 ... Seizure of Manchuria in 1931 ... Invasion of China in 1937.

In 1937, Imperial Japanese troops soldiers massacred 300,000 in Nanking, China. Pro-American General Chiang Kai–shek and his Republic of China army fought Imperial Japan on one side and Mao Zedong's Communist People's Republic of China on the other.

In 1946, President Truman cut off aid to Chiang Kai–shek. This allowed Communist Party leader Mao Zedong to gain strength and drive Chang Kai-shek's army out of mainland China onto the Island of Taiwan.

Beginning in 1949, mainland China was separated from the western world by what has been called the "Bamboo Curtain." Mao Zedong introduced the "continuous revolution theory," and editing China's historical identity through a Cultural Revolution. Purges resulted in an estimated 80 million deaths.

A person who lived through this was Xi Van Fleet, a mother who gave testimony at a Loudoun County School Board meeting in Virginia, regarding CRT–Critical Race Theory being taught to students (Michael Ruiz, FoxNews, therightscoop.com, Rumble.com, MPM-Mr Producer Media, published June 9, 2021):

> I've been very alarmed about what's been going on in our school. You are now training our children to be social justice warriors and to

loathe our country and our history. Growing up in Mao's China, all this seems very familiar. The Communist regime used the same critical theory to divide people. The only difference is they used classes instead of race.

During the cultural revolution I witnessed students and teachers again turn against each other. We change the school names to be politically correct. We were taught to denounce our heritage; the red guards destroyed anything that is not communist. Statues, books and anything else. We were also encouraged to report on each other just like the student equity ambassador program and the bias reporting system.

This is indeed the American version of the Chinese cultural revolution. The Critical Race Theory has its roots in cultural marxism; it should have NO PLACE in our schools.

Mao Zedong stated:

Chinese socialism is founded upon Darwin and the theory of evolution.

In the article "Nationalism in the Slave States of Soviet Russia, Nazi Germany and now, China" (December 23, 2010), Lev Navrozov, an immigrant from the U.S.S.R. who worked with the Center for the Survival of Western Democracies, stated:

Once upon a time it was assumed that a slave should fulfill the slave-owners' order as efficiently as a machine. But after Stalin, Hitler, and Mao ... slaves must relive the order, and hence scream in their delight to kill and be killed.

Reagan stated in Beijing, China, April 27, 1984:

I have seen the rise of fascism and communism. Both philosophies glorify the arbitrary power of the state ... But both theories fail. Both deny those God-given liberties that are the inalienable right of each person on this planet, indeed, they deny the existence of God

George H.W. Bush acknowledged March 22, 1989:

> Barbara and I went to China ... in 1974, and we had wondered about the family in China – Communist country, totalitarian ... We knew that there had been almost entire banning on practicing and teaching Christianity ... This was right after the Cultural Revolution.

Eisenhower stated (*TIME Magazine,* June 16, 1952):

> China was lost to the free world in one of the greatest international disasters of our time – a type of tragedy that must not be repeated.

❧

CHAPTER 63
ROMANIA

In 1947, communists forced Romanian King Michael I to abdicate. In 1965, Nicolae Ceauşescu came to power. He ruled as an autocratic dictator and imposed a cult of personality using Securitate secret police. He was finally overthrown in 1989.

Warning against the communist threat to Romania was Lutheran minister Richard Wurmbrand. He was arrested in 1948 and tortured for 14 years in prison. His wife, Sabina, was sent to a labor camp.

International pressure secured their amnesty, and in 1965, they testified before the U.S. Senate's Internal Security Subcommittee. In 1967, the Wurmbrand's formed "Jesus to the Communist World," renamed "Voice of the Martyrs."

Rev. Richard Wurmbrand stated:

> America is the hope of every enslaved man, because it is the last bastion of freedom in the world. Only America has the power and spiritual resources to stand as a barrier between militant communism and the people of the world.

> It is the last "dike" holding back the rampaging flood waters of militant communism. If it crumples, there is no other dike, no other dam; no other line of defense to fall back upon ...

Rev. Wurmbrand ended:

> America is the last hope of millions of enslaved peoples. They look to it as their second fatherland. In it lies their hopes and prayers.

> I have seen fellow-prisoners in communist prisons beaten, tortured, with 50 pounds of chains on their legs – praying for America ... that the dike will not crumple; that it will remain free.

❦

CHAPTER 64
HUNGARY

In 1949, Hungary became a satellite of the Soviet Union. In 1956, a student protest against the communists mushroomed into a national revolt.

In November 1956, Soviet communists crushed the revolt in Hungary, mercilessly killing 2,500, wounding 13,000, and causing 200,000 to flee as refugees.

President John F. Kennedy stated October 23, 1960:

> Americans will never ... recognize Soviet domination of Hungary. Hungary's claim to independence and liberty is not based on sentiment or politics. It is deeply rooted in history, in culture and in law.

> No matter what sort of puppet government they may maintain, we do not mean to see that claim abandoned. Americans intend to hasten ... the day when the men and women of Hungary will stand again in freedom and justice.

Cardinal József Mindszenty was arrested in 1949 and tortured by communists. Eisenhower wrote to the United Catholic Organization for Freeing Cardinal Mindszenty, February 1, 1954:

> The communist assault upon religious liberty and leadership in Hungary has failed to turn the Hungarian people from their faith in God.

> The plight of Cardinal Mindszenty and of other churchmen who have suffered at the hands of the

communists has not been forgotten ...

The spirit of these men has defied confinement by the totalitarian state. It has become, indeed, a symbol of faith and freedom for our times.

∽

CHAPTER 65
POLAND

Nazi and Soviet troops invaded Poland in 1939 and carried away thousands, killing them in the Katyn Massacre, while the rest of the world did nothing.

Hitler set up six extermination camps in Poland, killing 3 million Jews and nearly 3 million ethnic Poles.

Though Poland contributed the fourth largest amount of troops to the Allied effort in Europe in World War II, they were betrayed.

At the Yalta Conference, February 4–11, 1945, Franklin Roosevelt and Winston Churchill let Stalin take control of Poland, putting it under communist control.

In 1979, Pope John Paul II visited communist Poland, where he was welcomed by hundreds of thousands. The enthusiasm spread and in 1980, with the leadership of labor leader Lech Wałęsa, the Polish people rejected communism and set up a free government.

Pope John Paul II stated:

The fundamental error of socialism is (it) considers the individual person simply as an element, a molecule within the social organism, so that the good of the individual is completely subordinated to the functioning of the socio-economic mechanism.

He wrote in his encyclical *Centesimus Annus,* 1991:

In recent years the range of such intervention has vastly expanded, to the point of creating a new type of state, the so-called "welfare state" ...

The principle of subsidiarity must be respected: a community of a higher order should not interfere in the internal life of a community of a lower order ...

An inordinate increase of public agencies, which are dominated more by bureaucratic thinking ... are accompanied by an enormous increase in spending ...

Needs are best understood and satisfied by people who are closest to them who act as neighbors to those in need.

It should be added that certain kinds of demands often call for a response which is not simply material but which is capable of perceiving the deeper human need.

∾

CHAPTER 66
KOREA

"FREEDOM IS NOT FREE" is the inscription on the Korean War Memorial 1 in Washington, D.C.

The Korean War started June 25, 1950. Communist North Korea invaded South Korea, killing thousands.

Outnumbered South Korean and American troops, as part of a U.N. police action, fought courageously against the communist Chinese and North Korean troops, who were supplied with arms and MIG fighters from the Soviet Union.

Five-star General Douglas MacArthur was Supreme U.N. Commander, leading the United Nations Command from 1950 to 1951. He made a daring landing of troops at Inchon, deep behind North Korean lines, and recaptured the city of Seoul.

With temperatures sometimes forty degrees below zero in the Korean mountains, and Washington politicians limiting the use of air power against the communists, there were nearly 140,000 American casualties:

in the defense of the Pusan Perimeter and Taego; in the landing at Inchon and the freeing of Seoul; in the capture of Pyongyang; in the Yalu

River where nearly a million Communist Chinese soldiers invaded; in the Battles of Changjin Reservoir, Old Baldy, White Horse Mountain, Heartbreak Ridge, Pork Chop Hill, T–Bone Hill, and Siberia Hill.

Harry S Truman stated April 3, 1951:

> Every day our newspapers tell us about the fighting in Korea. Our men there are making heroic sacrifices. They are fighting and suffering in an effort to prevent the tide of aggression from sweeping across the world ...

> Our young men are offering their lives for us in the hills of Korea – and yet too many of us are chiefly concerned over whether or not we can buy a television set next week ...

> This is a failure to understand the moral principles upon which our Nation is founded.

President Eisenhower told Congress, February 2, 1953:

> I must make special mention of the war in Korea. This war is, for Americans, the most painful phase of communist aggression throughout the world.

> It is clearly a part of the same calculated assault that the aggressor is simultaneously pressing in Indochina and in Malaya.

Fighting in Korea was halted July 27, 1953, with the signing of an armistice with North Korea at Panmunjom. This separation grew more hostile after the Korean War and setting of the demarcation of the North Korea Demilitarized Zone.

⤚৯⤙

CHAPTER 67

MEXICO

In 1920, Mexico's 38th President, Adolfo de la Huerta, was defeated by Álvaro Obregón, Mexico's 39th President, who reportedly ordered the death Pancho Villa. Huerta started revolt against Obregón, but it was crushed and Huerta fled in exile.

In 1924, Obregón was succeeded by the aggressively anti-Christian freemason, Plutarco Elías Calles, Mexico's 40th President. He promoted a gang-style socialism in Mexico, and in 1924, had Mexico host the U.S.S.R.'s first embassy in the Western Hemisphere.

In 1936, socialist politician Leon Trotsky fled to Mexico. Stalin sent assassins to kill Trotsky, and after several attempts, finally accomplished it in 1940.

Calles violently closed and confiscated churches, schools, convents, hospitals, seminaries, missions and monasteries. He imposed radical atheist "Calles Laws" which made it illegal for clerical garb to be worn outside a church, imposed a 5–year prison sentence on pastors who criticized the government, and limited the number of clergy per state.

This began the Cristero War, 1926–29, where over 90,000 were killed. Mexico's priests, ministers, and faithful laity were harassed, arrested and murdered. Catholic women and girls were assaulted and raped.

Obregón was re-elected in 1928, but at a banquet in his honor he was assassinated, allowing Calles to return to power.

Calles was nicknamed "Grand Turk" and "Jefe Máximo" (political chieftain). He started Mexico's PNR party, the predecessor to the PRI party.

President Portes Gil, Mexico's 41st President, agreed not to enforce the "Calles Laws" but left them on the books.

In 1936, Mexico's 44th President, Lázaro Cárdenas, deported Calles and repealed the "Calles Laws," thereby restoring a degree of freedom of religion.

In the 1950, Marxists creatively borrowed Christian terminology to create political methods labeled "liberation theology" and "social justice movement."

This opened the door for socialist and communist

infiltration of the predominately Catholic countries in Central and South America.

Mexico's power struggle continues, as CNN reported July 2, 2018:

> Mexico goes to the polls this weekend: 132 politicians have been killed since campaigning began.

✧

CHAPTER 68
COMMUNISM VS. DEMOCRACY

Harry S Truman compared communism and democracy in his Inaugural Address, January 20, 1949:

> We believe that all men are created equal because they are created in the image of God. From this faith we will not be moved ...
>
> Communism is based on the belief that man is so weak and inadequate that he is unable to govern himself, and therefore requires the rule of strong masters.
>
> Democracy is based on the conviction that man has the moral and intellectual capacity, as well as the inalienable right, to govern himself with reason and justice.
>
> Communism subjects the individual to arrest without lawful cause, punishment without trial, and forced labor as a chattel of the state. It decrees what information he shall receive, what art he shall produce, what leaders he shall follow, and what thoughts he shall think.
>
> Democracy maintains that government is established for the benefit of the individual, and is charged with the responsibility of protecting the rights of the individual and his freedom ...
>
> These differences between communism and democracy do not concern the United States alone. People everywhere are coming to realize that what is involved is material well-being, human dignity, and the right to believe in and worship God.

A comparison similar to Truman's was written by Tocqueville after France's Revolution of 1848:

Democracy extends the sphere of individual freedom, socialism restricts it. Democracy attaches all possible value to each man; socialism makes each man a mere agent, a mere number.

Democracy and socialism have nothing in common but one word: equality. But notice the difference: while democracy seeks equality in liberty, socialism seeks equality in restraint and servitude.

Truman stated at the New York Avenue Presbyterian Church, Washington, D.C., April 3, 1951:

The international communist movement is based on a fierce and terrible fanaticism. It denies the existence of God and, wherever it can, it stamps out the worship of God. Our religious faith gives us the answer to the false beliefs of communism.

Our faith shows us the way to create a society where man can find his greatest happiness under God.

Surely, we can follow that faith with the same devotion and determination the communists give to their godless creed.

Truman told the Attorney General's Conference, February 15, 1950:

The fundamental basis of this nation's laws was given to Moses on the Mount. The fundamental basis of our Bill of Rights comes from the teachings we get from Exodus and St. Matthew, from Isaiah and St. Paul. I don't think we emphasize that enough these days.

If we don't have a proper fundamental moral background, we will finally end up with a totalitarian government which does not believe in rights for anybody except the state!"

Truman stated at Gonzaga University in Spokane, May 11, 1950:

The greatest obstacle to peace is a modern tyranny led by a small group who have abandoned their faith in God. These tyrants have forsaken ethical and moral beliefs. They believe that only force makes right.

They are aggressively seeking to expand the area of their domination. Our effort to resist and overcome this tyranny is essentially a moral effort.

✄

CHAPTER 69
DWIGHT D. EISENHOWER

Dwight Eisenhower was quoted in the *Religious Herald,* Virginia, January 25, 1952:

> What is our battle against communism if it is not a fight between anti-God and a belief in the Almighty? ... Communists ... have to eliminate God from their system. When God comes, communism has to go.

At the College of William and Mary, May 15, 1953, Eisenhower stated:

> It is necessary that we earnestly seek out and uproot any traces of communism at any place where it can affect our national life ... The true way to uproot communism in this country is to understand what freedom means, and thus develop an impregnable wall, that no thought of communism can enter.

Eisenhower addressed Congress, February 2, 1953:

> Our country has come through a painful period of trial and disillusionment since the victory of 1945 ... The calculated pressures of aggressive communism have forced us ... to live in a world of turmoil.

He stated at a News Conference, March 9, 1953:

> Our churches ... should be the greatest possible opponents to communism ... The church, with its testimony of the existence of an Almighty God, is the last thing that ... would be preaching, teaching or tolerating communism.

Eisenhower told the National Conference on the

Spiritual Foundation of Democracy, November 9, 1954:

> We are attacked by the communists who in their own documents state that capitalism – democracy – carries within itself the seeds of its own destruction ...

> Fundamentally, democracy is nothing in the world but a spiritual conviction ... that each of us is enormously valuable because of a certain standing before our own God.

Laying the cornerstone of the Eisenhower Museum, Dwight Eisenhower stated, as recorded in *TIME Magazine*, June 5, 1952:

> If each of us in his own mind would dwell more upon those simple virtues – integrity, courage, self-confidence and unshakable belief in his Bible – would not some of these problems tend to simplify themselves? ...

> Free government is the political expression of a deeply felt religious faith.

TIME Magazine published an article titled "Faith of the Candidates," September 22, 1952, in which Dwight Eisenhower stated:

> You can't explain free government in any other terms than religious. The founding fathers had to refer to the Creator in order to make their revolutionary experiment make sense; it was because all men are "endowed by their Creator with certain inalienable rights" that men could dare to be free.

❧

CHAPTER 70
PRAYER

During the Cold War, Dwight Eisenhower stated December 24, 1953:

> The world still stands divided in two antagonistic parts. Prayer places freedom and communism in opposition one to the other.

The communist can find no reserve of strength in prayer because his doctrine of materialism and statism denies the dignity of man and consequently the existence of God.

But in America ... religious faith is the foundation of free government, so is prayer an indispensable part of that faith ... The founders of this, our country, came first to these shores in search of freedom ... to live ... beyond the yoke of tyranny.

Conrad Hilton, founder of the hotel chain, spoke at a Prayer Breakfast at the Mayflower Hotel, following addresses by Congressmen, Senators, and Vice-President Nixon. He stated:

It took a war to put prayer at the center of the lives of our fighting men. It took a war, and the frightening evil of communism, to show the world that this whole business of prayer is not a sissy, a counterfeit thing that man can do or not as he wishes.

Prayer ... is a part of man's personality, without which he limps ... Men grope in darkness unless they believe that God, in His kindness, is willing to lift the shadows if we ask Him in prayer.

In *Lessons of History* (NY: Simon and Schuster, 1968), Will and Ariel Durant wrote:

The greatest question of our time is not communism versus individualism, not even East versus West; it is whether man can live without God.

President Eisenhower stated February 20, 1955:

Without God, there could be no American form of government, nor an American way of life. Recognition of the Supreme Being is the first – the most basic – expression of Americanism.

In 1960, Madalyn Murray O'Hair, an atheist proponent of socialism, attempted to defect to the Union of Soviet Socialist Republics, but was refused entry, as reported by her son, William J. Murray.

Returning to Maryland, Madalyn Murray O'Hair

sued the Baltimore City Public School System (*Murray v. Curlett*) to have "mandatory" Bible reading taken out of public schools, using her 14 year old son, William J. Murray, as the plaintiff.

The case went to the Supreme Court where it was combined with the case of *Abington Township v. Schempp*. As a result, "mandatory" Bible reading was stopped in America's public schools. Not long after Justice Hugo Black wrote his 1962 *Engel v. Vitale* decision ending official school prayer.

Twenty years later, President Reagan pushed Congress to pass a bill to allow children the freedom to voluntarily pray in school. He commented August 23, 1984 at Reunion Arena, Dallas, Texas:

> We even had to pass a special law in the Congress just a few weeks ago to allow student prayer groups the same access to school rooms after classes that a Young Marxist Society ... would already enjoy.

Of note is that William J. Murray eventually disassociated himself from his mother. He became a minister and author, writing of his atheist upbringing and conversion to Christ in *My Life Without God* (2012).

Reagan stated in a Ceremony for Prayer in Schools, September 25, 1982:

> In the last two decades we've experienced an onslaught of such twisted logic that if Alice were visiting America, she might think she'd never left Wonderland.

> We're told that it somehow violates the rights of others to permit students in school who desire to pray to do so. Clearly, this infringes on the freedom of those who choose to pray.

Rep. Nick Joe Rahall introduced a bill in 1992, to declare November 22–28, "America's Christian Heritage Week," stating:

> While ... emerging democracies ... turn from

the long held atheism of communism to true religious freedoms, we find ourselves, with heavy hearts, watching our own government succumb to pressures to distant itself from God and religion ...

Bans against the simple freedom as ... representations of the Ten Commandments on government buildings ...

Such a standard of religious exclusion is absolutely and unequivocally counter to the intention of those who designed our government.

Ronald Reagan stated at the Conservative Political Action Conference Dinner, Mayflower Hotel, Washington, DC, March 20, 1981:

Evil is powerless if the good are unafraid.

That's why the Marxist vision of man without God must eventually be seen as an empty and a false faith – the second oldest in the world – first proclaimed in the Garden of Eden with whispered words ..."Ye shall be as gods."

The crisis of the Western world ... exists to the degree in which it is indifferent to God.

◈

CHAPTER 71
CUBA

In the early 1920s, Cuba was a prosperous country. The very popular Gerardo Machado was elected President in 1925. Then there was a global drop in sugar prices, followed by the 1929 Stock Market Crash.

Machado broke his promise of only serving one term, which violated the Cuban Constitution and led to protests. Machado censored free speech and used repressive police state tactics, including murders and assassinations of opposition leaders.

After several attempts on his life, Machado fled to the Bahamas in 1933, and then Miami, where he died.

Taking advantage of the domestic unrest, communists

began infiltrating student groups at the University of Havana, and formed the Cuban Communist Party.

In August of 1933, Cubans elected Carlos Manuel de Céspedes y Quesada, the son of the "Padre de la Patria" (Father of the Country) who led Cuba in 1868.

Unfortunately, he only served one month before being forced out by Sergeant Fulgencio Batista and the Democrat Socialist Coalition. Batista appointed himself chief of the military.

Over the next seven years, though there were a half-dozen presidents, Batista clandestinely ran the nation's politics.

The President in 1939 was Federico Laredo Brú, infamously remembered for turning away the *MS St. Louis*, May 27, 1939, which was carrying 930 Jews fleeing Hitler's persecutions.

Batista was elected Cuba's President in 1940. After a four year term, he moved to Florida.

In 1952, Batista returned and formed the Progressive Action Party. He ran for President again. Facing defeat, he staged a coup and set up a military dictatorship. He also began working closely with the American mafia.

At this time, casinos and baseball brought tourism to Cuba, resulting in two-thirds of the country enjoying the highest standard of living in Latin America.

The remaining third, though, suffered in rural poverty and unemployment.

In 1956, Fidel Castro stirred up and organized the rural poor to begin a rebellion. Batista cracked down with arrests, imprisonments, and executions.

Senator John F. Kennedy stated October 6, 1960:

> Batista murdered 20,000 Cubans in seven years ... and he turned Democratic Cuba into a complete police state – destroying every individual liberty.

Castro was hailed as a rising leader who would

stamp out corruption. He was even invited to speak at Harvard University.

In 1959, Castro forced Batista to flee. Once in power, Castro ignored his promises that he would give citizens equality, and instead set up a communist dictatorship. He seized thousands of acres of farmland from Cuban citizens and arrested anti-revolutionaries.

An observable pattern in history is, that whenever a tyrannical government is overthrown, unless citizens have been trained in Judeo-Christian principles of self-restraint, the country succumbs to internal chaos, out of which a worse tyrannical dictator seizes power.

George Orwell explained in *1984,* (part 2, chap. 9):

> Socialism, a theory which appeared in the early nineteenth century and was the last link in a chain of thought stretching back to the slave rebellions of antiquity, was still deeply infected by the utopianism of past ages.

> But in each variant of socialism that appeared from about 1900 onwards the aim of establishing liberty and equality was more and more openly abandoned. The new movements which appeared in the middle years of the century, Ingsoc (English Socialism) in Oceania, Neo-Bolshevism in Eurasia, Death-Worship ... in Eastasia, had the conscious aim of perpetuating unfreedom and inequality.

> These new movements, of course, grew out of the old ones and tended to keep their names and pay lip-service to their ideology. But the purpose of all of them was to arrest progress and freeze history at a chosen moment.

> The familiar pendulum swing was to happen once more, and then stop. As usual, the High were to be turned out by the Middle, who would then become the High; but this time, by conscious strategy, the High would be able to maintain their position permanently.

Castro removed anyone associate with the old leadership, imprisoned dissidents, and made agreements with the Soviets.

CIA Director Allen Dulles and CIA planner Richard Bissell arranged the Bay of Pigs invasion which failed. Kennedy fired them and threatened to "shatter the CIA into a thousand pieces and scatter it to the winds."

In 1964, Castro worked with the KGB to create the National Liberation Army of Columbia (FARC), and the National Liberation Army of Bolivia (ELN).

Thousands of Cubans, including church leaders, were tortured and executed by Castro's men. His main enforcer was Che Guevara, who wrote:

> We executed many people by firing squad without knowing if they were fully guilty. At times, the revolution cannot be stop to conduct much investigation ...

> Hatred (was) an element of the struggle ... transforming (the soldier) into an effective, violent, selective, and cold killing machine. Our soldiers must be thus; a people without hatred cannot vanquish a brutal enemy ...

> I'd like to confess ... I discovered that I really like killing.

Leftist writers awkwardly defend statements made by Che Guevara in his 1952 *The Motorcycle Diaries*:

> The blacks, those magnificent examples of the African race who have maintained their racial purity thanks to their lack of an affinity with bathing ...

> The black is indolent and a dreamer; spending his meager wage on frivolity or drink; the European has a tradition of work and saving, which has pursued him as far as this corner of America and drives him to advance himself, even independently of his own individual aspirations.

In 1959, Guevara wrote:

We're going to do for blacks exactly what blacks did for the revolution. By which I mean: nothing.

During Castro's reign, over 1.5 million Cubans fled to the United States. President Reagan stated:

What's happening in Cuba is not a failure of the Cuban people. It's a failure of Fidel Castro and the Communists.

Che Guevara traveled the world exporting socialist revolution, including the African Congo and Bolivia, where he was captured and executed October 9, 1967.

David P. Goldman wrote in "Fidel Castro's Mass Murder by the Numbers" (PJ Media, November 28, 2016):

Fidel Castro shed blood on a scale unimaginable in American terms. His butchers executed perhaps 15,000 prisoners ...

British historian Hugh Thomas, in his study Cuba for the pursuit of freedom stated that "perhaps" 5,000 executions had taken place by 1970, while *The World Handbook of Political and Social Indicators* ascertained that there had been 2,113 political executions between the years of 1958–1967.

Professor of political science at the University of Hawaii, Rudolph J. Rummel estimated the number of political executions at between 4,000 and 33,000 from 1958–87, with a mid-range of 15,000 ...

Stalin, Hitler, Mao and Pol Pot killed more people in relative terms. After that, it's hard to find a tyrant with a bigger body count than Fidel. To speak of him with anything but a curse is an insult to the memory of his victims.

Democrat Senator John F. Kennedy condemned Castro's communism, stating October 6, 1960:

Two years ago, in September of 1958 – bands of bearded rebels descended from Cuba's Sierra Maestra Mountains and began their long march on Havana – a march which ended in the overthrow of the brutal, bloody, and despotic dictatorship of Fulgencio Batista.

The slogans, the manifestos, and the broadcasts of this revolution reflected the deepest aspirations of the Cuban people.

They promised individual liberty and free elections. They promised an end to harsh police-state tactics. They promised a better life for a people long oppressed by both economic and political tyranny ...

Kennedy continued:

But in the two years since that revolution swept Fidel Castro into power, those promises have all been broken. There have been no free elections – and there will be none as long as Castro rules.

All political parties – with the exception of the Communist Party – have been destroyed.

All political dissenters have been executed, imprisoned, or exiled. All academic freedom has been eliminated ... All major newspapers and radio stations have been seized.

And all of Cuba is in the iron grip of a communist-oriented police state. Castro and his gang have betrayed ... the Cuban people.

The United States reopened its embassy in Havana, Cuba, on July 20, 2015. Castro died November 25, 2016. Though socialism promised equality, the average citizen in Cuba made $20 a month, while Castro's personal worth was estimated at $900 million.

⤚⥓

CHAPTER 72

NIXON ON COMMUNISM

Richard Nixon was Vice-President under Dwight Eisenhower and was immensely popular for his stand against communism. He gave an address, "The Meaning of Communism to Americans," August 21, 1960:

The major problem confronting the people of the United States ... is ... communism ... The test is one not so much of arms but of faith ... Communism denies God, enslaves men, and destroys justice ...

The appeal of the communist idea is not to the masses ... but ... to an intelligent minority ... It has failed in its promise of equality in abundance ... It has produced ... disillusionment and a steady stream of men, women, and children seeking to escape its blight ... Communism is a false idea ...

Nixon continued:

Communism inevitably supplants and destroys capitalism ... free trade, free selling and buying ... The Soviet Union ... started by attempting to root out ... every vestige of the market principle ...

Production and distribution of goods were put under central direction ... It was a catastrophic failure ... in appalling shortages of the most elementary necessities ...

Communist theory ... says nothing about how the economy shall be run except that it shall not be by the market principle ...

Nixon added regarding truth:

Communism starts with the proposition that there are no universal truths or general truths of human nature ...

The high priest of this doctrine was Eugene Pashukanis. His reign came to an abrupt end ... With an irony befitting the career of one who predicted that communism would bring an end to law and legal processes, Pashukanis was quietly taken off and shot without even the semblance of a trial ...

Nixon commented on communist elections:

Voters are in the end permitted only to vote for the candidates chosen by the only political party permitted to exist ... the electorate is given no choice ... Knowing that it cannot achieve representative democracy, it seems to feel better if it adopts its empty forms ...

Nixon continued discussing power:

Throughout the ages, among men of all nations and creeds, law has generally been thought of as a curb on arbitrary power. It has been conceived as a way of substituting reason for force ...

Law in the Soviet Union is not conceived as a check on power, it is openly and proudly an expression of power. In this conception ... the bankruptcy of communism as a moral philosophy openly declares itself ...

Nixon added regarding freedom:

Communist philosophy is basically inconsistent with the ideal of freedom because it denies that there can be any standard of moral truth by which the actions of any given social order may be judged ...

If the individual says to government, "Thus far may you go, but no farther," he necessarily appeals to some principle of rightness that stands above his particular form of government.

It is precisely the possibility of any such standard that communism radically ... denies. Marx and Engels had nothing but sneers for the idea that there are "eternal truths, such as freedom, justice, etc., that are common to all states of society." They contend that there are no eternal truths (*Manifesto of Communist Party,* 1848, Chapter II. Proletarians & Communists) ...

If that system requires tyranny and oppression, then tyranny and oppression must within that system be accepted; there can be no higher court of appeal ...

A sense of freedom can never develop under the Soviet regime.

Despite the promises of socialism and communism promises, statistics reveal that more people have been killed under such atheistic regimes – estimated at over 150 million – than any other political system, except fundamental Islam at 270 million. Nixon continued:

Communism has appeared as a kind of

nightmare ... Communist faith ... tells men to forget all the teachings of the ages about government, law, and morality ...

There is only one rule: Smash the existing "bourgeois" economic and legal order and leave the rest to the "spontaneous class organization of the proletariat (working class)."

Nixon's warning echoed a *Chicago Tribune,* April 21, 1934, editorial cartoon depicting communist "psychological projection," with "Young Pinkies from Columbia and Harvard," and Leon Trotsky writing:

– Plan of Action for U.S.

– SPEND! SPEND! SPEND! under the guise of recovery,

– BUST the government,

– BLAME the capitalists for the failure,

– JUNK the constitution and DECLARE A DICTATORSHIP.

– It worked in Russia!

Richard Nixon added in his 1960 warning that without "eternal truth" tyranny inevitably repeats itself, with the dragon-slayer becoming the dragon:

How, following the overthrow of a tyranny, do you suggest steps that will prevent an interim dictatorship from hardening into a second tyranny? ...

A cruel dictatorship has been overthrown ... because it permitted no elections or never counted the vote honestly. Following the successful revolt ... order is kept by something approaching a dictatorship.

Nixon described what communist dictators do to those "useful idiots" who helped them get into power:

Men who were once united in overthrowing plain injustice become divided on the question of what constitutes a just new order.

Militant zealots, useful in the barricades, are too rough for civil government and must be curbed. If curbed too severely, they may take up arms against the new government. Etc., etc ...

The shift in power when it comes may involve only a few quick maneuvers within the apparatus of the party ...

The fate of millions will be determined by processes which take no account of their interests or wishes, in which they are granted no participation, and which they are not even permitted to observe.

∽

CHAPTER 73

VIETNAM

The Gulf of Tonkin Incident involved an alleged attack on the *USS Maddox* on August 2, 1964, after which the U.S. directly engaged in the Vietnam War to stop the spread of communism in Asia.

U.S. forces inflicted over a million enemy fatalities, yet peace demonstrations, left-leaning media coverage and socialist political maneuvering thwarted victory.

As a result, U.S. backed South Vietnam surrendered unconditionally to the communist North Vietnamese on April 30, 1975.

Colonel Bui Tin, who reportedly received the surrender, explained how protests by "anti-war peace demonstrators" was key to the communist victory:

Every day our leadership would listen to world news over the radio at 9 a.m. to follow the growth of the American antiwar movement ...

Visits to Hanoi by people like Jane Fonda and former Attorney General Ramsey Clark and ministers gave us confidence that we should hold on in the face of battlefield reverses ...

We were elated when Jane Fonda, wearing a red Vietnamese dress, said at a press conference that she was ashamed of American actions in the war and that she would struggle along with us.

Award-winner actor John Wayne commented:

> I would think somebody like Jane Fonda and
> her idiot husband would be terribly ashamed and
> saddened that they were a part of causing us to
> stop helping the South Vietnamese. Now look
> what's happening. They're getting killed by the
> millions. Murdered by the millions. How the hell
> can she and her husband sleep at night?

After the war, Bui Tin became vice chief editor
of the Communist Party's official newspaper in
Vietnam, *People's Daily*, but he grew disillusioned with
communist corruption and defected to Paris in 1990.

In an interview, Bui Tin stated:

> The roots of the Vietnam War – its all-
> encompassing and underlying nature – lie in a
> confrontation between two ideological worlds:
> socialism versus capitalism ... totalitarianism
> versus democracy ...
>
> The conscience of America was part of its
> war-making capability, and we were turning that
> power in our favor. America lost because of its
> democracy; through dissent and protest it lost the
> ability to mobilize a will to win.

Commenting on the "will to win" was retired Major
General Patrick Brady, considered the most decorated
living veteran. He received the Medal of Honor
for flying over 2,500 combat missions in Vietnam,
rescuing over 5,000 wounded.

In *Dead Men Flying*, Brady described rescuing 51
wounded in one day, flying 3 different helicopters shot
up by enemy fire with 400 holes. Major General Brady
wrote, June 4, 2013:

> The greatest danger (is) ... the feminization,
> emasculation and dismantling of our military.
>
> The two most important elements of national
> survival are the media and the military ... We
> know the media are failing – God help us if the
> military does also ...

He added:

> Let's begin with Benghazi. It is incomprehensible that any commander, let alone the commander-in-chief (President Obama) would go AWOL during a crisis such as Benghazi, but he was.

Brady warned of:

> Unprecedented rates of suicide ... cut benefits to veterans ... quad-sexual military with all the health, readiness and moral issues that come with exalting sodomy ... sexual assault ... women will be tasked to lead bayonet charges ... billions of defense dollars are unaccounted for ... Christianity is under military attack, and Bibles have been burned to appease Muslims ...

General Brady concluded:

> Just as the way forward for America is a return to the morality and values of the past, so too must the military return to the readiness standards and common sense of the past.

❧

CHAPTER 74
WEATHERMAN

"Weatherman" was a reference to an anarchist group led by radicals including Mark Rudd, Eric Mann and Bill Ayers, son of Chicago philanthropist Thomas Ayers, former CEO of Chicago Edison electric utility company.

In the late 1960's, Bill Ayers helped start the New Left, SDS and the militant group "Weatherman Underground," whose name was inspired by a line in Bob Dylan's 1965 song "Subterranean Homesick Blues." Ayers supposedly asked John Lennon to write a theme song for their revolution movement, but was disappointed when Lennon released *Revolution* in 1968:

> You say you want a revolution, Well you know, We all want to change the world; You tell me that it's evolution, Well you know, We all want to change the world; But when you talk about destruction, Don't you

know you can count me out ...

You say you got a real solution, Well you know, We'd all love to see the plan; You ask me for a contribution, Well you know, We're doing what we can; But when you want money for people with minds that hate, All I can tell you is brother you have to wait ...

You say you'll change the constitution, Well you know, We all want to change your head; You tell me it's the institution, Well you know, You better free your mind instead; But if you go carrying pictures of Chairman Mao, You ain't going to make it with anyone anyhow.

Interestingly enough, Lennon's son, Sean Lennon, wrote (DailyWire.com, 8/2/20): "I'm unsure how this 'fight racism with racism' and 'fight fascism with fascism' strategy is supposed to succeed in anything but destruction and chaos. But maybe I'm just a Luddite."

On October 6, 1969, Ayers bombed the statue dedicated to the police who died in the 1886 Haymarket Riot. The statue was rebuilt, only to be blown up again by the Weatherman Underground on October 6, 1970.

In 1970, the Federal Government filed charges against Bill Ayers after members of his group died when a nail bomb they were assembling exploded. That same year, they bombed New York City's Police Headquarters, San Francisco's Police Department and on March 1, 1971, the U.S. Capitol building.

In 1970, the Beatles disbanded. In 1971, John Lennon and his second wife, Yoko Ono, co-wrote the song *Imagine,* with socialist-themed lyrics: "Imagine no possessions ... And no religion too."

On May 19, 1972, the Weatherman Underground bombed the Pentagon "in retaliation for the U.S. bombing raid in Hanoi." In July of 1972, Jane Fonda visited Communist North Vietnam.

Ayers was quoted in *Sixties Radicals, Then and Now: Candid Conversations With Those Who Shaped the Era,* by Ron Chepesiuk (Jefferson, NC: McFarland & Co, 1995, "Bill Ayers: Radical Educator"):

> I am a radical, Leftist, small "c" communist ... Maybe I'm the last communist who is willing to admit it ... The ethics of communism still appeal to me. I don't like Lenin as much as the early Marx.

In 1995, Bill Ayers helped launch Barack Obama's political career by hosting a fund-raiser for him at his home in the Hyde Park neighborhood of Chicago.

Ayers helped start the Chicago Annenberg Challenge, a 501(c)3 education-related nonprofit of which Barack Obama served as the president of the board from 1995 to 2001.

From 1999 to 2002, Ayers served with Obama on the board of the Woods Fund of Chicago, which had been funding the Developing Communities Project, where Obama was a community organizer from 1985 to 1988. Ayers donated to the Obama campaign in 2001.

Ayers' friend was Mark Rudd, who was mentioned in the article "Another Weatherman terrorist a player in Obama campaign" (*WorldNetDaily.com*, 9/2708):

> Among the signatories and endorsers to Progressives for Obama is Mark Rudd, one of the main founders of the Weatherman terrorist organization. Rudd worked closely for years with Weatherman terrorist William Ayers ... In 1968, Rudd traveled with the SDS to Cuba, defying U.S. travel bans, where he says he was heavily influenced by the legacy of Che Guevara and by Cuban-style revolution.

Weatherman Eric Mann recruited and trained Patrisse Cullors, co-founder of Black Lives Matter, who stated in a 2015 interview with Jared Ball of the Real News Network:

> The first thing, I think, is that we actually do have an ideological frame. Myself and Alicia in particular are trained organizers ... We are trained Marxists. We are super-versed on, sort of, ideological theories.

CHAPTER 75
CAMBODIA

Pol Pot's communist Khmer Rouge killed 2 million Cambodians in "killing fields" between 1975 and 1979.

Just as the French Revolution made 1792 year one, Pol Pot made 1975 year zero, with everything before that being irrelevant. To erase Cambodia's pre-communist identity, he killed anyone who wore glasses, figuring if someone could read, they knew history.

With Darwinian–utilitarian logic, Pol Pot stated:

> Keeping you is no gain. Losing you is no loss.

President Gerald Ford requested Congress assist Cambodia and Vietnam, January 28, 1975:

> Communists ... violated the political provisions of the Paris Agreement. They have refused all South Vietnamese offers to set a specific date for free elections ...

> North Vietnamese forces captured an entire province, the population centers of which were clearly under the control of the South Vietnamese Government ... Communists have intensified hostilities by attacking on the outskirts of Phnom Penh and attempting to cut the land and water routes to the capital.

> We must continue to aid the Cambodian Government in the face of externally supported military attacks. Unless such assistance is provided, the Cambodian army will run out of ammunition ... The Cambodian people are totally dependent on us for their only means of resistance to aggression ... If additional military assistance is withheld ... government forces will be forced, within weeks, to surrender.

Gerald Ford wrote to the Speaker of the House urging assistance, February 25, 1975:

An independent Cambodia cannot survive unless the Congress acts very soon ... Refugees forced to flee their homes by the communists' repressive measures and scorched earth policies have poured into Phnom Penh ... Severe food shortages are already beginning ... Millions of innocent people will suffer – people who depend on us for their bare survival.

On March 6, 1975, Ford spoke about:

I would like to be able to say that the killing would cease if we were to stop our aid, but that is not the case. The record shows, in both Vietnam and Cambodia, that communist takeover of an area does not bring an end to violence, but on the contrary, subjects the innocent to new horrors.

Unfortunately, the United States did not help and the Soviet-backed People's Republic of Kampuchea took over Cambodia in 1979.

∽

CHAPTER 76
YUGOSLAVIA, CROATIA, BOSNIA WAR

In 1991-1992, Yugoslavia suffer a civil war which broke up the nation. A detailed account of what led up to it was recorded by a Yugoslavian woman in a YouTube video that went viral in 2020:

To establish national socialism, you must first install hatred in people ... You must divide people of one country into well-defined groups ... by ethnicity, by race, by religion ...

Since Yugoslavs were white and practicably indistinguishable among themselves, the only card they could play was the religion card.

Yugoslavia was very mixed religion-wise. We had Orthodox Christian Serbs, Catholic Croats and Slovenes, and Muslim Bosnians ...

In the next phase ... you must start claiming that the cause of ... inequalities is nothing but discrimination and hatred of one group towards another ... and ... must be corrected by favoring the "oppressed discriminated group" over the "oppressor group" ...

The mainstream media in Yugoslavia were government controlled and were fueling the narrative about mutual discrimination and hatred relentlessly ...

Growing fear and feeling of insecurity destroyed relationships, marriages, and friendships ... people started retreating and isolating within their own group because they did not feel safe anymore with the individuals from the other group.

All of a sudden, staged and very well-organized mass protests started all over the country ... against oppression ... At first those protests were peaceful, but soon ... rioting and burning started.

Now ... you need ... a spark ... a convenient event of murdering a random member of one group by a hateful member of another ...

At this point, people were still not completely divided ... Reasonable people ... understood we are all one nation ... and that we will not kill each other under any circumstances. They went out ... singing for peace and holding their hands.

But the hunger for absolute power of socialist was stronger than our love for each other And shootings and attacks at protesters continued.

In the next phase, the tipping point of no return was reached. People started erecting barricades at the entrances of their cities, their neighborhoods, even on highways and roads. Barricades were guarded by armed civilians ... Every attempt of the law enforcement to remove barricades and to de-escalate the situation was in vain since they would be ambushed and killed.

Peace could not be restored anymore because headlines, photos, and videos of those incidents propagated by mass media became too explicit and horrifying.

Even those hardcore idealists who believed in one nation under God, peace and love, snapped under the pressure.

At this point, our army was deployed to restore order, but they could not do much because they were clueless about who was the perpetrator and who was the victim simply because there were perpetrators and victims on both sides.

In the final stages, even the army was attacked during the negotiated retreat, with 50 to 100 soldiers killed.

And just like that Yugoslavia found itself in a civil war, city against city, village against village, family against family, and so on until each territory became cleansed of the members of the enemy group.

Genocide, ethnic cleansing, dislocation of hundreds of thousands of people were everyday news. It lasted four years. One hundred thousand people died, five hundred thousand displaced ... People lost everything. Yugoslavia was drowned in the blood of thousands of innocent people and destroyed forever.

You might wonder how we let this happen ... That was because we did not realize who were the real enemies ... of the Yugoslav people as a whole.

We were brainwashed into buying the story we the people are the enemies of each other, while our true enemies were advancing with their sick demented agenda which had as the ultimate goal of total and unlimited power.

∽

CHAPTER 77
VENEZUELA

In 1970, Venezuela was the richest country in Latin America and one of the 20 richest countries in the world. FoxNews reported September 24, 2019:

Home to the world's largest oil reserves, Venezuela was for decades an economic leader in the western hemisphere and, despite a massive gap between rich and poor, was a major destination for neighboring Colombians and other Latin Americans fleeing their less prosperous and more troubled homelands.

In 2002, Hugo Chavez was elected President by making appealing promises of democratic socialism, but in a short time, he transformed the country into a totalitarian socialist state. He established ties with the fundamentalist Islamic State of Iran, ended freedom of the press and expression, and silenced church leaders.

The organization, Reporters Without Borders, noting in their 2009 Press Freedom Index that: "Venezuela is now among the region's worst press freedom offenders"; and Freedom House listed Venezuela's press in 2011 as being "Not Free."

America's Hollywood elite nevertheless praised Hugo Chavez, with Oliver Stone releasing a tribute documentary titled, *Mi amigo Hugo.*

In 2013, socialist politician Nicolas Maduro was elected President of Venezuela, and the nation's recession escalated. Hyperinflation brought factory closures, shortages of food, medicine and basic necessities.

John Hopkins University Professor Steve Hanke considered its currency as being "in a death spiral and things will get worse." With inflation estimated at 10 million per cent in 2019, the United Nations reported some 2.3 million people fled Venezuela since 2015.

There has been reports of corruption, black market, soring murder rate, censored media, restricted churches, and rigged elections. All channels of political dissent are closed and protesters are killed.

FoxNews reported September 24, 2019:

Socialist policies of Maduro and his close ties to leaders in Cuba along with the practice of detaining political prisoners and reports of extrajudicial killings by death squads linked to leaders in Caracas.

"According to a recent report by the United Nation Human Rights Council, women in Venezuela stand in line for 10 hours every day waiting for food, over 15,000 people have been detained as political prisoners, modern day death squads are carrying out thousands of extrajudicial killings," Trump said.

He added: "The dictator Maduro is a Cuban puppet, protected by Cuban bodyguards, hiding from his own people, while Cubans plunder Venezuela's oil wealth to sustain its own corrupt communist rule."

In 2015, Venezuela was visited by BLM co-founder Opal Tometi, who spoke highly of Maduro's rule as "a place where there is intelligent political discourse" (Breitbart, 6/13/20 "Black Lives Matter founder an open supporter of socialist Venezuelan dictator Maduro").

∾

CHAPTER 78
SURRENDER FREEDOM FOR SECURITY

From the beginning of history, in times of crises, people gave up freedom for security. Stalin stated:

Crisis alone permitted the authorities to demand – and obtain – total submission and all necessary sacrifices from its citizens.

Mao Zedong developed the concept of a perpetual crisis with his "continuous revolution."

The first recorded invention was the plow. The Bible described Cain as a "tiller of the soil." Then people made weapons and started hitting each other.

Fear and insecurity caused people give up the independence living on farms to gravitate together for protection, creating the first cities. They looked for someone who was good at fighting to be their captain.

One of the earliest was Gilgamesh, who built the

first wall around a city, Uruk.

An example from the Bible of fearful people wanting a captain is in Book of Judges 11:

> And it was so, that when the children of Ammon made war against Israel, the elders of Gilead went … unto Jephthah, Come, and be our captain, that we may fight with the children of Ammon.

After captains won victories, people showed favoritism to them and their families, leading to a concentration of power in the hands of kings. After Gideon led Israelites to victory (Judges 8):

> Then the men of Israel said unto Gideon, Rule thou over us, both thou, and thy son, and thy son's son also: for thou hast delivered us from the hand of Midian.

Over time, a leader's sons and grandsons became a political machine, controlling those in their cities.

Another example is the Roman Republic, ruled by 600 senators. For centuries, whenever there was a serious national emergency, such as an enemy attack, Rome had a one-year position called a "dictator" who would be given complete charge of the country.

After the year passed and the crisis was over, the dictator would step down and the Republic would go back business as usual under the senators.

Julius Caesar took the unprecedented step of making himself dictator *for life*. Lucan wrote in *Pharsalia*, or *On The Civil War* (61 AD):

> Then for the first time was Rome poorer than a Caesar.

Cicero, a political opponent of Caesar, stated:

> When a government becomes powerful it ... takes bread from innocent mouths and deprives honorable men of their substance, for votes with which to perpetuate itself.

In 2010, a panic was created when President Obama set an arbitrary deadline for Congress to pass the

Affordable Healthcare Act. When the media fanned the public into a frenzy, Speaker of the House Nancy Pelosi hurriedly rushed it to a voice vote, exclaiming:

> We have to pass the bill so you can find out what is in it.

A crisis could be a natural disaster, such as the famine in Egypt where people surrendered their cattle, land, and lives to the Pharaoh in exchange for food. A crisis could also be planned famine for political purposes, such as Stalin's.

In either case, individual are inclined to surrender their freedom during crises.

Actor John Wayne said of socialism, May 1971:

> In the late Twenties, when I was a sophomore at USC, I was a socialist myself – but not when I left. The average college kid idealistically wishes everybody could have ice cream and cake for every meal.

> But as he gets older and gives more thought to his and his fellow man's responsibilities, he finds that it can't work out that way – that some people just won't carry their load ...

> I believe in welfare – a welfare work program. I don't think a fella should be able to sit on his backside and receive welfare.

> I'd like to know why well-educated idiots keep apologizing for lazy and complaining people who think the world owes them a living.

> I'd like to know why they make excuses for cowards who spit in the faces of the police and then run behind the judicial sob sisters.

> I can't understand these people who carry placards to save the life of some criminal, yet have no thought for the innocent victim.

It can take a lifetime to build a mansion and one irresponsible match to burn it down in a day. It took centuries of brilliant minds and courageous hearts to create the freedoms experienced in America, but one irresponsible response to a panic could give it all up in a day.

Frederick Douglass stated April 16, 1888:

> It is well said that "a people may lose its liberty in a day and not miss it in half a century."

Ronald Reagan stated in his speech, "A Time for Choosing," October 27, 1964:

> I suggest to you there is no left or right. There is only an up or down. Up to the maximum of individual freedom consistent with law and order, or down to the ant heap of totalitarianism;
>
> and regardless of their humanitarian purpose, those who would sacrifice freedom for security have, whether they know it or not, chosen this downward path.

∽

CHAPTER 79
THE ENDS JUSTIFIES THE MEANS

Leaders who usurp power in times of crises justify it by promising the final result will be good, giving rise to the phrase, "the end justifies the means."

One of the earliest records of "the end justifies the means" was in India after Alexander the Great retreated.

During the 3rd century BC, King Chandragupta ruled the Maurya Empire, the largest empire in the world for a time. His political advisor Kautilya, also called Chanakya, utilized mafia–style tactics to the extent he was described as "India's Machiavelli."

In the pragmatic spirit as Sun Tzu's *Art of War* (5th century BC), Kautilya wrote a book titled *Arthashastra,* which gives shrewd advice on statecraft to accumulate power. Kautilya counseled the King to use spies to create crises of rivalry, where subjects would fight among themselves, allowing him to usurp control.

Max Weber wrote in *Politics as a Vocation* (1919):

He who seeks the salvation of the soul, of his own and of others, should not seek it along the avenue of politics ...

Radical "Machiavellianism," in the popular sense of this word, is classically represented in Indian literature, in the Kauṭilya's *Arthasastra* ... allegedly dating from Chandragupta's time.

In contrast with this document, Machiavelli's *Prince* is harmless.

Roger Boesche wrote "Kautilya's *Arthashastra* on War and Diplomacy in Ancient India" (*The Journal of Military History*, 2003), which he described:

Is there any other book that talks so openly about when using violence is justified? When assassinating an enemy is useful? When killing domestic opponents is wise?

How one uses secret agents? When one needs to sacrifice one's own secret agent?

How the king can use women and children as spies and even assassins? When a nation should violate a treaty and invade its neighbor?

Kautilya ... addresses all those questions.

In what cases must a king spy on his own people? How should a king test his ministers, even his own family members, to see if they are worthy of trust? When must a king kill a prince, his own son, who is heir to the throne?

How does one protect a king from poison? What precautions must a king take against assassination by one's own wife? When is it appropriate to arrest a troublemaker on suspicion alone? When is torture justified?

At some point, every reader wonders: Is there not one question that Kautilya found immoral, too terrible to ask in a book? No, not one.

And this is what brings a frightful chill. But this is also why Kautilya was the first great, unrelenting political realist.

Centuries later, the British took over India in a similar fashion, stirring up animosities between kingdoms, then taking advantage of the unrest to seize power.

American colonies indicted King George, July 4, 1776:

> He has excited domestic insurrections amongst us, and has endeavored to bring on the inhabitants of our frontiers, the merciless Indian Savages, whose known rule of warfare, is an undistinguished destruction of all ages, sexes and conditions.

A historical marker at Fort Mims, Alabama, states:

> ... the most brutal massacre in American history. Indians took fort ... then killed all but about 36 of some 550 in the fort. Creeks had been armed by British at Pensacola in this phase of War of 1812.

The Bible condemns such behavior (Proverbs 1):

> My son, if sinners entice you, do not yield to them. If they say, "Come along, let us lie in wait for blood, let us ambush the innocent ... We will fill our houses with plunder. Throw in your lot with us; let us all share one purse"— My son, do not walk the road with them ... They lie in wait for their own blood; they ambush their own lives.

Apostle Paul also wrote in Romans, chapter 6:

> Shall we continue in sin, that grace may abound? God forbid ... Neither yield ye your members as instruments of unrighteousness ... For the wages of sin is death; but the gift of God is eternal life through Jesus Christ our Lord.

As long as humans interact, the fallen nature of the human heart will manifest on the political stage.

❦

CHAPTER 80
MACHIAVELLI

The "ends justifies the means" and "everything is permitted" were amoral political tactics explained by Niccolò Machiavelli in his book, *The Prince*, 1515, based on the devious tactics of Cesare Borgia.

Five hundred years ago, Italy consisted of many independent city-states:

Venice, Genoa, Naples, Florence, Sienna, Amalfi, Milan, Corsica, Pisa, San Marino, Cospaia, Gaeta, Lucca, Noli, Trani and Papal States.

These were primarily nobleman's republics, each with their own armies and navies, and they continually fought. Machiavelli thought that if one prince could control all of Italy, it would stop the in-fighting.

He observed the tactics of Cesare Borgia (1475–1507), who reputedly used intrigue, deceit, seduction, incest, poisoning and assassination to usurp power.

Lord Acton wrote:

> Machiavelli supplied the immoral theory needful for the consummation of royal absolutism ... [He] analyzed the wants and resources of aristocracy, and made known that its best security is poison ...

> The central idea of Machiavelli is that the state power is not bound by the moral law. The law is not above the state, but below it.

Machiavelli wrote that in politics, "one must consider the final result," a phrase more succinctly remembered as "the end justifies the means," an adage which dates back to Ovid's *Heroides*, 10 BC.

Called "consequentialism," it replaces absolute standards of right and wrong with subjective reasoning that the rightness of an action is based on whether the consequence or end result is good.

But since every criminal and ambitious politician defines "good" as benefiting themselves or advancing their agenda, it gives them license to lie under oath, deceitfully usurp freedoms, and commit the most reprehensible injustices and atrocities.

The "end," of one prince controlling all of Italy, was such a good end that any "means" necessary to get there was justified.

According to Machiavelli, if a prince wanted to conquer a city, in his quest to unify Italy, the people would hate him. But if the prince secretly paid agitators and criminals under the table to burn barns, kill cows, smash windows and set buildings on fire, thus creating crises and terror in the streets, the people would cry out for help.

The prince would come in, get rid of the "useful idiot" criminals he paid, and nobody would know the better for it. The naive citizens, unaware of his subterfuge, would praise the prince as a hero.

It is good marketing – create the need and fill it. Go around the back of a house and set it on fire, then go around to the front door and sell them a fire extinguisher – they will pay anything for it and thank you for being there.

Jezebel hired "sons of Belial" to create a crisis by falsely accuse Naboth.

Hitler used "Brownshirts" to create crises by disrupting the meetings of his opponents, then once in power, Hitler had the Brownshirts killed in the Night of the Long Knives, and the people praised Hitler for restoring order.

In numerous Democrat-run cities across America, homeless persons were allowed to camp on the streets. During the COVID pandemic, these cities released criminals, including MS13 gang members who illegally crossed borders or ISIS members who accompanied unvetted Middle Eastern immigrants. Soon, crime increased, compounded by the defunding of police.

COVID responses also closed schools, releasing high school and college students indoctrinated with "hate America" views and organized by leftist professors to participate in "indivisible" Antifa protests.

COVID responses also included the unprecedented shutting down of small businesses.

An observation is that when crime goes up in big cities, some people feel insecure; and when businesses are shut down, some people lose their livelihood.

Many of these people decide to leave, especially if they have children or are small business owners. And if churches were shut down, pro-life conservatives would have difficulty organizing.

Statistically, pro-life, pro-family and pro-business citizens are a higher percentage Republican. If these people leave, who is left in the cities? Perhaps more people who are dependent on government entitlements and benefits, being a higher percentage Democrat.

So when crime and unemployment go up, and when churches are restricted, Republicans leave and Democrats end up with a monopoly on city politics. Voter fraud would be more feasible in such a situation.

In elections, whoever wins the big cities usually wins the state, and whoever wins the state gets all the electoral votes for the state, and the President is elected by electoral votes.

There is clear Democrat political advantage to have crime and unemployment go up in big cities. Could this be an example of the end justifies the means?

⤧

CHAPTER 81

NEVER WASTE A CRISIS

The term "Machiavellianism" means, whether a crises is created or coincidental it can be capitalized upon to consolidate control.

A crisis could be anything from organizing riots, to an orchestrated financial collapse; or a virus, as depicted in movies: *Mission Impossible II* (2000); *Twelve Monkeys* (1995); *Outbreak* (1995); *The Hot Zone* (2019 mini–series); *Pandemic* (mini–series 2020); *Contagion* (2011).

Henry Louis Mencken wrote in *Notebooks*, 1956:

> The urge to save humanity is almost always only
> a false-face for the urge to rule it. Power is what
> all messiahs really seek: not the chance to serve.

When normal people experience a crisis, they just want to help people get through it; when ambitious politicians see a crisis, they look at it as an opportunity to seize power and push their agenda.

Rahm Emanuel, President Obama's chief of staff, was quoted in the *New York Times*, November 7, 2008:

> You don't ever want a crisis to go to waste; it's
> an opportunity to do important things that you
> would otherwise avoid.

Rahm Emanuel stated in an interview with *The Wall Street Journal*, November 19, 2008:

> You never want a serious crisis to go to waste
> ... It is an opportunity to do things that you think
> you could not do before.

Secretary of State Hillary Clinton addressed the European Parliament in Brussels, March 6, 2009:

> I'm actually excited by this ... The chief of staff
> for President Obama is an old friend of mine and
> my husband's ... and he said, you know, never
> waste a good crisis.

Clinton viewed the coronavirus pandemic as an opportunity to advance a political agenda, April 28, 2020:

> This is a high-stakes time, because of the pandemic.
> But this is also a really high-stakes election ... I can
> only say, "Amen," to everything you're saying, but
> also to, again, enlist people – that this would be a
> terrible crisis to waste, as the old saying goes.

Bill Domenech stated (FoxNews "PrimeTime" 8/5/21)

> If you are wide awake, you understand that the
> authoritarian left is using the permanent pandemic
> to achieve as many ends as they can imagine ...
> This is Rahm Emmanuel's famous dictum 'never
> let a crisis go to waste' ...

Normal times don't produce the outcomes that the authoritarian left wants because people are not scared enough to give them the limitless power they crave. Crises are necessary. And so, if there aren't any on offer, they manufacture them ... as an opportunity to exploit the moment to achieve their authoritarian aims ...

The left's only answer to the crisis is ... their boot on your neck. But they can't do that if you are wide awake. So are you?

In "Democrats willing to tank the economy to defeat Trump" (FoxNews, 01/14/20), Andy Puzder stated:

At least one anti-Trump leftist was honest ... comedian Bill Maher ... When asked if he really wanted a recession, Maher responded "I do." Why? Well, because "one way you get rid of Trump is a crashing economy."

Such politicians studied Machiavelli, as *Washington Post* reporter David Broder wrote, May 16, 1994:

A year ago ... President Bill Clinton gave an interview to several of us from *The Washington Post* ... At the end of the interview, he stood before the fireplace in the Oval Office and recited to us a passage from Machiavelli's *The Prince*.

Machiavelli gave his diabolical counsel:

One who deceives will always find those who allow themselves to be deceived ...

... Men are so simple and yield so readily to the desires of the moment that he who will trick will always find another who will suffer to be tricked ...

... Men are so simple and so much inclined to obey immediate needs that a deceiver will never lack victims for his deceptions ...

... It is double pleasure to deceive the deceiver ...

... A wise ruler ought never to keep faith when by doing so it would be against his interests ...

... A prince never lacks legitimate reasons to break his promise ...

... The promise given was a necessity of the past: the word broken is a necessity of the present.

This is similar to Talleyrand, the French Foreign Minister, who demanded millions in bribes and infamously spoke out of all sides of his mouth, stating:

We were given speech to hide our thoughts.

Machiavelli advised:

I'm not interested in preserving the status quo; I want to overthrow it.

Machiavellianism was adapted by Hegel into a triangular formula thesis–antithesis–synthesis: the "thesis" is the status quo, which is disrupted by the creation of a crisis or "antithesis," so people willingly accept the "synthesis" of big government control.

Understood politically, it takes people that are content with the way things are and creates a problem that is real bad so people will gladly accept the solution that is only half as bad.

This process is repeated over and over again, and with each solution, the people give up a little more of their freedom, till they are at last reduced to serfs.

Can human nature really be this diabolical?

Machiavelli said: "Politics have no relation to morals."

Sir Francis Bacon wrote in *Essay: Of Goodness* (1625), how Machiavelli opposed Christian values:

And one of the doctors of Italy, Nicholas Machiavelli, had the confidence to put in writing, almost in plain terms, That the Christian faith had given up good men in prey to those that are tyrannical and unjust.

Indeed, even Shakespeare's plays reveal such depths of evil lurking in the human heart. In the play *The Tragedy of Othello*, the revengeful Iago deceitfully gained Othello's trust, then insidiously made him suspicious of his wife's faithfulness till Othello, in blind jealously, strangled his innocent wife.

CHAPTER 82
HEGELIAN DIALECTIC

Machiavelli's capitalizing on crises to consolidate control was adapted by G.W.F. Hegel into "Hegelian Dialectics." It can be described as a triangle:

- one corner is the THESIS;
- the opposite corner it the ANTITHESIS; and
- the top corner is the SYNTHESIS.

Hegel's dialectic struggle influenced Darwin in his development of the theory of evolution and its survival of the fittest, and Hitler, who titled his book *Mein Kampf* (*My Struggle*).

Karl Marx translated Hegelian Dialectics into a political application, where people who are accepting of the status quo (thesis), are subjected to a created crisis that is real bad (antithesis), so that they will be relieved to surrender their freedoms for a solution that is only half as bad (synthesis).

Each synthesis then becomes the new thesis, and the process is repeated until all power is voluntarily relinquished by the people into the hands of a dictator who promises big government solutions.

To create an antithesis, there needs to be division in society. In *Communism–A History* (Random House, 2001) Richard Pipes described:

> As Fidel Castro, the leader of communist Cuba, would explain ... "The revolution needs the enemy ... The revolution needs for its development its antithesis" ... And if enemies were lacking, they had to be fabricated.

To create division, citizens must be made to stop thinking of themselves as citizens, and instead, be made to identify with subgroups which can be pitted against each other to create division – the antithesis.

Subgroups can be social, ethnic, racial, sexual, economic or religious. David Horowitz explained:

> An SDS radical once wrote, "The issue is never the issue. The issue is always the revolution."
>
> In other words ... civil rights or women's rights – is never the real cause; women, blacks ... are only instruments in the larger cause, which is power.
>
> Battles over rights and other issues, according to Alinsky, should never be seen as more than occasions to advance the real agenda, which is the accumulation of power.

Malcolm X exposed this liberal power tactic in 1963:

> The white liberal ... is more deceitful, more hypocritical than the conservative ...
>
> The American Negro is nothing but a political football and the white liberals control this ball through ... false promises.

Once Marx's "critical theory" divides a country into subgroups of victims and oppressors, "haves and have nots," then crisis incidents are manufactured to cause the groups to attack each other, weakening and destabilizing society. It is like a lab-created virus injected into the body politic which causes an autoimmune response of the body attacking itself.

In the weakened, desabilized state, people panic in fear and easily surrender their freedoms to any politician who promises to restore order and security.

The phenomenon of millions of people manipulated into mass panic was when Orson Welles read the 1938 radio drama based on H.G. Wells' *War of the Worlds,* "NEW JERSEY is being INVADED by MARTIANS!!!"

Austrian–American economist Ludwig von Mises described in his 1947 book, *Planned Chaos,* how naive youth can easily be manipulated into a panic to focus on minor divisive issues, not aware they are pawns in bringing about the major issue – a revolution so a dictator can seize power. They are "useful innocents" organized into "confused and misguided sympathizers."

President Ford warned against division, July 4, 1975:

> We are not Americans alone by birth or blood, by oath or creed ... We are Americans because we deliberately chose to be one nation, indivisible, and for 199 years, with God's help, we have gone forward together, and we will in the future.

∽

CHAPTER 83
REVOLUTION NEEDS THE ENEMY

Karl Marx and Friedrich Engels explained (*Marx and Engels Collected Works,* Vol. 10, p. 318):

> It goes without saying that these conspirators by no means confine themselves to organizing the revolutionary proletariat (working class) ...
>
> Their business consists in ... spurring it into artificial crises ...
>
> For them the only condition required for the revolution is a sufficient organization of their own conspiracy. They are the alchemists of the revolution.

Attorney General William P. Barr remarked February 26, 2020:

> Totalitarian(ism) ... requires an all-knowing elite to guide the masses toward their determined end, and that elite relies on whipping up mass enthusiasm to preserve its power and achieve its goals.

Crises can be economic. Friedrich Engels proposed financial crises to bankrupt small businesses (London: W.O. Henderson, *The Life of Friedrich Engels,* 1976; *Outlines of a Critique of Political Economy,* 1844):

> Every new crisis must be more serious and more universal than the last. Every fresh slump must ruin more small capitalists and increase the workers who live only by their labor.
>
> This will increase the number of the unemployed and this is the main problem that worries economists.

In the end commercial crises will lead to a social revolution far beyond the comprehension of the economists with their scholastic wisdom.

William Barr noted February 26, 2020:

The progressive program is to use the public purse to provide ever-increasing benefits to the public ... to ... build a permanent constituency of supporters who are also dependents. They want able-bodied citizens to become more dependent, subject to greater control, and increasingly supportive of dependency.

The tacit goal of this project is to convert all of us into 25 year-olds living in the government's basement, focusing our energies on obtaining a larger allowance rather than getting a job and moving out.

He continued:

Alexis de Tocqueville foresaw that American democracy would be susceptible to this ... a soft despotism wherein the majority would gradually let itself be taken care of by the state – much like dependent children ...

The tyranny that results, Tocqueville wrote, "does not break wills, but it softens them, bends them and directs them ... and finally it reduces [people] to being nothing more than a flock of timid and industrious animals, of which the government is the shepherd."

As Tocqueville summed it up: "By this system the people shake off their state of dependence just long enough to select their master and then relapse into it again."

This was hinted at by the rock band The Who, in their song, "We Won't Get Fooled Again":

Meet the new boss; Same as the old boss.

In *Communism–A History* (Random House, 2001) author Richard Pipes described how Stalin fabricated a crisis – which he shifted the blame onto his opponents, and used it as an excuse for the government to eliminate his enemies and seize more power:

Stalin's regime needed another crisis ... as Fidel

Castro, the leader of Communist Cuba, would explain ... "The revolution needs the enemy ... The revolution needs for its development its antithesis" ... And if enemies were lacking, they had to be fabricated ...

Pipes continued:

In 1934, a prominent Bolshevik, Sergei Kirov, the party boss of Leningrad, was assassinated under mysterious conditions ... evidence points to Stalin ...

Kirov was gaining too much popularity in party ranks for Stalin's comfort. His assassination brought Stalin two advantages: it rid him of a potential rival and provided a rationale for instigating a vast campaign against alleged anti-Soviet conspirators ...

Pipes concluded:

Purges of the 1930's were a terror campaign that in indiscriminate ferocity and number of victims had no parallel in world history ... Authorities ... beat them until they confess to crimes they have not committed.

Regarding a government lying to its citizens, Solzhenitsyn stated (*The Observer,* December 29, 1974):

In our country the lie has become not just a moral category but a pillar of the state.

❧

CHAPTER 84

SAUL ALINSKY

Saul Alinsky rode around Chicago with Al Capone's hitman Frank Nitti, and saw how all he had to do was kill a few people and smash a few windows and the entire neighborhood would become fearful and agree to pay the mob "protection money."

Alinsky adapted this into his political technique of "community organizing."

In 1969, Hillary Clinton's senior thesis at Wellesley College was "'There Is Only the Fight': An Analysis of the Alinsky Model." It was based on Saul Alinsky's book *Reveille for Radicals* (1946). Barak Obama taught Alinsky's *Rules for Radicals* (1971), beginning his political career as a community organizer in Chicago.

Alinsky taught how to identify tension "fault lines" in a society and fan real or perceived injustices into emotional flames. When they reach the boiling point and anarchy breaks out, everyone is so desperate to have order restored that they will "knee-jerk reaction" relinquish their rights. He wrote in *Rules for Radicals*:

> The first step in community organization is community disorganization. The disruption of the present organization is the first step ...

> The organizer must first rub raw the resentments of the people of the community; fan the latent hostilities of many of the people to the point of overt expression ...

> He must search out controversy and issues, rather than avoid them, for unless there is controversy people are not concerned enough to act ...

> The organizer's first job is to create the issues or problems ...

> An organizer must stir up dissatisfaction and discontent; provide a channel into which the people can angrily pour their frustrations ...

> The organizer ... polarizes the issue ...

> The organizer helps to lead his forces into conflict ... The real arena is corrupt and bloody... In war the end justifies almost any means ...

> The question of morality would never arise ... Ethics are determined by whether one is losing or winning ...

> In the arena of action, a threat or a crisis becomes almost a precondition.

Author David Horowitz explained:

> An SDS radical once wrote, "The issue is never the issue. The issue is always the revolution" ...

Battles over rights and other issues, according to Alinsky, should never be seen as more than occasions to advance the real agenda, which is the accumulation of power.

Where Psalm 113:1 declares "How good and how pleasant it is for brethren to dwell together in unity," Proverbs 6 states "A wicked man ... soweth discord ... The Lord hates ... he that soweth discord among brethren."

In the introductory pages of *Rules for Radicals*, Alinsky mentioned Lucifer, who sowed discord in heaven:

Lest we forget at least an over-the-shoulder acknowledgment to ... the first radical known to man who rebelled against the establishment and did it so effectively that he at least won his own kingdom — Lucifer.

∽

CHAPTER 85
CRISES

As mentioned earlier, crises, whether created or coincidental, can be consistently capitalized upon to concentrate control. Some crises include:

•AIDS Crisis •Anthrax Crisis •Avian Flu Crisis •Mad Cow Disease Crisis •West Nile Virus Crisis •Swine Flu Crisis •E. Coli Crisis •SARS Crisis •MERS Crisis •Ebola Crisis •Zika Crisis •COVID19 Crisis •Prescription Drug Crisis •Healthcare Crisis •Y2K Crisis •National Debt Crisis •Sub-Prime Mortgage Crisis •Unemployment Crisis •911 & ISIS Crisis •Terrorism Crisis •Patriot Act & NSA Surveillance Crisis •Oil Embargo Crisis •BP Gulf Oil Spill Crisis •Environmental Crisis •Global Warming Crisis •Climate Change Crisis •North Korea Missile Crisis •Internet Virus Cyber Attacks •Computer Hacking Crisis •Identity Theft Crisis •Border Crisis •Immigration Crisis •Homeless Crisis •Occupy Wall Street •School Shooting Crisis •Gun Violence Crisis •"Hands Up Don't Shoot" •BLM (Black Lives Matter) •Ferguson Riots •Baltimore Riots •Charlotte Riots •March for Our Lives •Confederate Statue Protests.

Crises may be psychologically induced:

- students needing safe-spaces so as not be traumatized by hearing triggering views;

- being offended by micro-aggressions, intersectionality, or hearing wrong pronouns;

- hateful organizations projecting their hate onto innocent opponents;

- intolerant sharia adherents claiming to be victims of intolerance";

- violent "peace" demonstrators and aggressive social justice activists;

- occupy Wall Street protests, Flag protests, National Anthem protests, Pledge of Allegiance protests, autonomous zones;

- school or other shootings capitalized upon to advance political agendas;

- predictions of fearful climate crisis with urgent deadlines that pass unfulfilled; or

- virus pandemic crisis with economic shut-downs, governor ordered home confinement and church designation of non-essential.

The media irresistibly exacerbates crises to an urgency where people almost believe the world will end. Crises can be used to advance a political agenda.

✖

CHAPTER 86
UTOPIA A DANGEROUS IDEAL

Michael Shermer wrote in "Utopia Is a Dangerous Ideal" (Aeon, April 2020):

> People act on their beliefs, and if you believe that the only thing preventing you and/or your family, clan, tribe, race or religion from going to heaven (or achieving heaven on Earth) is someone else or some other group, then actions know no bounds.

> From homicide to genocide, the murder of others in the name of ... ideological belief accounts for the

high body counts in history ...

Shermer explained what happens to those "blocking the road to paradise":

> We can see that calculus behind the utopian logic in the now famous "trolley problem" in which most people say they would be willing to kill one person in order to save five. Here's the set-up: you are standing next to a fork in a railroad line with a switch to divert a trolley car that is about to kill five workers on the track.
>
> If you pull the switch, it will divert the trolley down a side track where it will kill one worker. If you do nothing, the trolley kills the five. What would you do? Most people say that they would pull the switch.
>
> If even people in Western enlightened countries today agree that it is morally permissible to kill one person to save five, imagine how easy it is to convince people living in autocratic states with utopian aspirations to kill 1,000 to save 5,000, or to exterminate 1,000,000 so that 5,000,000 might prosper.
>
> What's a few zeros when we're talking about infinite happiness and eternal bliss?
>
> The fatal flaw in utilitarian utopianism is found in another thought experiment: you are a healthy bystander in a hospital waiting room in which an ER physician has five patients dying from different conditions, all of which can be saved by sacrificing you and harvesting your organs.
>
> Would anyone want to live in a society in which they might be that innocent bystander?
>
> Of course not, which is why any doctor who attempted such an atrocity would be tried and convicted for murder.
>
> Yet this is precisely what happened with the grand 20th–century experiments in utopian socialist ideologies as manifested in Marxist/Leninist/Stalinist Russia (1917–1989), Fascist Italy (1922–1943) and Nazi Germany (1933–1945) ...

All (are) large-scale attempts to achieve political, economic, social (and even racial) perfection, resulting in tens of millions of people murdered by their own states or killed in conflict with other states perceived to be blocking the road to paradise ...

Shermer added:

The Marxist theorist and revolutionary Leon Trotsky ... gained power as one of the first seven members of the founding Soviet Politburo ...

He established concentration camps for those who refused to join in this grand utopian experiment, ultimately leading to the gulag archipelago that killed millions of Russian citizens who were also believed to be standing in the way of the imagined utopian paradise to come.

When his own theory of Trotskyism opposed that of Stalinism, the dictator had Trotsky assassinated in Mexico in 1940. Sic semper tyrannis.

Shermer concluded:

In the second half of the 20th century, revolutionary Marxism in Cambodia, North Korea and numerous states in South America and Africa led to murders, pogroms, genocides, ethnic cleansings, revolutions, civil wars and state-sponsored conflicts, all in the name of establishing a heaven on Earth that required the elimination of recalcitrant dissenters.

All told, some 94 million people died at the hands of revolutionary Marxists and utopian communists in Russia, China, North Korea and other states, a staggering number compared with the 28 million killed by the fascists.

When you have to murder people by the tens of millions to achieve your utopian dream, you have instantiated only a dystopian nightmare.

CHAPTER 87
INFILTRATION

John F. Kennedy cautioned, April 27, 1961:

We are as a people inherently and historically opposed to secret societies ... We are opposed around the world by a ... ruthless conspiracy that relies primarily on covert means for expanding its sphere of influence – on infiltration ... tightly knit, highly efficient ... political operations.

Eisenhower spoke in Abilene's Plaza Theater (*TIME Magazine,* June 16, 1952):

Any kind of communistic, subversive or pinkish influence (must) be uprooted from the responsible places in our government.

At the College of William and Mary, May 15, 1953, Eisenhower stated:

It is necessary that we earnestly seek out and uproot any traces of communism at any place where it can affect our national life ...

The true way to uproot communism in this country is to understand what freedom means, and thus develop an impregnable wall, that no thought of communism can enter.

Eisenhower stated February 25, 1953:

Almost 100 percent of Americans would like to stamp out all traces of communism in our country ...

I went to Columbia University as its President and I insisted on one thing ... If we had a known communist in our faculty and he could not be discharged ... I was automatically discharged.

I personally would not be a party to an organization where there was a known card-carrying communist in such a responsible position as teaching our young

Lyndon B. Johnson supported Franklin Roosevelt's collectivist New Deal programs, which he later expanded with his Great Society Welfare State.

Prior to his reelection to the Senate, a 501(c)3 non-profit, the Committee for Constitution Government, circulated a pamphlet in 1954, calling out Johnson.

In the pamphlet, Willis Ballinger wrote:

> A vote for Johnson – many Texans feel – will be a vote for more centralization of power and socialism in Washington; for more of the internationalism which is designed to abolish the U.S.A.; and for more covering up of communist infiltration.

Johnson wanted to silence this group, so he proposed the IRS censor the freedom of speech of 501(c)3 non-profit organizations from speaking on politics.

∽

CHAPTER 88
COMMUNIST GOALS

During World War II, the United States won a two front war, Europe and the Pacific. In the Cold War, the U.S.S.R. realized it could not be successful against the U.S. on the battlefield, so the strategy was to weaken it from within.

A list of these subversive communist goals for America was disclosed by Rep. Albert S. Herlong, Jr., of Florida, who read into the *Congressional Record*, January 10, 1963 (Vol 109, 88th Congress, 1st Session, Appendix, pp. A34–A35). Excerpts of the list include:

12. Resist any attempt to outlaw the Communist Party.

13. Do away with all loyalty oaths ...

15. Capture one or both of the political parties in the U.S.

16. Use technical decisions of the courts to weaken basic American institutions by claiming their activities violate civil rights.

17. Get control of the schools. Use them as transmission belts for socialism and current communist propaganda. Soften the curriculum. Get control of teachers' associations. Put the party line in textbooks.

18. Gain control of all student newspapers.

19. Use student riots to foment public protests against programs or organizations which are under

communist attack.

20. Infiltrate the press. Get control of book-review assignments, editorial writing, policymaking positions.

21. Gain control of key positions in radio, TV, and motion pictures.

22. Continue discrediting American culture by degrading all forms of artistic expression ... eliminate all good sculpture from parks and buildings, substitute shapeless, awkward and meaningless forms.

23. Control art critics and directors of art museums. "Our plan is to promote ugliness, repulsive, meaningless art."

24. Eliminate all laws governing obscenity by calling them "censorship" and a violation of free speech and free press.

25. Break down cultural standards of morality by promoting pornography and obscenity in books, magazines, motion pictures, radio, and TV.

26. Present homosexuality, degeneracy and promiscuity as "normal, natural, healthy."

27. Infiltrate the churches and replace revealed religion with "social" religion. Discredit the Bible and emphasize the need for intellectual maturity which does not need a "religious crutch."

28. Eliminate prayer or any phase of religious expression in the schools on the ground that it violates the principle of "separation of church and state."

29. Discredit the American Constitution by calling it inadequate, old-fashioned, out of step with modern needs, a hindrance to cooperation between nations on a worldwide basis.

30. Discredit the American Founding Fathers. Present them as selfish aristocrats who had no concern for the "common man."

31. Belittle all forms of American culture and discourage the teaching of American history on the ground that it was only a minor part of the "big picture." Give more emphasis to Russian history

since the communists took over.

32. Support any socialist movement to give centralized control over any part of the culture–education, social agencies, welfare programs, mental health clinics, etc ...

36. Infiltrate and gain control of more unions.

37. Infiltrate and gain control of big business ...

40. Discredit the family as an institution. Encourage promiscuity and easy divorce.

41. Emphasize the need to raise children away from the negative influence of parents. Attribute prejudices, mental blocks and retarding of children to suppressive influence of parents.

42. Create the impression that violence and insurrection are legitimate aspects of the American tradition; that students and special-interest groups should rise up and use "united force" to solve economic, political or social problems.

&

CHAPTER 89
ROGER BALDWIN AND THE ACLU

A person who used legal means to advance socialist goals in America was Roger Baldwin, one of the founders of the American Civil Liberties Union (ACLU), a 501(c)3 tax-exempt Foundation.

Roger Baldwin graduated from Harvard in 1905. The editor of the *Harvard College Class 35th Anniversary Yearbook* sent him a questionnaire, to which Baldwin replied with a statement echoing Lenin's phrase, "the goal of socialism is communism":

> I am for socialism, disarmament, and ultimately, for abolishing the state itself as an instrument of violence and compulsion. I seek social ownership of property, the abolition of the propertied class, and sole control of those who produce wealth. Communism is the goal.

Baldwin twice visited the Soviet Union. He embraced Vietnamese Communist dictator Ho Chi Minh. In

Liberty Under the Soviets (NY: Vanguard Press, 1928), he unapologetically defended communist hypocrisy:

> Communists aid the workers in capitalist countries to the fullest possible expression of their class ... while suppressing in Russia the working class ...

> To communists, there is no inconsistency in denying civil liberties to all opponents in Soviet Russia, while demanding these liberties for their movement in capitalist countries ...

He concluded:

> I joined. I don't regret being a part of the communist tactic, which increased the effectiveness of a good cause. I knew what I was doing. I was not an innocent liberal. I wanted what the communists wanted.

The California Senate Fact Finding Committee on Un-American Activities stated in its 1948 report, p. 107:

> The ACLU may be definitely classified as a communist front or transmission belt organization ...

> At least 90 percent of its efforts are on behalf of communists who come in conflict with the law.

Baldwin's friend, Earl Browder, was general secretary of the Communist Party USA from 1930 to 1944. The Senate Internal Security Subcommittee reported, 1956:

> Founded in September 1919, the Communist Party of the United States of America is an organization unique in American history.

> It is not a true political party and differs fundamentally from all political parties in this country. It is in fact a Russian–inspired, Moscow–dominated military conspiracy against our government, our ideals, and our freedoms.

In 1982, FBI assistant director of intelligence, Edward O'Malley, testified the Communist Party USA was:

> One of the most loyal and pro-Soviet Communist Parties in the world and has unfalteringly accepted

Soviet direction and funding over the years.

In 1950, members of the Communist Party USA formed the Mattachine Society, the nation's first homosexual rights organization, which lobbied to repeal sodomy laws. Other organizations followed suit. The Black Lives Matter website (accessed 6/12/20):

> We make space for transgender .... and ... work ... to dismantle cisgender privilege and uplift ... trans folk, especially ... trans women ...

> We disrupt the Western-prescribed nuclear family structure requirement by supporting each other as extended families and "villages" that collectively care for ... children ...

> We foster a queer-affirming network. When we gather, we do so with the intention of freeing ourselves from the tight grip of heteronormative thinking, or rather, the belief that all in the world are heterosexual (unless s/he or they disclose otherwise).

Ruth Bader Ginsburg became a director at the ACLU in 1972. Bill Clinton appointed her to the Supreme Court in 1993.

The ACLU opposed the Bible, as Reagan told the National Religious Broadcasters, January 30, 1984:

> I was pleased last year to proclaim 1983 the Year of the Bible. But, you know, a group called the ACLU severely criticized me for doing that. Well, I wear their indictment like a badge of honor.

Franklin Roosevelt warned delegates of the American Youth Congress, February 10, 1940:

> Some of you are communists ... You have no American right, by act or deed of any kind, to subvert the Government and the Constitution of this Nation.

Eisenhower made a reference to ACLU efforts in *TIME Magazine*, October 13, 1952:

> The Bill of Rights contains no grant of privilege for a group of people to destroy the Bill of Rights.

A group – like the communist conspiracy – dedicated to the ultimate destruction of all civil liberties, cannot be allowed to claim civil liberties as its privileged sanctuary from which to carry on subversion of the government.

Eisenhower's view could likewise be a warning against sharia Islam, namely, the extending civil liberties to groups whose goal is to establish a fundamentalist Islamic system which denies civil liberties to non-Muslims.

࿇

CHAPTER 90
WHITTAKER CHAMBERS

Soviet infiltration tactics in Hollywood, media, education, politics, business, churches, seminaries, etc., were confirmed by Vasili Mitrokhin, senior archivist for the Soviet Union's foreign intelligence and the First Chief Directorate of the KGB.

After the Berlin Wall came down in 1989 and the disestablishment of the Soviet Union in 1991, Vasili Mitrokhin left Russia for Estonia, then traveled to England in 1992.

He brought with him over 25,000 pages of Soviet intelligence records, documented in *The Mitrokhin Archive: The KGB in Europe and the West* (1999).

One infiltration incident that shocked the nation was in 1948. *TIME Magazine* senior editor Whittaker Chambers confessed to being a Soviet spy.

Chambers had joined the communist underground in 1932 and worked with spies within Franklin D. Roosevelt's New Deal administration who leaked classified documents.

When fellow Soviet spy Walter Krivitsky was found murdered in 1941, Chambers feared for his life and decided to give himself up. He went to the FBI, but strangely, the FBI did not follow up on his lead.

It was not until another spy, Elizabeth Bentley, defected in 1945 and corroborated Chambers' story that his defection was given attention.

In 1948, Whittaker Chambers testified before the House Un-American Activities Committee, naming 18 current and former government employees who were communist spies or sympathizers.

One of those named was Alger Hiss, who worked in Roosevelt's Department of Justice and State Department, and who helped write the United Nation's Charter.

For his effort in exposing Soviet spies, Chambers was posthumously awarded the Medal of Freedom by Ronald Reagan, who stated March 6, 1984:

> Whittaker Chambers understood the struggle between totalitarianism and the West.
>
> He, himself, had turned to communism out of a sense of idealism in which he thought that might be the answer. And then he wrote ... "the communist vision is the vision of man without God" ...
>
> When men try to live in a world without God, it's only too easy for them to forget the rights that God bestows — too easy to suppress freedom of speech ... jail dissidents, and to put great thinkers in mental wards.

⤚

CHAPTER 91
FRANK MARSHALL DAVIS

In 1943, a journalist named Frank Marshall Davis joined the Communist Party in Chicago. In 1956, he was called to testify before the Senate Internal Security Subcommittee, then he moved to Hawaii.

In the article "Frank Marshall Davis: A Forgotten Voice in the Chicago Black Renaissance," written by ex-University of Hawaii professor Kathryn Takara (2002), Frank Marshall Davis is quoted as saying:

> From now on I knew I would be described as

a communist, but frankly I had reached the stage where I didn't give a damn.

In the Communist Party USA's journal *Political Affairs,* Gerald Horne wrote of "a history of the radical, communist and working-class movement in Hawaii":

> It is not well known, I'm afraid, that before statehood in 1959 probably the most vigorous, communist and radical trade union movement under the U.S. flag was in Hawaii.

Investor's Business Daily, August 5, 2008, wrote:

> Frank Marshall Davis was a member of the Moscow–controlled Communist Party USA, according to the 1953 report of the Commission of Subversive Activities of the Territory of Hawaii.

While in Hawaii, Davis wrote a weekly column, "Frankly Speaking," for the labor union paper *Honolulu Record,* headed by vocal communist Harry Bridges (*TIME Magazine,* July 19, 1937.)

In 1956, the House Un-American Activities Committee concluded that the *Honolulu Record* was "a front for the Communist Party," stating:

> Mr. Davis' column defends communists and attacks capitalism with the same vigor as columns appearing regularly in the *Daily Worker* and other frankly communist publications ...

> Mr. Davis constantly defended the 11 top United States Communist officials recently convicted in New York on charges of conspiracy to overthrow the government ...

> Mr. Davis comments ... as follows: "I feel strong sympathy for the communist minority."

While in Hawaii, Frank Marshall Davis became friends with Stanley Dunham, as the *Telegraph.co.uk* reported in the article "Frank Marshall Davis, alleged Communist," August 24, 2008:

> Frank never really did drugs, though he and Stan would smoke pot together.

On February 2, 1961, Stanley Dunham's daughter, Ann Dunham, married, a student from Kenya, Barack Hussein Obama, Sr, father of the 44th U.S. President.

✧

CHAPTER 92

DREAM VERSUS REALITY

Socialism exists in two separate phases: the dream and the reality. In the dream phase, it holds out the vision of a perfectly ordered society, where every need is met and every problem solved, but the reality phase brings a rude awakening of a nightmare.

If socialism's past failures are pointed out, naive youth blame them on the insincere efforts by inept leaders, but this time they are convinced it will work.

It is like the Children's Crusade of 1212, in which thousands of youth joined a frenzied march to free the Holy Land from the Saracens, only to be sold into slavery.

Or the Pied-Piper of Hamelin, who, in 1284, played his flute, leading the cheering children to follow him out of town. They were never to be seen again.

It is like dangling a carrot on a stick before a donkey, always out of reach; like a mirage in the desert that looks refreshing but evaporates as one gets near.

It is like the Greek sailor Ulysses sailing past the island of the sirens – mythical half-women creatures – whose singing lured sailors to come close to the shore only to be shipwrecked on the rocks.

Or Germany's Legend of the Lorelei, where an enchanting woman sat on a cliff overlooking a dangerous turn in the Rhine River. When sailors floated near to get a glimpse of her, the water current crashed their boats on submerged boulders.

Socialism is the dream for mankind to have heaven on earth without God, though what it delivers is nearer hell. To prevent this, after Adam and Eve sinned, God would not let them eat from the Tree of Life.

On a macro-societal scale, socialism is a grand bait and switch. It promises a perfect, utopian society, but delivers a totalitarian dictatorship, a top–down structured society, ruled by deep-state elites.

Imagine if older fish could pass history on to younger fish not yield to the temptation to bite shiny objects dangling in the water, but they cannot. Every new generation of fish is tempted to bite, only to find out too late the fatal hook.

Socialism is a shiny object. Free food, free healthcare, free education, free housing, free everything. Free is attractive, but there is a fatal hook. President Gerald Ford stated March 11, 1976:

> People say ... why don't you expand that program, why don't you spend more Federal money? ... I don't think they have understood one of the fundamentals ...
>
> I look them in the eye and I say, "Do you realize that a government big enough to give us everything we want is a government big enough to take from us everything we have?"

If you are friends with those in power you are more equal; if you are not, then you are less equal.

Those in the socialist ruling class are tempted to distribute benefits in exchange for favors. Pharaoh distributed grain in Egypt in exchange for people's cattle, land, and lives. Selfish human nature inclines the ruling class to funnel benefits to those who support them; and withhold them from those who do not.

Actor John Wayne observed:

> Government has no wealth, and when a politician promises to give you something for nothing, he must first confiscate that wealth from you – either by direct taxes, or by the cruelly indirect tax of inflation.

When socialism first takes over, there is a honeymoon

period where problems appear to turn around, but when the dust settles, citizens are shocked by the realization they gave away their rights. As well-intentioned as big government solutions are, they ends up with more control over people's lives. Washington warned in his Farewell Address, 1796:

> But let there be no change by usurpation; for though this, in one instance, may be the instrument of good, it is the customary weapon by which free governments are destroyed.

> The precedent [of usurpation to solve a crisis] must always greatly overbalance in permanent evil any partial or transient benefit which the use can at any time yield.

∾

CHAPTER 93
REAL PATRIOTS ATTACKED

Washington predicted in his Farewell Address, 1796:

> Real Patriots, who may resist the intrigues [secret plans] of the favorite, are liable to become suspected and odious; while its tools and dupes usurp the applause and confidence of the people, to surrender their interests.

President William Harrison compared "spirit of liberty" to the counterfeit "spirit of party":

> There is at times much difficulty in distinguishing the false from the true spirit, a calm investigation will detect the counterfeit ...

> The true spirit of liberty ... is mild and tolerant and scrupulous ... whilst the spirit of party, assuming to be that of liberty, is harsh, vindictive, and intolerant, and totally reckless as to the character of the allies which it brings to the aid of its cause ...

> The reign of an intolerant spirit of party amongst a free people seldom fails to result in a dangerous accession to the executive power introduced and established amidst unusual

professions of devotion to democracy.

George Washington warned further:

In contemplating the causes which may disturb our Union ... (are) parties ... (which) acquire influence ... to misrepresent the opinions and aims of other(s) ....

You cannot shield yourselves too much against the jealousies and heart burnings which spring from these misrepresentations ...

Washington continued:

And of fatal tendency ... to put, in the place of the delegated will of the nation, the will of a party; – often a small but artful and enterprising minority ...

They are likely, in the course of time and things, to become potent engines (mechanisms), by which cunning, ambitious, and unprincipled men will be enabled to subvert the power of the people and to usurp for the themselves the reins of government; destroying afterwards the very engines which have lifted them to unjust dominion ...

Washington stated further:

Let me ... warn you in the most solemn manner against the baneful effects of the spirit of party ... This spirit, unfortunately, is inseparable from our nature, having its roots in the strongest passions of the human mind.

It exists under different shapes in all governments ... but, in those of the popular form it is ... their worst enemy ...

Ill-founded jealousies and false alarms, kindles the animosity of one part against another, foments occasionally riot and insurrection ...

Domination of one faction over another, sharpened by the spirit of revenge natural to party dissension, which in different ages and countries has perpetrated the most horrid enormities ... leads at length to a more formal and permanent despotism.

CHAPTER 94
POWER GRAB

History has shown party rivalry, domestic unrest, mob emotions and national crises allow ambitious leaders to usurp power. A worldwide crisis would allow for a global power grab.

Deep state elitists claim to be more intelligent, and therefore should be trusted to take care of the world's population. George Orwell wrote in "The English People" (1947):

> In the last generation ... intelligentsia have tended to take their ideas from Europe and have been infected by habits of thought that derive ultimately from Machiavelli.

> All the cults that have been fashionable in the last dozen years, communism, fascism, and pacifism, are in the last analysis forms of power worship.

In Orwell's novel, *Nineteen Eighty–Four,* O'Brien tells Winston:

> "There is no way in which the Party can be overthrown. The rule of the Party is forever. Make that the starting-point of your thoughts ...

> The Party maintains itself in power. Now tell me why we cling to power. What is our motive? Why should we want power? Go on, speak,"

> Winston said feebly, "You are ruling over us for our own good ... You believe that human beings are not fit to govern themselves, and therefore --"

> "That was stupid, Winston, stupid!" O'Brien said. "You should know better than to say a thing like that ... I will tell you the answer to my question ...

> The Party seeks power entirely for its own sake. We are not interested in the good of others; we are interested solely in power ... pure power ...

> We are different from all the oligarchies of the past ... German Nazis and the Russian Communists came very close to us in their methods, but they never

had the courage to recognize their own motives.

They pretended, perhaps they even believed, that they had seized power unwillingly and for a limited time, and that just round the corner there lay a paradise where human beings would be free and equal.

We are not like that. We know that no one ever seizes power with the intention of relinquishing it. Power is not a means, it is an end.

One does not establish a dictatorship in order to safeguard a revolution; one makes the revolution in order to establish the dictatorship ...

The object of power is power. Now do you begin to understand me?"

David Horowitz wrote in *Rules for the Revolution–The Alinsky Model* (Freedom Center, 2009, p. 8–9):

The New Republic's Ryan Lizza nicely illustrates ... When Alinsky would ask new students why they wanted to organize, they would invariably respond with selfless bromides about wanting to help others. Alinsky would then scream back at them that there was a one-word answer: "You want to organize for POWER!"

World War I Fighter Ace Eddie Rickenbacker warned:

Every time the liberals discover ... a new way to circumvent the constitutional limits of the Federal power, they pile up more power in Washington at the expense of individual liberty across the land ...

The liberal would sweep aside the constitutional restraints upon government in a blind rush to supply food, clothes, houses and financial security from birth to death, from the cradle to the grave for everybody ... The conservative knows that to regard man of a part of an undifferentiated mass is to consign him to ultimate slavery ... Government is like fire: a dangerous servant and a fearful master ... (It needs) limits.

In his address "Americanism versus Communism,"

November 1, 1971, Rickenbacker warned:

> A government that is large enough to give you all you want is large enough to take all you own first.

President Gerald Ford stated October 19, 1974:

> What they don't tell us when they propose all these benefits that they are going to give you from our government ... that a government big enough to give us everything we want is a government big enough to take from us everything we have.

President Donald Trump warned February 18, 2019:

> The more power they get, the more they crave. They want to run healthcare, transportation, finance, energy, education ... Socialism is not about justice, it's not about equality, it's not about lifting up the poor ... it's about one thing only: power for the ruling class.

⤶

CHAPTER 95
GEORGE ORWELL'S DYSTOPIA

Every attempt at a "utopia" inevitably ends with the opposite, a "dystopia." Dystopian novels include:

- *A Modern Utopia* by H.G. Wells, 1905
- *Men Like Gods* by H.G. Wells, 1923
- *We* by Yevgeny Zamyatin, 1924;
- *Brave New World* by Aldous Huxley, 1931;
- *Kallocain* by Karin Boye, 1940;
- *Lord of the Flies* by William Golding, 1954;
- *THX 1138* by George Lucas, 1971.

The classic dystopian novel is *Animal Farm,* published in 1945 by George Orwell.

It tells a story of farm animals who rebel against their human farmer, hoping to create a society where the animals can be equal, free, and happy. Unfortunately, the rebellion is betrayed by the pigs, who declared:

> All animals are equal, but some animals are

more equal than others.

Despite socialist promises of a "classless" society, Orwell explained in *Animal Farm* how socialism always ends up being run by selfish bullies who set themselves up as the elite ruling-class, the new royalty.

A pig named Napoleon usurped control of the farm:

We pigs are brainworkers. The whole management and organization of this farm depend on us. Day and night we are watching over your welfare.

It is for YOUR sake that we drink that milk and eat those apples. Do you know what would happen if we pigs failed in our duty? ... The importance of keeping the pigs in good health was all too obvious.

So it was agreed without further argument that the milk and the windfall apples (and also the main crop of apples when they ripened) should be reserved for the pigs alone.

Socialist hierarchy is contrary to the Bible, which affirmed in Acts 10:34 "God is no respecter of persons."

Despite socialism's unrealistic utopian promises, what it delivers is a deep-state ruling class who control:

•land; •production; •distribution of food; •where one lives; •what job one works; •what clothes one wears; •what one can say; •what views one can express; and •what one must believe.

George Orwell's dystopian novel, *Nineteen Eighty–Four,* was written in 1949, at the beginning of the Cold War.

In it, he eerily predicted things to come, such as the government labeling those holding politically incorrect views as "hateful," continual crises, and state-controlled surveillance technology:

• "Thought crimes" (such as enforced on college campus with transgendered pronouns and intersectionality, etc.);

• "Thought police";

- "Newspeak" fake-news propaganda;
- "Doublethink" (believing contradictory thoughts in order to fit in);
- Continual crises and international tension;
- Cameras & listening devices everywhere (i.e. Alexa, Siri, Echo, 5G);
- Telescreens (i.e. Facial Recognition, FaceTime, Zoom, etc.)

East Germany's "Stasi" tracked every citizen. China installed 20 million AI equipped street cameras to track people; pandemic responses include "contact tracing"; and social media accounts are censored or suspended.

In ancient Israel people behaved fairly because God was watching. Modern socialist states are attempting to replace God and make people conform to their agenda with "Big Brother" government watching.

Orwell described a highly controlled socialized state with continual surveillance:

> On each landing, opposite the lift-shaft, the poster with the enormous face gazed from the wall. It was one of those pictures which was contrived that the eyes follow you about when you move. BIG BROTHER IS WATCHING YOU, the caption beneath it ran.

Orwell wrote to H.J. Willmett, May 18, 1944:

> Everywhere the world movement seems to be in the direction of centralized economies which can be made to "work" in an economic sense, but which are not democratically organized, and which tend to establish a caste system.

Judge Learned Hand wrote to Supreme Court Justice Felix Frankfurter, March 24, 1945, warning:

> I confess it seems to me that we are pretty plainly headed for some fairly comprehensive collectivist ordering of industry; people don't want it ... Can you have a collectivist democracy?

The future has all sorts of creatures in its womb

... There seems to me great obstacles; a society in which the individual's fate is completely in the hands of the government can scarcely manifest itself as a succession of resultants of "pressure groups" – it won't stand up.

Orwell wrote in *The Observer*. April 9, 1944:

Collectivism leads to concentration camps, leader worship, and war.

∾

CHAPTER 96
WHO CONTROLS INFORMATION?

Democratic nations boast that what citizens agree upon is the law, but is this the case? In reality, those who control what information the citizens receive are really in control.

Edward Bernays, nephew of Sigmund Freud, explained in *Propaganda* (1928) how "public relations" used by businesses to get the public to buy products has been adapted to get the public to adopt political views:

A larger manufacturer ... of women's shoes ... (has) a popular actress ... wear the shoes. The fashion spreads ... The man who injected this idea into the shoe industry was ruling women in one department of their social lives ...

Today ... the minority has discovered a powerful help in influencing the majority ... to mold the mind of the masses ... They find in propaganda a tool which is increasingly powerful ... regimenting the public mind.

It has a domino effect:

- the country is controlled by laws;
- laws are controlled by politicians;
- politicians are controlled by voters;
- voters are controlled by public opinion;
- public opinion is controlled by media, education, church, & Internet censorship;

• therefore, whoever controls media, education, church & the Internet controls the country.

Oswald Spengler wrote in *The Decline of the West. 1923*:

Democracy has become a weapon of the moneyed interests. It uses the media to create the illusion that there is consent from the governed.

The press today is an army with carefully organized weapons, the journalists its officers, the readers its soldiers. The reader neither knows nor is supposed to know the purposes for which he is used and the role he is to play ... Democracy is often ... a government of wealthy elites.

There is a computer term "gigo"–"garbage in garbage out." Social planners have discovered that by controlling what information goes into voters' minds they can determine the outcome of how they vote.

Joseph Goebbels, a master at manipulation, stated:

It is the absolute right of the state to supervise the formation of public opinion ... Think of the press as a great keyboard on which the government can play.

False "experts" are used, as noted in *Manufacturing Consent: The Political Economy of the Mass Media* (1988) by Edward Herman and Noam Chomsky:

The propaganda model also incorporates ... "experts" to confirm the official slant on the news ... taken for granted by media personnel and the elite, but are often resisted by the general population.

Pope John Paul II stated August 15, 1993:

Vast sectors of society are confused about what is right and what is wrong and are at the mercy of those with the power to "create" opinion and impose it on others.

Will and Ariel Durant wrote in the *Lessons of History* (Simon & Schuster, 1968, p. 77):

Ignorance ... lends itself to manipulation by the forces that mold public opinion.

Jim Morrison, lead singer of The Doors, said: "Whoever controls the media, controls the mind."

Mark Twain stated December 2, 1906 (*Autobiography of Mark Twain, Vol. 2*, Univ. of California Press, 2013):

How easy it is to make people believe a lie, and how hard it is to undo that work again!

Orwell wrote in his book *Nineteen Eighty–Four*:

In the long run, a hierarchical society was only possible on a basis of poverty and ignorance.

Thomas Sowell, a Senior Fellow at the Hoover Institution at Stanford University, who stated:

Ours may become the first civilization destroyed, not by the power of our enemies, but by the ignorance of our teachers and the dangerous nonsense they are teaching our children. In an age of artificial intelligence, they are creating artificial stupidity.

Hegel wrote in *Philosophy of Law* (J. Loewenberg, ed., *Hegel: Selections,* NY: C. Scribner's Sons, 1929):

Public opinion deserves ... to be esteemed as much as to be despised ... The definition of the freedom of the press as freedom to say and write what one pleases ... such a view belongs to the uneducated crudity and superficiality of naive thinking.

Controlled media can favor or malign candidates. It can spread false polling data prior to an election to prepare voters to accept a fraudulent election. During the Cold War, the CIA's Operation Mockingbird recruited journalists and news media outlets to disseminate propaganda to influence public opinion.

Washington Post reporter Carl Bernstein, who uncovered the Watergate Scandal, said in a 1977 *Rolling Stone* article, "The CIA and the Media," that by 1953, CIA Director Allen Dulles had 25 newspapers and wire agencies carry manipulated stories which were repeated by cooperating or unwitting reporters.

On May 28, 2020, President Donald Trump signed an executive order to curb Internet tech censorship:

They've had unchecked power to censor, restrict, edit, shape, hide, alter, virtually any form of communication between private citizens or large public audiences ... There's no precedent in American history for so small a number of corporations to control so large a sphere of interaction ,..

The choices that Twitter makes, when it chooses to suppress, edit, blacklist, or shadowban, are editorial decisions pure and simple.

U.S. Attorney General William Barr stated:

These companies grew because they held themselves out as public forums ... Now that they've become these very powerful networks ... they've ... switched and they are using that market power to force particular viewpoints.

Solzhenitsyn stated at Harvard, June 8, 1978:

The press (media) ... enjoys the widest freedom ... If they have misled public opinion by inaccurate information or wrong conclusions, even if they have contributed to mistakes on a state level, do we know of any case of open regret voiced by the same journalist or the same newspaper?

No ... A nation may be the worse for such a mistake, but the journalist always gets away with it ... Rumors and suppositions ... settle into the readers' memory ...

The press can act the role of public opinion or miseducate it ... Terrorists heroized, or secret matters pertaining to the nation's defense publicly revealed ... The press has become the greatest power within Western countries, exceeding that of the legislature, the executive, and the judiciary.

General MacArthur stated July 25, 1951:

The scourge of imperialistic communism ... has infiltrated into positions of public trust and responsibility – into journalism, the press, the radio and the school.

It seeks through covert manipulation of the civil power and the media of public information and education to pervert the truth, impair respect for moral values, suppress human freedom and representative government, and in the end destroy our faith in our religious teachings ... the type of pressure which has caused many Christian nations abroad to fall ...

There can be no compromise with atheistic communism, no halfway in the preservation of freedom and religion. It must be all or nothing.

President William Harrison warned, March 4, 1841:

As long as the understanding of men can be warped and their affections changed by operations upon their passions and prejudices, so long will the liberties of a people depend on their constant attention to its preservation.

Washington warned in his Farewell Address, 1796:

Ambitious, corrupted, or deluded citizens ... facility to betray, or sacrifice the interests of their own country ... sometimes even with popularity ...

How many opportunities do they afford to tamper with domestic factions, to practice the arts of seduction, to mislead public opinion, to influence or awe the public councils.

Solzhenitsyn warned, June 30, 1975:

There is a ... Russian proverb: "The yes–man is your enemy, but your friend will argue with you" ... I am the friend ... I have come to tell you ...

One of your leading newspapers, after the end of Vietnam, had a full headline: "The Blessed Silence." I would not wish that kind of "blessed silence" on my worst enemy ... I spent 11 years in the Archipelago (labor camps).

CHAPTER 97
PEER PRESSURE & GROUP DYNAMICS

Military boot camps utilize group dynamics to break down individuals and then rebuild them into a cohesive fighting unit. This technique has been adapted by socialist governments to control their populations.

Government manipulated peer pressure is also a substitute for ancient Israel's concept of God watching you, replacing it with the eyes of neighbors watching you.

The concept of "the individual" is foundational in the Christian worldview. Each person is unique with inherent worth simply because they are made in the image of the Creator, not because of what they contribute to society. Socialist governments seek to eliminate the concept of the individual and replace it with citizens identifying only with "a group."

Antonio Gramsci, founder of the Italian Communist Party, wrote in his prison notebooks, 1929-1935:

> Any country grounded in Judaeo-Christian values can't be overthrown until those roots are cut ...

> Socialism is precisely the religion that must overwhelm Christianity ... In the new order, socialism will triumph by first capturing the culture via infiltration of schools, universities, churches, and the media by transforming the consciousness of society.

The group is controlled by the dynamics of peer pressure, where a person modifies their behavior in order to "fit in." If the group likes them, their worth increases; if the group shuns them, their worth decreases.

Bertrand Russell stated December 11, 1950:

> Vanity is a motive of immense potency. Anyone who has much to do with children knows how they are constantly performing some antic and saying, "Look at me."

> "Look at me" is one of the most fundamental desires of the human heart. It can take innumerable forms, from

buffoonery to the pursuit of posthumous fame ...

It is scarcely possible to exaggerate the influence of vanity throughout the range of human life, from the child of three to the potentate at whose frown the world trembles ...

What vanity needs for its satisfaction is glory ... Many people prefer glory to power.

Critics of homeschooling argue that a child taught at home misses out on "socialization," but what is "socialization" other than learning to fit in with the group.

Home schooled children are more independent and achievement oriented as compared to "socialized" classroom educated children who draw self-worth from approval or disapproval of their fellow classmates.

Dr. Ben Carson explained:

The more solid the family foundation, the more likely you are to be able to resist peer pressure. Human beings are social creatures. We all want to belong, we all have that desire, and we will belong, one way or another.

If the family doesn't provide that, the peers will, or a gang will, or you will find something to belong to. That's why it becomes so critical for families with young children to understand what a critical anchor they are.

If one draws their self-esteem from the group, then being ignored or bullied by the group brings a loss of self-worth, with some even committing suicide.

Group rejection is the ultimate fear. From preschool to senior high to online communities everyone wants to be "liked" and no one wants to be "unfriended."

Adults seek this as well, from Oscar and Grammy Awards, to Dancing with the Stars, to American Idol, to athletic championships, to recognition from professional associations.

CHAPTER 98
HONOR–SHAME CULTURES

Asian and Middle–Eastern countries are largely "honor–shame" cultures. Where Western Judeo–Christian civilization were based on an absolute right and wrong – the Ten Commandments, "honor–shame" cultures define "right" as what brings honor to a person or family, and "wrong" is what brings shame.

China is implementing a "social credit" system to shame those who do not conform to the communist state.

In some sharia Islamic communities, parents will even kill their own daughter if she embarrasses or "shames" the family in front of their community.

A sharia professor from Indiana University, Dr. Mohammad Khalifa, published an "equity" document (3/27/17), "shaming" those who disagree with him, demanding schools stop teaching Western Civilization's concept of "the individual," which he labeled "White privilege" and "Christian privilege":

> Christian privilege can encompass much more complex issues such as community vs. individual epistemologies.

In its place, Khalifa wants schools to promote the "group" concept of umma – the Muslim community:

> Empower Muslim student identities ... measuring Muslim student belongingness ... Infuse curriculum and school activities with traditions that originate in the Muslim world ... Invite local Muslim leaders ... from the Muslim community.

Honor in front of a peer group is among the highest of human aspirations and being rejected or humiliated, even online, is among the greatest of human fears.

During COVID-19, some wore masks in public thinking it would keep them healthy, but others did so simply because they wanted to avoid being shamed.

Plato and Montesquieu explain how leaders can

manipulate a person's desire to be honored and their fear of being shamed in order to bring conformity.

Authority figures, such as teachers, imams, news anchors, talk show panelists, late-night comedians, and online influencers, determine what fashions, behavior, speech, and beliefs are acceptable or unacceptable.

This explains the left's preoccupation with being cultural trend-setters and academic authorities.

Yale President Timothy Dwight wrote of Voltaire and his followers prior to the French Revolution:

> The appropriation to themselves ... the places and honors of members of the French Academy ... In this way they ... dictate all literary opinions to the nation.

In ancient Greece, statues, epic poems, and heroic ballads memorialized those in the past who exhibited acceptable behavior for the next generation to emulate.

Greek plays, comedies, tragedies and satires, honored some behaviors and ridiculed others, causing citizens to adjust their behavior accordingly. Pericles let the poor of Athens attend the theater for free, as he knew it would exert pressure on them to conform.

The ultimate Greek punishment for those exhibiting unacceptable behavior was "ostracizing," a process in which 6,000 citizens of Athens could vote to banish someone for ten years.

George Orwell wrote in *Nineteen Eighty–Four*:

> Power is in inflicting pain and humiliation.

Saul Alinsky explained how people would rather conform in order to be accepted and honored by other people than face shame, humiliation, or ridicule:

> Pick the target, freeze it, personalize it, and polarize it. Cut off the support network and isolate the target from sympathy.
>
> Go after people and not institutions; people hurt faster than institutions. (This is cruel, but very effective. Direct, personalized criticism and

ridicule works.)

The opposite of "fear of God" is "fear of man" – living in fear of what others say about you. It is rooted in pride, the sin of Satan (Isaiah 14; Ezekiel 28).

When Cain offered his works and they were rejected, his countenance fell, his pride was hurt.

Rather than humbly repenting and trust in the sacrifice of the lamb, like his brother Abel, Cain channeled his offended feelings into anger and hatred and avenged himself by killing his brother (Genesis 4).

King Saul disobeyed the Prophet Samuel when he did not wait to offer sacrifice, "Then Saul said to Samuel, 'I have sinned ... I feared the people and listened to their voice.'"

When Samuel turned to depart, Saul grabbed his coat, saying "I have sinned: yet honor me now, I pray thee, before the elders of my people." (I Samuel 15).

Aaron had the courage to confront Pharaoh with Moses, but later, when Moses was on top of Mount Sinai for 40 days, Aaron caved to the pressure of the mob and made them a golden calf. (Exodus 32)

Similarly, King Joash served the Lord as long as the old priest Jehoiada was alive, but "... after the death of Jehoiada came the princes of Judah, and made obeisance to the king. Then the king hearkened unto them." (2Chronicles 24:17)

Scriptures call us to come out from the fear of man:

• "You shall not fear man, for the judgment is God's." (Deuteronomy 1:17);

• "The fear of man brings a snare, But he who trusts in the LORD will be exalted." (Proverbs 29:25);

• "Do not be afraid of those who kill the body and after that have no more that they can do." (Luke 12:4);

• "In God have I put my trust: I will not be afraid what man can do unto me." (Psalm 56:11)

- "Many believed on him; but because of the Pharisees they did not confess him, lest they should be put out of the synagogue." (John 12:42);

- "Pilate wanted to please the crowd, so he set Barabbas free for them. Then he had Jesus whipped and handed him over to be crucified." (Mark 15:15)

- "Jesus asked: 'How can ye believe, which receive honor from one another, and seek not the honor that cometh from God only?'" (John 5:44)

☙

CHAPTER 99
ASCH CONFORMITY STUDY

Joseph Goebbels, Hitler's Minister of Propaganda and National Enlightenment, pioneered "fake news" to manipulate mob emotions, stating:

> The most brilliant propagandist technique will yield no success unless one fundamental principle is borne in mind constantly – it must confine itself to a few points and repeat them over and over ...

> If you tell a lie big enough and keep repeating it, people will eventually come to believe it. The lie can be maintained only for such time as the state can shield the people from the political, economic and/or military consequences of the lie.

> It thus becomes vitally important for the state to use all of its powers to repress dissent, for the truth is the mortal enemy of the lie, and thus by extension, the truth is the greatest enemy of the state.

One who believed Goebbels' cliches was Adolph Eichmann, architect of the Holocaust. Observing Eichmann's trial after the war, Hannah Arendt described him as having "authentic inability to think" critically.

Goebbels' propaganda methods utilized cinema and immense Super Bowl–size choreographed gatherings to exert massive peer pressure to conform and give the Nazi salute, a method more recently adapted to pressure individuals into the universal act of submission – kneeling.

Goebbels understood that there existed a psychological predisposition for individuals to behave as they perceive everyone else behaving.

This phenomenon was examined post-WWII in the notable Solomon Asch Conformity Experiment. Eight students were invited into a classroom. Seven were actors and one was a naive, unsuspecting participant.

Two cards were placed on the teacher's desk:

• the first card had one line on it, and

• the second card had three lines, one the same length as the first card, another longer and another shorter.

Students were asked to choose which of the three lines on the second card were the same length as the one line on the first card. The paid actors went first, intentionally giving the identical wrong answer. Then it was the naive participant's turn.

So strong was the desire to fit in, that 30 percent of naive students denied their own eyes and gave the incorrect answer in order to go along with the group.

This method of manipulation has since been integrated into classroom education, television sitcoms, revisionist docudramas, news reporting, social media platforms, and political campaigning.

The idea is to make one's agenda appear like everyone is doing it, that it is the "in" thing, that it is perfectly normal, that it is "trending." This acts upon the psyche of impressionable people, manipulating their deep-seated human craving to be accepted.

It also manipulates the human fear of rejection, the phobia of being left out, the stigma of being labeled uncaring, intolerant, hateful, bigot, chauvinist, or racist.

Jesse Jackson was known for "shake downs" of corporations, threatening to label them as racists and organize nationwide boycotts unless they gave millions of dollars to his Rainbow PUSH Coalition. Black Lives Matter has used this method against entire industries.

It most recently is seen in the advancement of sexual agendas. Television programs include characters holding novel alternative sexual views and have the other characters respond like it is normal and accepted.

People who privately hold the biological view of sexuality, male and female, are then afraid to express their views publicly for fear of being shamed, ridiculed, isolated, or ostracized.

✑

CHAPTER 100
THE SPIRAL OF SILENCE

Similar to the Asch experiment was another conducted in 1984 by German sociologist Elisabeth Noelle–Neumann, who wrote *The Spiral of Silence: Public Opinion–Our Social Skin.*

It found that individuals will self-censor their views if they think they are in the minority in order to conform to what they perceive to be the majority public views, thus avoiding "negative social judgment."

Chuck Colson commented on this adult version of peer pressure in his *BreakPoint* commentary, November 2, 2011, "The Emperor's New Clothes, Breaking the Spiral of Silence":

> Inspired by Hans Christian Andersen's "The Emperor's New Clothes," researchers Rob Willer, Ko Kuwabara and Michael Macy devised a set of ingenious experiments that showed how distressingly easy it is to make people go against what they believe to be true.
>
> One of the experiments involved wine-tasting ... The participants were given three samples of wine. In reality, all three samples were from the same bottle. One had even been tainted with vinegar!
>
> Before they delivered their evaluation, they listened to other participants, who were plants, who praised the vinegar-laced wine as the best. Half of the participants went against their own taste buds and joined in praising the vinegary concoction.

Colson went on to explain that once people come to believe the lie, they participate in enforcing it on others:

> Researchers call this phenomenon "false enforcement," which they define as "the public enforcement of a norm that is not privately endorsed."

Nick Chater, Professor of Behavioral Science at the University of Warwick, wrote in "Would You Stand up to an Oppressive Regime?" (*The Conversation*, 6/6/20):

> The vast majority of people aren't prepared to rebel against totalitarian rulers ... A now classic analysis by American organizational theorist James March and Norwegian political scientist Johan Olsen from 2004 ... argued that human behavior is governed by ... our tendency to conform to unwritten rules of appropriate behavior ...

> Most of us ... don't cheat when playing board games and follow etiquette ... We even conform to arbitrary norms ... We disapprove of, ostracize or report people who lie or cheat ... Children as young as three will protest if arbitrary "rules" of a game are violated.

> An oppressive state's main tools are ... rewarding conformity and punishing even a hint of rebellion ... (In) self-policed norms ... "good" party comrade or a member of a religious cult or terrorist group will learn that they are supposed to obey orders, root out opposition and not question authority – and enforce these norms on their fellows ...

> Philosopher Hannah Arendt famously argued, the atrocities of the Holocaust were made possible by normal people, manipulated into conforming to a horribly abnormal set of behavioral norms.

Chuck Colson continued:

> What sustains the norm? ... The desire to "avoid a negative social judgment from one's peers," according to the report ...

> Simply stated, out of a desire to avoid reprisal or isolation, people go along with what they think is the popular opinion — even if they object to

that opinion personally. Instead of voicing their objections, they remain silent ...

The result is the "spiral of silence." People keep their supposedly "wrong-thinking" opinions to themselves.

The *Washington Post* article "Mass surveillance silences minority opinions according to study," by Karen Turner, March 28, 2016, revealed:

A new study shows that knowledge of government surveillance causes people to self-censor their dissenting opinions online ...

The study, published in *Journalism and Mass Communication Quarterly,* studied the effects of subtle reminders of mass surveillance on its subjects ... Participants reacted by suppressing opinions that they perceived to be in the minority ...

The "spiral of silence" is a well-researched phenomenon in which people suppress unpopular opinions to fit in and avoid social isolation.

It has been looked at in the context of social media and the echo-chamber effect, in which we tailor our opinions to fit the online activity of our Facebook and Twitter friends.

But this study adds a new layer by explicitly examining how government surveillance affects self-censorship.

∾

CHAPTER 101
PUBLIC OPINION & ELECTIONS

Greek playwright Sophocles wrote: "What people believe prevails over the truth." Henry Kissinger wrote: "It is not a matter of what is true that counts, but a matter of what is perceived to be true."

Voters can be swayed by false pre-election polling which causes some to alter their views in order to "fit in" with the perceived group consensus. Schools, media, and the Internet influence public opinion.

In elections, some voters are committed Republicans, some are committed Democrats, and some are undecided. The undecided voters go to the Internet and most likely do a Google search on the candidates to see what others are saying about them. They are inclined to conform to the consensus in the search results.

Search engines and social media platforms use algorithms which identify key words and are able to bring up only good articles about one candidate and only bad articles about the other. They can censor political views, suspend accounts and even ban users.

Being that many elections are won by small margins, if Tech Giants sway a small percentage of undecided voters, it could interfere with election results.

George Orwell wrote in "Politics vs. Literature: An Examination of Gulliver's Travels" (*Polemic*: September/October 1946):

> In a society in which there is no law ... the only arbiter of behavior is public opinion. But public opinion, because of the tremendous urge to conformity in gregarious animals, is less tolerant than any system of law.

Orwell called humans "gregarious," meaning they love being accepted by others. He continued:

> When human beings are governed by "thou shalt not," the individual can practice a certain amount of eccentricity (freedom): when they are supposedly governed by ... "reason," he is under continuous pressure to ... behave and think in exactly the same way as everyone else.

❧

CHAPTER 102
MANIPULATING VOTERS

As more people exercise the right to vote, more tactics emerge to manipulate voters, including:

• media ignoring, censoring, or publishing "fake news" about a candidate;

- persuading more candidates to run to divide the opposing party's voter base;

- getting more voters to become dependent on government entitlement handouts;

- fear-mongering that voters might loose entitlements;

- street money to pay people to vote;

- psychological projection, where a candidate guilty of a crime accuses their opponent of committing it;

- "October Surprise" the week before the November elections, including planned political attacks ads, mailers, saved up "shocking revelations";

- prepared "breaking news" stories to grab the headlines and disrupt the momentum of a winning candidate; or engineered financial distress and "national emergencies" intended to alter the outcome of an election;

- race-baiting, Black Panther, Black Lives Matter, Antifa-type violence or intimidation at polls;

- using community organizers, agitators, agent provocateurs, undercover FBI stings, to incite riots.

Thomas Sowell of the Hoover Institute, wrote:

Racism is not dead, but it is on life support – kept alive by politicians, race hustlers, and people who get a sense of superiority by denouncing others as 'racists' ...

The civil rights movement, despite its honorable and courageous past, has over the years degenerated into a demagogic hustle, promoting the mindless racism they once fought against.

Archbishop Carlo Maria Viganò, Former Apostolic Nuncio to the United States, wrote June 7, 2020:

We will also discover that the riots in these days were provoked by those who, seeing that the virus is inevitably fading ... social alarm of the pandemic is waning, necessarily have had to provoke civil disturbances ...

The use of street protests is instrumental to the purposes of those who would like to see someone elected in the upcoming presidential elections who embodies the goals of the deep state ...

Behind these acts of vandalism ... are those who hope to profit from the dissolution of the social order so as to build a world without freedom.

∽

CHAPTER 103
VOTER FRAUD TO SEIZE POWER

In addition to silencing opposing viewpoints, there are many ways to manipulate the "counting" of votes.

Joseph Stalin remarked in 1923, (*The Memoirs of Stalin's Former Secretary by Boris Bazhanov,* 2002):

> I consider it completely unimportant who in the party will vote, or how; but what is extraordinarily important is this — who will count the votes, and how.

Would politicians stoop to voter fraud?

A question to ponder is, if a politician could justify an agenda which included killing unborn babies, is there anything that politician could not justify? What is lying, cheating, slander, or voter fraud, in comparison to that? Saul Alinsky wrote:

> In war, the end justifies almost any means.

As the restraining influence of moral virtue decreases in a country, methods of voter fraud increase:

- losing ballots;
- voting multiple times;
- mail-in ballots lost, altered or added to;
- delay in counting military ballots;
- same-day registration fraud;
- inaccurate ballot preparation;
- allowing non-citizens to vote;
- refusal to purge voter rolls of those who died or moved;
- orchestrated computer glitches;
- rigging of electronic voting machines;

- hacking into state election systems by Department of Homeland Security and blame on foreign interference (Georgia, *U.S. News*, 12/18/16; Indiana, *The Daily Caller*, 2/21/17).

False polling data published prior to an election prepares voters to accept fraudulent election results.

If, by chance, voter fraud is discovered, politicians promise to "investigate," and in the course of the investigation, they have the opportunity to destroy any evidence which could convict them.

If public pressure mounts, excuses are made that the fraud was unintentional, unauthorized, or a result of ineptness. Ultimately, a low-level scapegoat is blamed, allowing the politicians to stay in office.

Another concern is a one Party's push for universal mail-in voting. Millions of new ballots could overload the postal system causing the counting of them to drag on for weeks, especially if there are demands for recounts and legal challenges. What happens if the counting is not done by noon on January 20th, when the 20th Amendment requires the President and the Vice-President vacate Office?

According to interpretations of the Presidential Succession Acts of 1792, 1886, and 1947, and the Constitution's Article 2, Section 1, and Amendments 12, 22 and 25, the Speaker of the House would become the "acting President."

Since the potential for corruption lies in the human heart, the remedy is to exercise eternal vigilance.

Irish statesman John Philpot Curran said July 10, 1790:

> The whole body of citizens … should have a share in electing those magistrates who were to govern them, as it was their birthright to be ruled only by laws which they had a share in enacting.
>
> The Aldermen, however, soon became jealous of this participation, encroached by degrees … contrary to so evident principles of natural justice

and constitutional right ...

> It is the common fate of the indolent (slothful) to see their rights become a prey (victim) to the active. The condition upon which God hath given liberty to man is eternal vigilance.

Abolitionist Frederick Douglass wrote in *The North Star* newspaper, March 17, 1848:

> "The price of liberty is eternal vigilance." It can only be maintained by a sacred regard for the rights of all men.

Andrew Jackson stated in his Farewell Address, March 4, 1837:

> But you must remember, my fellow-citizens, that eternal vigilance by the people is the price of liberty ... You must pay the price if you wish to secure the blessing.

∾

CHAPTER 104
BATTLE FOR MINDS OF STUDENTS

Socialist author Antonio Gramsci wrote:

> In the new order, socialism will triumph by first capturing the culture via infiltration of schools, universities, churches and the media by transforming the consciousness of society.

Plato explained that in the perfect society, the governing class would not only dictate what is acceptable behavior, but also determine each child's skills and abilities and assign them their work for life.

Just like in computer terminology, there is hardware and software, a child's body and brain is the hardware, but the ideology they are taught is the software, which gives them their identity and purpose.

Just as the Bible, in one aspect, is like a behavioral software program (i.e. love your neighbor as yourself; love your enemies, etc.), so atheistic socialism is like a software virus. The battle for the future is over who gets to load the software on the next generation's brains.

Malware, viruses, and corrupted files loaded on children's brains produce narcissistic, selfish behavior. Students must abandon their parent's morals and adopt ever-evolving government–dictated beliefs.

Yale President Timothy Dwight warned that Voltaire's atheistic agenda included controlling the education:

> Education of youth ... books replete with infidelity, irreligion, immorality, and obscenity.

William T. Harris, U.S. Commissioner of Education, 1889–1906, drawing from the socialist philosophies of Hegel, Kant, Fichte, Fröbel and Pestalozzi, stated:

> Our schools have been scientifically designed to prevent over-education from happening. The average American should be content with their humble role in life, they're not tempted to think about any other role.

John Dewey wrote in *The Middle Works* (1915, vol. 8, p. 398):

> Education which trains children to docility and obedience, to the careful performance of imposed tasks because they are imposed, regardless of where they lead, is suited to an autocratic society. These are the traits needed in a state where there is one head to plan and care for the lives and institutions of the people.

Marx stated:

> The education of all children, from the moment that they can get along without a mother's care, shall be in state institutions at state expense.

Antonio Gramsci wrote:

> Before puberty the child's personality has not yet formed and it is easier to guide its life and make it acquire specific habits of order, discipline, and work.

Lenin stated:

> Give me four years to teach the children and

the seed I have sown will never be uprooted.

Stalin stated:

> Education is a weapon, whose effect depends on who holds it in his hands and at whom it is aimed.

Communist Party Education Workers Congress stated in 1918:

> We must create out of the younger generation a generation of communists. We must turn children, who can be shaped like wax, into real, good communists ...

> We must remove the children from the crude influence of their families. We must take them over and, to speak frankly, nationalize them.

> From the first days of their lives they will be under the healthy influence of communist children's nurseries and schools. There they will grow up to be real communists.

Hitler stated November 6, 1933:

> When an opponent declares, "I will not come over to your side," I calmly say,

> "Your child belongs to us already ... What are you? You will pass on. Your descendants, however, now stand in the new camp. In a short time they will know nothing else but this new community."

Hitler stated of the National Socialist Workers Party, May 1, 1937 (William Shirer, *Rise and Fall of the Third Reich,* NY: Simon & Schuster, 1960, p. 249):

> The youth of today is ever the people of tomorrow.

> For this reason we have set before ourselves the task of inoculating our youth with the spirit of this community of the people at a very early age, at an age when human beings are still unperverted and therefore unspoiled ...

> This Reich stands, and it is building itself up for the future, upon its youth.

And this new Reich will give its youth to no one but will itself take youth and give to youth its own education and its own upbringing.

Rep. Albert S. Herlong, Jr., read into the U.S. *Congressional Record,* January 10, 1963, a list of communist goals, which included:

Discredit the family as an institution ... Emphasize the need to raise children away from the negative influence of parents ...

Control schools. Use them as transmission belts for socialism and current communist propaganda. Soften curriculum.

Get control of teachers' associations. Put party line in textbooks ... Gain control of all student newspapers ...

Belittle all forms of American culture and discourage the teaching of American history ... Discredit the American Founding Fathers.

J. Edgar Hoover wrote in 1954:

The American home ... ceased to be a school of moral and spiritual education. When spiritual guidance is at a low ebb, moral principles are in a state of deterioration. Secularism advances when men forget God.

Leon Trotsky stated:

If our generation happens to be too weak to establish socialism over the earth, we will hand the spotless banner down to our children ... It is the struggle for the future of all mankind.

In Paris, John Adams wrote in his diary, June 2, 1778:

In vain are schools, academies, and universities instituted, if loose principles and licentious habits are impressed upon children in their earliest years ... The vices and examples of the parents cannot be concealed from the children.

How is it possible that children can have any just sense of the sacred obligations of morality or religion if, from their earliest infancy ... their fathers (are) in as constant infidelity to their mothers?

Henry A Giroux wrote in an op-ed "How Disney Magic and the Corporate Media Shape Youth Identity in the Digital Age," August 21, 2011:

Childhood ideals increasingly give way to a market-driven politics in which young people are prepared for a life of "objectification" (to treat a person as a thing) that will simultaneously drain them of any viable sense of moral and political agency.

Dr. James Dobson addressed the National Religious Broadcasters, February 16, 2002:

If they can get control of children ... they can change the whole culture in one generation ... There is a concerted effort to manipulate the minds of kids ...

A stem cell is a cell in the human being ... that in the very early stages of development it is undifferentiated. In other words, it's not yet other kinds of tissue, but it can go any direction depending on the environment that it's in ... Do you understand that children are the stem cells for the culture?

∽

CHAPTER 105
DECONSTRUCTION & BRAINWASHING

In more recent times, there has been the adaptation of a socialist tactic called "deconstruction."

This is where a country's past heroes are portrayed in a negative light so that people emotionally detach from them and their values. Then there is a period of disillusionment and searching. Finally, there is the introduction of rewritten history with socialist values.

Dystopian writer George Orwell, in his novel *1984*, had the character Winston working in the "Ministry of Truth," with the job of editing history and putting all evidence of the real past down a "memory hole":

Every record has been destroyed or falsified, every book rewritten, every picture has been repainted, every statue and street building has been renamed, every date has been altered ...

History has stopped. Nothing exists except an endless present in which the Party is always right. I know, of course, that the past is falsified, but it would never be possible for me to prove it, even when I did the falsification myself.

After the thing is done, no evidence ever remains. The only evidence is inside my own mind, and I don't know ... that any other human being shares my memories ... Everything faded into mist. The past was erased, the erasure was forgotten, the lie became truth.

A example of this is when Judge Amy Coney Barrett was criticized during her confirmation hearing, October 14, 2020, by Democrat Senator Mazie Hirono for using the term "sexual preference," though even Democrats had used the term. Senator Hirono claimed its meaning had evolved to be offensive. Withing hours after the hearing, Merriam-Webster changed its definition.

Orwell explained how to alter a nation's trajectory:

Those who control the past control the future, and those who control the present control the past.

It is actually a sales technique:

- first the salesman points out the negative aspects of the old product a customer is using;
- then the customer becomes dissatisfied with it and curious about new options;
- then the salesman presents the positive aspects of a new product.

Deconstruction does this on a national scale. It is a Drive–Neutral–Reverse method used in classrooms:

- separate students from their past by portraying negatively the country's founders;
- get students into a neutral point of view where

they are open-minded;

- then brainwash students by presenting positively a socialist future.

Socialist historian Howard Zinn's *A People's History of the United States* (1980) is of this genre.

Senate Chaplain Peter Marshall said of deconstruction:

Along with our higher education came a debunking contest ... a sort of national sport ... It was smarter to revile than to revere ... more fashionable to depreciate than to appreciate ... Debunking is ... a sign of decaying foundations.

Deconstruction is a cultural identity theft. It is a type of gene-replacement therapy for a civilization – take out the citizens' old identity and replace it with an edited gene.

It is a process of editing the collective memory of a society, making people believe something existed that never did, a process called the "Mandela Effect." Cognitive psychologists have even carried out experiments of implanting false memories into people's minds, making them believe that they remember events that never happened.

Deconstruction, or "cancel culture," involves selectively re-editing or ridiculing *past* individuals or events in order to advance a *future* political agenda – altering a nation's past in order to change its future.

Bill Maher of HBO's "Real Time," stated (07/30/21):

This is ... a purge ... that belongs in Stalin's Russia. How bad does ... have to get before the people who say cancel culture is overblown admit that it is in fact an insanity that is swallowing up the world? ... This is yet another example of how the woke invert the very thing that used to make liberals liberals ...

This new idea that each culture must remain in its own separate silo is not better, and it's not progress. And in fact, it's messing with one of the few ideas that still really does make this melting pot called America great ... Cultural mixing makes things better for everyone ... I can get kimchi on a taco, isn't that better ...

I thought walls were supposed to be bad. But we're living now in a world where ... white novelists aren't allowed to imagine what it would be like to be a Mexican immigrant, even though trying to inhabit the life of someone else is almost the very definition of empathy, the bedrock of liberalism.

One cannot be proud of their heritage and ashamed of it at the same time. A scriptwriter for Hollywood sitcoms confided how they were told to "make people laugh at what they held sacred." The movie, *Monty Python and the Holy Grail*, 1975, was in this vein, mocking England's noble legend of King Arthur.

Separating people from their past is mentioned in a quote attributed to Karl Marx:

Take away the heritage of a people and they are easily conquered.

Yang Berhorma, Minister of Culture of Borneo, wrote in *The Brunei Times,* August 29, 2013:

A nation or generation that does not know the history of their nation is a nation that lost its identity and can be easily manipulated.

This is why the first emperor of China, Qin Shi Huangdi, who conquered kingdoms to unify China in 221 BC, destroyed all history books. *The Basic Annals of the First Emperor of Qin* reported Chancellor Li Si told the Emperor in 213 BC:

I, your servant, propose that all historians' records other than those of Qin's be burned ... If anyone under heaven has copies of the *Classics of History [Shu Jing]* ... they shall deliver them to the governor ... for burning.

Anyone who dares to discuss the *Classics of History* shall be publicly executed. Anyone who uses history to criticize the present shall have his family executed ...

Anyone who has failed to burn the books after thirty days of this announcement shall be subjected to tattooing and be sent to build the Great Wall.

President Jimmy Carter started the Department of Education in 1979, and from that time on, proficiency in math, literature and history began to decline.

Lawrence W. Reed examined this trend in his article "The Myth that Americans Were Poorly Educated before Mass Government Schooling" (FEE, April 29, 2020).

The process of stripping away a people's past identity so they will accept a new identity was described by Edward Hunter in *Brainwashed* (NY: 1956)

Brainwashing was made up of two processes. One is the conditioning, or softening-up, process primarily for control purposes. The other is an indoctrination or persuasion process for conversion purposes ...

Brainwashing is a system of befogging the brain so a person can be seduced into acceptance of what otherwise would be abhorrent to him. He loses touch with reality. Facts and fancy whirl round and change places ...

This was war ... psychological warfare ... brain warfare. Formerly weapons were aimed principally at bodies, to incapacitate and destroy them, whereas now they were aimed mainly at minds, so subvert and control them. In brain warfare ultimate victory lay in the conquest of attitudes and feelings ...

In journalism ... news was now a weapon ... Reporters knew... that the new authorities didn't hesitate to alter details according to what they wanted to prove, and even to cut the news out of a whole cloth when it suited their purpose.

Hunter's term "brainwashing" was derived from a Buddhist practice. Communists used it on American prisoners during the Korean War, subjecting them to deprivation, trauma, pain, fear, shaming, then re-education:

> ... meetings were being held in vacant rooms and open spaces wherever a group could gather to discuss, self-criticize, and confess ...

> They went about this in the "democratic discussion" manner this was the new principle of unanimity (solidarity) ... He felt so tired that his minds did tricks on him.... God knows how little sleep he got ... What was truth anyway? Nobody knew. What was false? ... Everyone couldn't be wrong. Could they? ...

> They work then on persuading the prisoner to rid his mind of the "bourgeois poison" he had been carrying about of seeing good on all sides ... They point out to this weary mind. Their patient then is taught that there is good only on one side, that the other is "all bad" and the enemy.

> When an individual reaches this upside-down stage in his theorizing, he can then be freed ...

> The truly indoctrinated communist must be part of the collective ... Everyone has to participate ... learning means only political teaching from the communist standpoint. Confession is an integral part of the rites.

> In China there are no exceptions ... for attendance at "learning" classes. The retention of his own individuality by a single person is recognized as a deadly menace by the whole monolithic structure ...

> Communism is sheer power system, gang rule with modern appliances. So long as the individual submits unquestioningly, he is what is referred to as a "disciplined Party member."

The 1944 movie *Gaslight*, starred Ingrid Bergman as the niece of a famous actress who was murdered in an attempt to get her jewels. The murderer changes his identity, then, after a whirlwind courtship, marries Ingrid so he can secretly dig through the attic at night looking for the jewels.

When he turns on the gas lamp in the attic, the gas lamp in her bedroom noticeably dims. She tells him about it, but he convinces her that her mind is playing tricks on her, that she is seeing things, that she is going crazy. He nearly committed to an insane asylum when the diabolical plot is exposed.

Psychology Today (accessed 5/30/21) described:

> Victims of gaslighting are deliberately and systematically fed false information that leads them to question what they know to be true, often about themselves. They may end up doubting their memory, their perception, and even their sanity. Over time, a gaslighter's manipulations can grow more complex and potent, making it increasingly difficult for the victim to see the truth.

Gaslighting and brainwashing techniques are similar to an unruly dog being isolated in a dark room, starved nearly to death, and after it barks itself out, it is scared, emotionally spent and disoriented, it will gladly receive food and water from the person who locked it up, new looking upon that person as its new benefactor.

These steps are listed on Biderman's Chart of Coercion:

1. ISOLATION: deprive victim of all social interaction and emotional support, make them dependent on a controlled information source;

2. MONOPOLIZATION OF PERCEPTION: make victim ever conscience of their predicament, restrict their movement, force them to become introspective, eliminate all mental stimuli other than that which is controlled by captor;

3. INDUCE DEBILITATION: weaken them physically and mentally to the point of emotional exhaustion, sleep deprivation, prolonged interrogation, eroding their will to resist;

4. THREATS of endless isolation, never-ending interrogation, of death, against family members, vague, cultivating anxiety and despair;

5. OCCASIONAL INDULGENCES: providing positive reward for compliance but disrupting their mental adjustment to deprivation;

6. DEMONSTRATE OMNIPOTENCE & OMNISCIENCE: showing complete control over victim's fate and the futility of resistance, demoralize;

7. DEGRADATION: shame, destroy self-esteem, prevent personal hygiene, subject them to demeaning punishments, insults, taunts, no privacy, force them to admit their mistakes and "confess" to being bad;

8. ENFORCE TRIVIAL DEMANDS: require minute obedience till victim stops thinking critically or logically, and just surrenders to blind compliance.

A CBN News Report by Dan Andros, April 11, 2021, stated "China Forcing Detained Christians to Undergo 'Basement Brainwashing Sessions'":

A new report from Radio Free Asia outlines serious human rights abuses allegedly happening to Christians ... including detaining them in "secretive, mobile 'transformation' facilities to make them renounce their faith."

A Chinese Christian, speaking under a pseudonym in order to protect their identity, told RFA he had been held by the Communist ruling party's "United Front Work Department" for 10 months after the government had conducted a raid on their church:

"It was a mobile facility, that could just set up in some basement somewhere," Li said. "It was staffed by people from several different government departments." "It had its own (CCP) political and legal affairs committee working group, and they mainly target Christians who are members of house churches" ...

During those 10 months in captivity he suffered horrific treatment, claiming to be "beaten, verbally abused and mentally tortured" by officials. "They use really underhand methods" he said ...

A BBC reporter caught on tape when Chinese officials allowed him to tour one of their 'thought education' facilities.

Clearly, these religious minorities were being held against their will, and given the mental abuse reporters were allowed to see, it's not difficult to imagine what's going on behind closed doors.

"A police officer in my village told me to get enrolled in 'school' and transform my thoughts," one of the young men said on camera.

The new report from RFA alleges "basement brainwashing sessions" for the 'crime' of participating in church activities. "They threaten, insult and intimidate you. These were United Front officials, men, women, sometimes unidentified, usually in plain clothes ... "You have to accept the statement they prepare for you," he said. "If you refuse, you will be seen as having a bad attitude and they will keep you in detention and keep on beating you."

These "thought transformation" facilities are used when the offender hasn't done anything to warrant being charged with criminal prosecution, so they send them off to have their thoughts rewired.

The whistle-blower ... went on to describe the torture endured during these brainwashing sessions. "There were two plainclothes officers in my room, and a uniformed officer was in another room," Li said. "There were no windows, no ventilation and no time allowed outside," he said. "I was given just two meals a day, which were brought to the room by a designated person."

Inmates who refused to "admit their mistakes" were held in solitary confinement for prolonged periods. "There is no time limit for the brainwashing process," he said. "I don't know the longest time anyone has been held there, but I was detained for eight or nine months." "You can't see the sun, so you lose all concept of time."

The whistle-blower said after enduring so much mental and physical torture, thoughts of self-harm, including suicide, set in quickly.

CHAPTER 106
NORTH KOREAN DEFECTOR

YahooNews reported (*Insider,* June 15, 2021):

Yeonmi Park, 27, escaped from North Korea at the age of 13 and is now a US citizen. In 2016, she transferred to Columbia University and said the experience was jarring. She told *Fox News* the culture of political correctness reminded her of living under the oppressive Kim regime ...

Park has appeared often in the news to speak about life in North Korea, and to criticize Kim Jong Un's regime, as well as comment on Asian and American politics.

She has been interviewed by the *New York Post, The Sun, NBC News, The Guardian, NPR, and The Telegraph. She has also written op-eds for The New York Times* and *The Washington Post ...*

She described a culture of political correctness at the Ivy League institution that she said rivaled the thought-policing that happened in her native country ...

"I was paying this fortune, all this time and energy ... but they are forcing you to think the way they want you to think," Park told *Fox News.* "I realized, 'Wow, this is insane.' I thought America was different, but I saw so many similarities to what I saw in North Korea that I started worrying."

In one example, Park said she was scolded by a staff member for expressing a like for Jane Austen's novels. "I said, 'I love those books.' I thought it was a good thing," Park said.

"Then she said, 'Did you know those writers had a colonial mindset? They were racists and bigots and are subconsciously brainwashing you.'"

Columbia University did not immediately respond to *Insider's* request for comment on this story.

Park said she also found it bizarre that professors asked students what their pronouns were, and complained about using gender-neutral pronouns.

"English is my third language. I learned it as an adult. I sometimes still say 'he' or 'she' by mistake, and now they are going to ask me to call them 'they'?" she said. "How the heck do I incorporate that into my sentences?"

"It was chaos. It felt like the regression in civilization," Park said. "Even North Korea is not this nuts" ...

Park said her experience at Columbia made her believe that American students were losing the ability to think critically, something she said she is all too familiar with from her time in North Korea.

"In North Korea I literally believed that my Dear Leader was starving," she said. "He's the fattest guy - how can anyone believe that? And then somebody showed me a photo and said, 'Look at him. He's the fattest guy. Other people are all thin.' And I was like, 'Oh my God, why did I not notice that he was fat?' Because I never learned how to think critically."

"That is what is happening in America," she said.

∾

CHAPTER 107
WHEN A NATION LOSES ITS MEMORY

Sun Tzu's *Art of War* defined "Supreme excellence consists of breaking the enemy's resistance without fighting." The next level, called "fifth generation warfare" is getting your enemy to surrender without them being aware they were in a war.

Pulitzer Prize-winning historian Arthur M. Schlesinger, Jr., wrote in an op-ed titled "Folly's Antidote" (*The New York Times,* January 1, 2007):

History is to the nation as memory is to the individual. As persons deprived of memory become disoriented and lost, not knowing where they have been and where they are going, so a nation denied a conception of the past will be disabled in dealing with its present and its future.

"The longer you look back," said Winston Churchill, "the farther you can look forward" ... I believe a consciousness of history is a moral necessity for a nation.

John F. Kennedy wrote in the Introduction to the *American Heritage New Illustrated History of the United States* (1960):

History, after all, is the memory of a nation. Just as memory enables the individual to learn, to choose goals and stick to them, to avoid making the same mistake twice – in short, to grow – so history is the means by which a nation establishes its sense of identity and purpose.

If history is a nation's memory, then America has national Alzheimer's. Pulitzer Prize-winning poet Carl Sandburg wrote:

When a nation goes down, or a society perishes, one condition may always be found; they forgot where they came from.

Harvard Professor George Santayana wrote in *Reason in Common Sense* (Vol. I of The Life of Reason, 1905):

Those who cannot remember the past are condemned to repeat it.

Solzhenitsyn stated:

If we don't know our own history, we will simply have to endure all the same mistakes, sacrifices, and absurdities all over again.

Judge Learned Hand wrote:

The use of history is to tell us ... past themes, else we should have to repeat, each in his own experience, the successes and the failures of our forebears.

Aristotle, in his book *Rhetoric* (4th century BC), called this "deliberative rhetoric," using examples from the past to predict future outcomes:

The political orator is concerned with the

future: it is about things to be done hereafter that he advises, for or against.

Lord Acton wrote in 1877:

The story of the future is written in the past.

Patrick Henry stated March 23, 1775:

I know of no way of judging the future but by the past.

Edmund Burke wrote in *Reflections on the Revolution in France,* 1790:

People will not look forward to posterity who never look backward to their ancestors.

Cicero stated in *Ad M. Brutum,* 46 BC:

Not to know what happened before you were born is to be a child forever.

Will & Ariel Durant wrote in *The Story of Civilization,* 1967:

History is an excellent teacher with few pupils.

The Durants wrote in *The Lessons of History,* 1968:

Civilization is not inherited; it has to be learned and earned by each generation anew; if the transmission should be interrupted ... civilization would die, and we should be savages again.

Reagan warned the Phoenix Chamber of Commerce, March 30, 1961:

Freedom is never more than one generation away from extinction. We didn't pass it to our children in the bloodstream.

The only way they can inherit the freedom we have known is if we fight for it, protect it, defend it and then hand it to them with the well thought lessons of how they in their lifetime must do the same.

And if you and I don't do this, then you and I may well spend our sunset years telling our children and our children's children what it once was like in America when men were free.

CHAPTER 108
FORGETTING GOD

J. Edgar Hoover stated in the introduction to Edward L.R. Elson's book, *America's Spiritual Recovery,* 1954:

> We can see all too clearly the devastating effects of secularism on our Christian way of life. The period when it was smart to "debunk" our traditions undermined ... high standards of conduct. A rising emphasis on materialism caused a decline of "God-centered" deeds and thoughts.

This echoed an earlier Russian author, Dostoevsky, who wrote *The Brothers Karamazov,* 1880. In it, there was a character named Ivan Karamazov who contended that if there is no God, "everything is permitted."

"Everything is permitted" not only gives license to criminals on the street, but it also to gives license to criminals in the government, deep state individuals who seek to subvert from the inside. Such was the attitude of the Jacobins, a left-wing anarchist movement during the French Revolution. Solzhenitsyn explained:

> Over a half century ago, while I was still a child, I recall hearing a number of old people offer the following explanation for the great disasters that had befallen Russia: "Men have forgotten God; that's why all this has happened" ...

> Since then I have spent well-nigh 50 years working on the history of our revolution; in the process I have read hundreds of books, collected hundreds of personal testimonies ...

> But if I were asked today to formulate as concisely as possible the main cause of the ruinous revolution that swallowed up some 60 million of our people, I could not put it more accurately than to repeat: "Men have forgotten God; that's why all this has happened."

Attorney Chris Banescu, a contributor to OrthodoxyToday.org , wrote July 18, 2011:

As a survivor of the Communist Holocaust I am horrified to witness how my beloved America, my adopted country, is gradually being transformed into a secularist and atheistic utopia, where communist ideals are glorified and promoted, while ...

God has been progressively erased from our public and educational institutions ...

Those of us who have experienced and witnessed first-hand the atrocities and terror of communism understand fully why such evil takes root, how it grows and deceives, and the kind of hell it will ultimately unleash ...

Godlessness is always the first step towards tyranny and oppression!

Patrick Henry gave the same warning:

It is when a people forget God that tyrants forge their chains.

William Holmes McGuffey warned in his *Newly Revised Rhetorical Guide,* 1853:

If you can induce a community to doubt the ... authenticity of the Scriptures ... you have broken down the barriers of moral virtue and hoisted the flood-gates of immorality and crime.

Rose Wilder Lane, daughter of Laura Ingalls Wilder, visited Russia, writing in *Give Me Liberty* (1936):

In 1919 I was a communist ... We must eliminate the capitalist ... take his current profits, distribute his accumulated wealth ... When the capitalist is gone, who will manage production? The state ... It was at this point that the first doubt pierced my communist faith ... The lives, the livelihoods, of common men were once more subject to dictators... Every advance toward personal liberty which had been gained ... was lost by the collectivist economic reaction ...

Centralized economic control over multitudes of human beings...must become such minute and rigorous control of details of individual life as no people will accept without compulsion.

What I saw was not an extension of human freedom, but the establishment of tyranny on a new, widely extended and deeper base. The Soviet government ... suppressed personal freedom; freedom of movement, of choice of work, freedom of self-expression in ways of life, freedom of speech, freedom of conscience ...

I came out of the Soviet Union no longer a communist, because I believed in personal freedom ... I understood at last that every human being is free; that I am endowed by the Creator with inalienable liberty ... with individual self-control and responsibility...

Individualism. In less than a century, it created our America ... America's brief experiment in individualism has not only created ... an unimaginable multiplication of forms of wealth in goods and services, but it has also distributed these forms of wealth to an unprecedented and elsewhere unequaled degree.

∽

CHAPTER 109
IS "PROPERTY" A TOPIC IN THE BIBLE?

The opposite of individuals owning property is social ownership of property, which, in application, is no different from a feudal lord holding the land in trust and dividing it among his loyal knights and vassals, who in turn collect taxes from the poor peasants.

Webster's 1828 Dictionary defined "property" as:

The exclusive right of possessing, enjoying and disposing of a thing; ownership. In the beginning of the world, the Creator gave to man dominion over the earth ... It is one of the greatest blessings of civil society that the property of citizens is well secured.

Where John Locke believed natural law affirmed private property rights prior to the formation of any state, Jean-Jacques Rousseau believed the state's "social contract" preceded property rights.

Socialist writers such as Plato, Sir Thomas More, Sir Francis Bacon, and others advocated "social ownership" of property, or "communal property."

Karl Marx wrote:

> The theory of the communists may be summed up in the single sentence: Abolition of private property.

ACLU founder Roger Baldwin wrote in 1935 at his Harvard class 30th reunion:

> I am for socialism ... I seek social ownership of property.

Reagan explained October 27, 1964, how government regulations effectively take away property:

> Now it doesn't require ... confiscation of private property or business to impose socialism ... What does it mean whether you hold the deed to ... your business or property ...
>
> Machinery already exists (where)... the government can find some charge to bring against any concern it chooses to prosecute. Every businessman has his own tale of harassment.

What does the Bible say about property? In Scriptures, God gave men and women property which they were to be good stewards over. Genesis 2:15 states:

> And the LORD God took the man, and put him into the garden of Eden to work it and to keep it.

Abraham purchased a plot of land in which to bury his wife Sarah. (Genesis 23:20)

Moses divided up the Promised Land into family lots (Numbers 34), inherited by children (Deuteronomy 21:16; Proverbs 19:14; Luke 12:13; Luke 15:11–32).

Boaz bought the field from Naomi:

> At this, Boaz said to the elders and all the people, "You are witnesses today that I am buying from Naomi all that belonged to Elimelech, Chilion, and Mahlon." (Ruth 4:9)

The Ten Commandments affirm private property with the command "Thou shalt not steal" (Exodus 20:15), nor "covet" your neighbor's property (Deuteronomy 5:21):

Neither shalt thou covet thy neighbor's house, his field ... his ox, or his ass, or anything that is thy neighbor's.

Naboth refused to sell his property to King Ahab:

Ahab spake unto Naboth, saying, Give me thy vineyard, that I may have it for a garden ... I will give thee the worth of it in money. And Naboth said to Ahab, The Lord forbid it me, that I should give the inheritance of my fathers unto thee ...

But Jezebel his wife came to him ... and he said unto her ... I spake unto Naboth the Jezreelite, and said unto him, Give me thy vineyard for money ... and he answered, I will not. (I Kings 21)

An employer can negotiate to pay a worker wages, and once the work is complete, the wages are the worker's property. Jesus explained in a parable:

Friend, I do thee no wrong: didst not thou agree with me for a penny? Take that thine is and go thy way: I will give unto this last, even as unto thee. Is it not lawful for me to do what I will with mine own? Is thine eye evil because I am good? (Matthew 20:13–15)

It is criminal for an employer to hold back wages:

Thou shalt not defraud thy neighbor, neither rob him: the wages of him that is hired shall not abide with thee all night until the morning" (Leviticus 19:13); and

Behold, the hire of the laborers who have reaped down your fields, which is of you kept back by fraud, crieth: and the cries of them which have reaped are entered into the ears of the Lord of Hosts. (James 5:4)

John Adams explained in *Defense of the Constitutions of Government of the United States*, 1787, the consequence if private property is not protected:

Property is surely a right of mankind ... Perhaps, at first ... principle or religion, would restrain the poor from attacking the rich ... but the time would not be long before courage and enterprise would come, and pretexts be invented by degrees, to countenance the majority in dividing all the property among them, or at least, in sharing it equally with its present possessors.

Debts would be abolished first; taxes laid heavy on the rich, and not at all on the others; and at last a downright equal division of everything be demanded, and voted ...

Adams continued:

What would be the consequence of this? The idle, the vicious, the intemperate, would rush into the utmost extravagance of debauchery, sell and spend all their share, and then demand a new division of those who purchased from them.

The moment the idea is admitted into society, that property is not as sacred as the laws of God, and that there is not a force of law and public justice to protect it, anarchy and tyranny commence.

If "Thou shalt not covet," and "Thou shalt not steal," were not commandments of Heaven, they must be made inviolable (secure) precepts in every society before it can be civilized or made free.

∞

CHAPTER 110
PROPERTY AND CHARITY

When men and women have property, they have the freewill opportunity to express their hearts, voluntarily giving to those in need and for the work of the Lord.

In gathering materials for building the Tabernacle in the Wilderness, the Lord told Moses:

Speak unto the children of Israel, that they bring me an offering: of every man that giveth it willingly with his heart ye shall take my offering. (Exodus 25:2)

SOCIALISM: THE TRUE HISTORY

When King David was assembling materials for his son Solomon to use in building the Temple, he said:

> Who then is willing to consecrate his service this day unto the Lord?

> Then the chief of the fathers and princes of the tribes of Israel ... offered willingly, and gave for the service of the house of God of gold five thousand talents ... of silver ten thousand talents ... of brass eighteen thousand talents ... The people rejoiced, for that they offered willingly ...

> David blessed the Lord ...Who am I, and what is my people, that we should be able to offer so willingly after this sort? For all things come of Thee, and of Thine own have we given Thee. (I Chronicles 29)

When Cyrus let Jewish exiles return to Jerusalem:

> They ... offered freely for the house of God to set it up in his place. (Ezra 2:68)

Peter affirmed that a person's property is their's to do with as they wish (Acts 5:4):

> While it remained unsold, did it not remain your own? And after it was sold, was it not at your disposal?

The Bible talks much about charity. It is defined as voluntarily giving what is yours to someone else. If you do not own any property you cannot give away property. It is not charity to take property from someone against their will – theft – and redistribute it. If the government owns all property, individuals have none with which to be charitable. Pope John Paul II stated:

> Socialism ... maintains that the good of the individual can be realized without reference to his free choice ... The concept of the person as the autonomous subject of moral decision disappears ...

> From this mistaken conception of the person there arise(s) ... an opposition to private property.

> A person who is deprived of something he can call "his own," and of the possibility of earning a living through his own initiative, comes to depend

on the social machine and on those who control it.

This makes it much more difficult for him to recognize his dignity as a person and hinders progress towards the building up of an authentic human community.

King David rejected government confiscation and insisted on buying the threshing floor:

And Araunah said, Wherefore is my lord the king come to his servant? And David said, To buy the threshing floor of thee, to build an altar unto the Lord ...

And Araunah said unto David, Let my lord the king take and offer up what seemeth good unto him: behold, here be oxen for burnt sacrifice, and threshing instruments ... for wood ...

And the king said unto Araunah, Nay; but I will surely buy it of thee at a price: neither will I offer burnt offerings unto the Lord my God of that which doth cost me nothing.

So David bought the threshing floor and the oxen for fifty shekels of silver. And David built there an altar unto the Lord. (2 Samuel 24:21-5)

Jesus told the rich young ruler (Matthew 19: 21):

Go and sell that thou hast, and give to the poor, and thou shalt have treasure in heaven.

Dr. Walter C. Kaiser, Jr., wrote in "Ownership and Property in the Old Testament Economy":

Private property is both a gift and a certain type of power God has entrusted to humanity as stewards.

☙

CHAPTER 111
REDISTRIBUTION IS NOT CHARITY

When the church helps, it is "disinterested benevolence," expecting nothing in return. When government helps, it is in exchange for something, such as the recipient's votes, political loyalty or freedoms.

When there was a famine in Egypt, the government gave grain in exchange for the people's cattle, land, freedom, children and their lives.

As well-intended as government programs may be, they are run by career politicians and bureaucrats who have an inherent conflict of interests. In addition to running the program, they do not want the program to end as they would lose the justification for their jobs.

If the poor stop being poor, the politicians would lose them as a voting block and may lose reelection. In other words, they want the poor to stay poor so they can champion the needs of the poor and get their votes.

Rep. J.C. Watts described such politicians: "But I have my thoughts. And I think they're race-hustling poverty pimps." Watts added, February 5, 1997:

> For the past 30 years our nation's spent $5 trillion trying to erase poverty, and the result, as you know, is that we didn't get rid of it at all. In fact, we spread it.

> We destroyed the self-esteem of millions of people, grinding them down in a welfare system that penalizes moms for wanting to marry the father of their children, and penalizes moms for wanting to save money. Friends, that's not right.

Politicians also may be tempted to redirect public funds as favors and pork projects to loyal party members and supporters who can help them stay in office.

James Buchanan, Jr., received the Nobel Prize in Economics in 1986, for his examination of how politicians make economic policy decisions.

He discovered that if politicians are up for reelection, they tend to vote to increase debt so they can direct money to their districts, as this will help them get reelected – but they will not vote for corresponding tax increases to pay for it – as this will hurt their reelection.

Buchanan discovered that rather than being disinterested public servants, a large percentage of career bureaucrats are primarily interested in self-preservation. It is natural for people to want to keep their jobs.

When millions of people work for the government, their is a collective desire for it to get bigger as job security, creating an enormous deep-state bureaucracy.

Government employees are tempted to use their positions to perpetuate their jobs, while harassing, auditing, leaking, investigating, and prosecuting those who threaten to eliminate their jobs.

Reagan stated October 27, 1964:

> No government ever voluntarily reduces itself in size. So, governments' programs, once launched, never disappear. Actually, a government bureau is the nearest thing to eternal life we'll ever see on this earth.

On the other hand, when church members give charity, they voluntarily give as unto the Lord and expect nothing in return. Their reward is in Heaven. Their desire is solely to improve the life of the recipient.

If the church helps a person, the goal is for the person to grow in faith, teaching them that they can do all things through Christ who strengthens them.

As the person rises above their situation, they develop responsibility and accountability, qualities necessary for success in any occupation or career, and hopefully will be willing and able to help others too.

∾

CHAPTER 112
CHARITY IS NOT GOVERNMENT'S JOB

An overlooked Biblical teaching is, that God gives commands to five major entities:

• INDIVIDUALS, are told, among other things, to be charitable to the poor, visit the sick and imprisoned, and act like the good Samaritan.

• FAMILIES are given relational commands, such as husbands love your wives, children submit to your parents, and provide for those of your own household.

• BUSINESS: employees are to give an honest day's work, and employers are to not hold back wages and also leave gleanings in the fields for the poor to collect.

• CHURCHES, among other things, are told be charitable, feed the hungry, visit the sick and the imprisoned, take care of the poor, infirm, widows, orphans, maimed soldiers, unwed mothers, shut-ins, homeless, juvenile delinquents, and immigrants, etc.

Historically, churches have fulfilled this command, starting hospitals, orphanages, missions, schools, universities, and other Christian aid organizations, with some even vowing to give their lives in such service.

• GOVERNMENT has the shortest command, namely, protect the innocent and punish the guilty.

There is no Biblical command for government to help the poor, take care of the sick, dispense healthcare, operate schools, provide jobs, or other entitlements.

When naive voters, politicians, and ministers get these five categories mixed up, they let the government usurp the roles of individuals, families, businesses and churches. Coolidge warned of this, May 15, 1926:

> The Federal Government ought to resist the tendency to be loaded up with duties which the states should perform. It does not follow that because something ought to be done the national government ought to do it.

James Madison explained to Congress, 1794:

> The government of the United States is a definite government, confined to specified objects ... Charity is no part of the legislative duty of the government.

Any money the government has, it took from the people. It defies the definition of charity to give away what was taken from someone else. Davy Crockett, a U.S. Representative, 1827-1835, who died at the Alamo in 1836, explained this to Congress.

During a debate on whether to use taxes collected from citizens to redistribute to a person in need, Davy Crockett gave a speech "Not Yours to Give":

Congress has not the power to appropriate this money as an act of charity. Every member on this floor knows it. We have the right as individuals, to give away as much of our own money as we please in charity; but as members of Congress we have no right to appropriate a dollar of the public money ... as charity.

Mr. Speaker, I have said we have the right to give as much money of our own as we please. I am the poorest man on this floor. I cannot vote for this bill, but I will give one week's pay to the object, and if every member of Congress will do the same, it will amount to more than the bill asks.

President Grover Cleveland opposed Federal welfare, vetoing of the Texas Seed Bill in 1887:

I do not believe that the power ... of the general government ought to be extended to the relief of individual suffering ... Tendency to disregard the limited mission of this power ... should ... be steadfastly resisted ...

Charity of our countrymen can always be relied upon to relieve their fellow-citizens in misfortune. This has been repeatedly demonstrated ...

Federal aid in such cases encourages the expectation of paternal care on the part of the government and weakens the sturdiness of our national character, while it prevents ... among our people of that kindly sentiment ... which strengthens the bonds of a common brotherhood.

❧

CHAPTER 113
THE APOSTLES OR PILATE?

Early Christians willingly sold their property and brought the money to the feet of the apostles for the church to distribute. They were not unwillingly forced to lay their money at the feet of Pilate for the Roman government to redistribute.

> For as many as were possessors of lands or houses sold them, and brought the prices of the things that were sold, and laid them down at the apostles' feet: and distribution was made unto every man according as he had need. (Acts 4:32–35)

Believers gave because they wanted to voluntarily show their love to God by showing love for others.

> Arrange in advance for the gift you have promised, so that it may be ready as a willing gift, not as an exaction ... Each one must give as he has decided in his heart, not reluctantly or under compulsion, for God loves a cheerful giver ... For ... this service is not only supplying the needs of the saints but is also overflowing in many thanksgivings to God. (2 Corinthians 9: 5–12 ESV)

This contrasts to a godless state taking your money – "an exaction" – and redistributing it against your will–"under compulsion." It is the difference between an individual's free will – the voluntary choice of believers to be charitable; versus socialism's involuntary forced participation.

Jefferson wrote in his Virginia Bill for Religious Liberty, January 16, 1786:

> To compel a man to furnish contributions of money for the propagation of opinions which he disbelieves and abhors, is sinful and tyrannical.

A superficial reading of the book of Acts shows the early church having "all things in common," but in context, this was: 1) *voluntary* charity, not an *involuntary* government seizure and welfare; 2) believers gave possessions to *the church* not to *the Roman Government*; 3) it was a *temporary* measure to start the church off, not a *permanent* economic model.

As an economic model, it was unsustainable. Just a few chapters after the church started, the Apostle Paul had to collect freewill offerings from Gentile believers to send as relief to the church in Jerusalem:

> • But now I go unto Jerusalem to minister unto the saints. For it hath pleased them of Macedonia and Achaia to make a certain contribution for the poor saints which are at Jerusalem. (Romans 15:25-26)

> • Concerning the collection for the saints ... On the first day of every week, each of you is to put something aside ... I will send those whom you accredit by letter to carry your gift to Jerusalem. (1 Corinthians 16:1–4 ESV)

> • Churches of Macedonia ... have overflowed in ... generosity ... For they gave ... beyond their means, of their own accord, begging us earnestly for the favor of taking part in the relief of the saints. (2 Corinthians 8:1–4)

In addition to providing domestic welfare, churches provide an important social service by instilling morals and virtues, which reduces crime, child abuse, broken homes, homelessness, and other social ills. As the church relinquishes this role, the government provides these services at an immense price tag, placing a major financial burdens on taxpayers, often the largest items on state budgets. This is in addition to robbing individuals of the opportunity to be charitable.

In ancient Egypt, government gave grain, but in exchange for cattle, land, and lives. Bureaucrats are tempted to require recipients to surrender more control of their lives in order to keep getting benefits, even demanding they adopt anti-Biblical social and sexual agendas. Patrick Henry said June 5, 1788:

> But now, Sir, the American spirit, assisted by the ropes and chains of consolidation, is about to convert this country to a powerful and mighty empire.

∽

CHAPTER 114
GOVERNMENT DEPENDENCY

A drug dealer can take over a neighborhood with guns, or by giving away free drugs and getting people hooked. President Gerald Ford stated October 19, 1974:

> A government big enough to give us everything we want is a government big enough to take from us everything we have.

When an individual gives to a person in need, the recipient is inclined to express gratitude, followed by the building of a friendship which strengthens society. The person's self-esteem rises in an atmosphere of caring love and empowering encouragement, followed by them growing in their desire to help others in need.

If the government takes from some to distribute to others, those from whom it is taken have no choice. It is not charity but coercion, and the recipients prefer that the interaction be impersonal with no accountability.

Recipients of government redistribution can fall into dependency and view handouts as a debt "owed" to them. There is not only a lack of gratefulness, they become demanding if an expected benefit is interrupted.

Ungratefulness is followed by another attitude – low self-esteem. If a person is dependent on handouts long enough, it lowers their self-worth. They become embarrassed around those successfully working and channel their resentment towards the entity making them feel bad–the government giving them a free living.

∽

CHAPTER 115
IS SOCIALISM COUNTERFEIT CHURCH?

Is socialism counterfeit church – an "anti-church? Is "woke" the counterfeit of being "born again"? Is government redistribution of wealth counterfeit of Christian charity? Is "love your enemies" replaced with "cancel" your enemies? Is "social justice" the counterfeit of Biblical justice? Is forgiving offenses replaced with inciting hate? Is the definition of sin reversed?

The Gospel is that God is just, and therefore must judge every sin. If He overlooks a sin, even the smallest,

His silence would effectively be giving consent to the sin, as in law silence equals consent (Numbers 30:3-8).

If God gave consent to sin, He would no longer a just God; He would deny His just nature – He would be denying Himself. But "God cannot deny Himself" (2 Timothy 2:13) therefore He must judge every sin.

God is love, in that He provided the Lamb to take the judgment for our sins. I John 4:9 "In this was manifested the love of God toward us ... He loved us, and sent His Son to be the propitiation for our sins."

In Genesis 22:7-8, Isaac asked his father: "Where is the lamb for the sacrifice? And Abraham said, My son, God will provide himself a lamb for burnt offering."

God "gave his only begotten Son" to take all our sins away. This was foreshadowed by the scapegoat on the Day of Atonement, Leviticus 16:21-22:

> Aaron shall lay both his hands on the head of the live goat, confess over it all the iniquities of the children of Israel, and all their transgressions, concerning all their sins, putting them on the head of the goat ... And the goat shall bear upon him all their iniquities unto a land not inhabited.

Similarly, Isaiah foreshadowed the suffering Messiah:

> He was led as a lamb to the slaughter ... For the transgressions of My people He was stricken ... My righteous Servant shall justify many, For He shall bear their iniquities ... He bore the sin of many. (Isaiah 53)

"A day with the Lord is as a thousand years and a thousand years as a day." (2 Peter 3:8) Jesus experienced the day on the cross as if it were a thousand years. In the divine scale of justice: The eternal Being, Jesus–the Son of God, who is innocent, suffering for a finite (limited) period of time is equal to all us finite beings (mankind), who are guilty, suffering for an eternal period of time. Infinity times finite equals finite times infinity.

Jesus suffered the equivalent of eternal judgment for

every person, so that every person could be accepted, free from sin, by God who is just.

An insight into what Jesus may have experienced is in Matthew 12, in Jesus' reply to those wanting a sign:

None will be given it except the sign of the prophet Jonah. For as Jonah was three days and three nights in the belly of the great fish, so the Son of Man will be three days and three nights in the heart of the earth.

The Book of Jonah records:

Jonah prayed unto the Lord his God out of the fish's belly ... 'Out of the belly of hell cried I, and thou heardest my voice. For thou hadst cast me into the deep ... I went down to the bottoms of the mountains; the earth with her bars was about me forever: yet hast thou brought up my life from corruption ... Salvation is of the Lord.' So the Lord spoke to the fish, and it vomited Jonah onto dry land.

When someone believes the Gospel – that Jesus took judgment in their place, that their sins have been taken away, and that they are accepted by God – they become grateful for what Jesus did. With joy, they enter into a personal relationship with God the Father through Jesus the Son, with the indwelling of the Holy Spirit, in accordance with the Scriptures.

The unconditional love they experience brings a behavioral change from the inside–out. "The goodness of God brings men to repentance." (Romans 2:4) They want to share God's love by caring for everyone, irregardless of race, sex, economic status, or past sinful behavior.

Mother Teresa of Calcutta cared for people abandoned to die in the street gutters of slums, saying:

I see Jesus in every human being. I say to myself, this is hungry Jesus, I must feed him. This is sick Jesus. This one has leprosy or gangrene; I must wash him and tend to him. I serve because I love Jesus.

But where Jesus said to "love your enemies," the woke culture says to cancel your enemies, silence them, ostracize them, erase them, banish them, fire them, sue them, end their careers, de-platform them, lock them out of their accounts, pressure banks to cease doing business with them, and force retailers to drop their products. They want to be tolerated but do not want to tolerate.

When Peter asked "How oft shall my brother sin against me, and I forgive him?" Jesus replied: "Seventy times seven" (Matthew 18:21-22); and "If you forgive other people for their offenses, your heavenly Father will also forgive you" (Matthew 6:14). Christians are to follow Jesus' example, who, when crucified, said: "Father, forgive them." (Luke 23:34)

He warned: "If you do not forgive, neither will your Father who is in heaven forgive your offenses." (Mark 11)

> Then his lord ... said unto him, O thou wicked servant, I forgave thee all that debt ... Shouldest not thou also have had compassion on thy fellow-servant ... And his lord was wroth, and delivered him to the tormentors ... So likewise shall my heavenly Father do also unto you, if ye from your hearts forgive not every one his brother their trespasses. (Matthew 18:32-35)

Where Jesus taught forgiveness, the woke culture teaches unforgiveness, to harbor offenses, to stoke grievances, and to retaliate.

Dr. Alan Keyes stated on his "Let's Talk America" program (April 2021): "Where Jesus taught: 'Do to others what you would have them do to you' (Matthew 7:12), the woke culture teaches 'do to others as they have done to you and your ancestors.'"

They violate Leviticus 19:18: "You shall not take vengeance or bear a grudge ... but you shall love your neighbor as yourself: I am the Lord."

Woke culture forces a behavioral change from the outside–in, through guilt and "shaming." Adherents must adjust their behavior to an ever changing set of woke rules out of the fear rejection. It is a religion of works of which one can never do enough to earn redemption. One must continually grovel in hopes of receiving fickle acceptance by others.

If one lets down their guard, even for a moment, in public or at a private party, and tweets or post a word that could be mistook as insensitive, or that someone may take offense at, or if a photo resurfaces from their unwoke past, then they are instantly shunned by friends, abandoned by followers, and banned for life.

A question: would you rather have someone exhibit caring behavior towards you because they love you, or because they are terrified of being canceled by a group?

Such fear is real, as even Peter, who had been with Jesus three years, publicly denied him when asked by an unnamed girl so he would not to be rejected by a group standing around the fire outside the High Priest Caiaphas' house. (Matthew 26:69-75)

After Jesus' resurrection, though, Peter was filled with the Holy Spirit and his behavior changed, he cared for beggars, and publicly prayed for their healing.

Instead of diversity training, critical race theory, intersectionality, confessing "privilege," shaming exercises, and sensitivity codes, there simply needs to be the presenting of the Gospel, helping people to be born again, then they would show their love for God by loving others. "Whoever loves has been born of God ... Anyone who does not love does not know God." (I John 4:7-8)

The Bible warns against the desire to be accepted. In fact, Jesus told his followers that they would be rejected, even by their own families: "If they hated me they will hate you," but He promised "I will never leave thee, nor forsake thee." (Hebrews 13:5)

Social justice treats different people differently, whereas Biblical justice treats everyone the same, without respect of persons, without partiality.

In the Book of Job, Satan accused God of being unjust by showing partiality to Job, to which God spent

42 chapters showing He did not. Abraham asked the Lord, "Shall not the judge of all the world do justly?" Acts 10:34 "Peter ... said, Of a truth I perceive that God is no respecter of persons." Leviticus 19:15 "You shall do no injustice in judgment. You shall not be partial to the poor, nor honor the person of the mighty." James 2:9 "If ye have respect to persons, ye commit sin."

The church cares for everyone without partiality, but social justice flips the definition of "justice" to "injustice" by promoting partiality, showing more respect to some than others, treating some better or giving some more, based on class, race, economic status, sexual behavior, identity, or treatment of ancestors.

Ezekiel 18:20 states "The child will not share the guilt of the parent" (Deut. 24:16), yet woke culture demands children pay reparations for the sins of their parents.

God's word identifies life as beginning at conception, as Jesus, himself, was in His mother Mary's womb from the moment of conception, as the Angel told Mary. "Behold, you will conceive in your womb ... The Holy Ghost shall come upon thee, and the power of the Highest shall overshadow thee." (Luke 1)

Woke culture requires not only acceptance of abortion, but government funding of it and the turning of a blind eye to the selling of baby body parts.

The Bible definition of sin is violating God's moral law. Jesus did not get rid of the law – He paid the penalty for us breaking it. He did not affirm or celebrate people in their sin. He forgive the adulterous woman, but then told her "Go, and sin no more." (John 8:11)

Jesus taught "God made them male and female" and "a man leave his father and mother, and cleave to his wife; And they twain shall be one flesh" (Mark 10:6-8); that sex outside of this union is sin (Mark 10:19); yet woke culture not only demands acceptance of every form of extramarital sex, but one must endorse, encourage and celebrate it. If you don't – "silence is violence," you have committed a woke sin.

Deuteronomy 22:5 addresses transgenderedism: "A woman shall not wear man's clothing, nor shall a man put on a woman's clothing; for whoever does these things is an abomination to the LORD," but in the woke world, if one even mentions this moral law of God it is a woke sin.

The woke culture has drag queen story hour, lax enforcement of child sex-trafficking laws, and classroom LGBTQ indoctrination, indistinguishable from the crime of "grooming" for sexual exploitation.

In contrast, God's law protects a child's innocence. Jesus warned "Whoever causes one of these little ones who believe in Me to sin, it would be better for him if a millstone were hung around his neck, and he were drowned in the depth of the sea." (Matthew 18:6)

✍

CHAPTER 116
DID JESUS TEACH SOCIALISM?

Where Marx taught government should redistribute "From each according to his ability, to each according to his needs," Jesus did not:

> And one ... said unto him, Master, speak to my brother, that he divide the inheritance with me. And he said unto him, Man, who made me a judge or a divider over you? And he said ... Beware of covetousness: for a man's life consisteth not in the abundance of the things which he possesseth. (Luke 12:13-15)

Instead of government redistribution, Jesus taught the industrious person would be rewarded with more:

> A man of noble birth ... called ten of his servants and gave them ten minas. "Put this money to work," he said, "until I come back" ... He ... returned home. Then he sent for the servants ... The first one came and said, "Sir, your mina has earned ten more." "Well done, my good servant!" his master replied. "Because you have been trustworthy in a very small matter, take charge of

ten cities." The second came and said, "Sir, your mina has earned five more." His master answered, "You take charge of five cities."

Then another servant came and said, "Sir, here is your mina; I have kept it laid away in a piece of cloth" ... His master replied ... "You wicked servant ..." He said to those standing by, "Take his mina away from him and give it to the one who has ten minas." "Sir," they said, "he already has ten!" He replied, "I tell you that to everyone who has, more will be given, but as for the one who has nothing, even what they have will be taken away."

Jesus did not say, take from the person who has ten and redistribute them equally among the others. Proverbs 12:24 states: "The hand of the diligent shall bear rule, but the slothful shall be under tribute."

But what is one to do with what they earned? Jesus taught charity, where those who had more could be moved upon in their hearts to voluntarily make a free will decision to give to the poor. Matthew 25:40:

Inasmuch as ye have done it unto one of the least of these my brethren, ye have done it unto me.

Voluntary free will is one of the major things that separates man from the rest of creation. Animals follow instinct. Man was created as a free moral agent, being given the choice as to whether or not to follow God's word.

There is a woke exercise of having students line up for a race, and as each "privilege" is mentioned, those possessing it get to take a step forward. This exercise ignores the most important item – the finish line!

If there is no God, the finish line is how much stuff one can accumulate before they die, but if there is a God, the finish line is standing before Him and giving an account of the voluntary choices one made in their life.

In the parable of the sheep and the goats, Jesus said:

The King will say to those on His right, "Come, you who are blessed by My Father, inherit the kingdom ...

For I was hungry and you gave Me something to eat, I was thirsty and you gave Me something to drink, I was a stranger and you took Me in, I was naked and you clothed Me, I was sick and you looked after Me, I was in prison and you visited Me."

Then the righteous will answer ... "Lord, when did we see You hungry and feed You, or thirsty and give You something to drink? When did we see You a stranger and take You in, or naked and clothe You? ... sick or in prison and visit You?"And the King will reply, "Truly I tell you, whatever you did for one of the least of these brothers of Mine, you did for Me." (Matthew 25)

∽

CHAPTER 117
COVENANT VERSUS COMMUNIST

At first glance, a biblical "covenant" system and a "communistic" system may appear similar, but so do the leaves of Boston Ivy and the leaves of Poison Ivy.

To the untrained eye, the leaves look the same, but all one has to do is naively touch the Poison Ivy leaf and inadvertently rub their eyes, and they will immediately regret not having noticed the difference, as itching, swelling, and blistering will incapacitate them for days.

Covenant is voluntary, willingly, not under compulsion, purposed in your heart, "government by the *consent* of the governed." Communism, on the other hand, is involuntary, under *compulsion*, an extraction.

Covenant and communism may look similar, but they are drastically different:

- Creator-given inalienable rights vs. state granted benefits;
- identity as an individual vs. identity as part of a group;
- personal initiative vs. guaranteed government welfare;
- charitable giving vs. compulsory government confiscation;
- voluntary vs. involuntary; generosity vs. theft;
- government exists to protect an individual's rights &

property vs. an individual existing to benefit & perpetuate big government.

Is a fence installed to keep people safe from intruders or to make people prisoners? Water may fill a pipe, but in which direction is it flowing? Is power flowing up from the people or down from the government?

Supreme Court Justice Robert Jackson wrote in *American Communications Association v. Douds* (1950):

> It is not the function of the government to keep the citizen from falling into error; it is the function of the citizen to keep the government from falling into error.

Without a Creator, government is the giver of rights, and the taker. Eisenhower stated February 20, 1955:

> The Founding Fathers ... recognizing God as the author of individual rights, declared that the purpose of government is to secure those rights ...

> In many lands the state claims to be the author of human rights ... If the state gives rights, it can – and inevitably will – take away those rights.

In a covenant government, citizens voluntarily enter into agreement with each other, getting individual rights from God and personally accountable to God to care for others and treat their neighbor fairly.

Without the concept of a God who wants everyone to be fair, and who will hold each individual personally accountable in a future life, then this present life is all there is, and any action is justifiable to prolong it in the attempt to set up a heaven on Earth without God.

CHAPTER 118
HE WHO DICTATES

Naive students are taught that with socialism, everyone owns everything equally. But does this ever happen?

Who decides what one's ability is, or what one's needs are? A question need simply be asked: "Who decides who lives in the nice house and who lives in the dumpy house?"

The answer is: "Someone in the government dictates those things." Well, whoever ultimately dictates those things is the dictator. As the maxim goes, "he who controls the purse strings has the power."

In practice, socialism and communism are nothing more than a monarchy makeover — a top–down system of government where one supreme leader forces his will on the others. President Harrison warned:

> The danger to all well-established free governments arises from the unwillingness of the people to believe in ... the influence of designing men ...
>
> This is the old trick of those who would usurp the government of their country. In the name of democracy they speak, warning the people against the influence of wealth and the danger of aristocracy.
>
> History, ancient and modern, is full of such examples ... It behooves the people to be most watchful of those to whom they have entrusted power.
>
> The great dread ... seems to have been ... a consolidated power ... that government ... be essentially and radically changed.

President Eisenhower stated June 24, 1957:

> The National Government was itself the creature of the states ... Yet today it is often made to appear that the creature, Frankenstein–like, is determined to destroy the creators.

President Reagan stated:

> All of us need to be reminded that the Federal Government did not create the states; the states created the Federal Government.

President Gerald Ford remarked July 4, 1975:

> A government too large and bureaucratic can stifle individual initiative by a frustrating statism. In America ... our sovereign is the citizen, and we

must never forget it. Governments exist to serve people. The state is the creature of the populace.

President Harrison wrote:

> It is the part of wisdom for a republic to limit the service of that officer ... to whom she has entrusted the management ... to a period so short as to prevent his forgetting that he is the accountable agent, not the principle; the servant, not the master.

President Woodrow Wilson addressed the New York Press Club, September 9, 1912:

> The history of liberty is a history of the limitation of governmental power, not the increase of it.

In contrast, President Obama disregarded limits of constitutional checks and balances, January 14, 2014:

> We are not just going to be waiting for legislation ... I've got a pen, and I've got a phone. And I can use that pen to sign executive orders.

Attempting a return to the original intent, President Trump stated:

> Today we are not merely transferring power from one Administration to another, or from one party to another – but we are transferring power from Washington, D.C. and giving it back to you, the American people ... January 20th 2017, will be remembered as the day the people became the rulers of this nation again.

∽

CHAPTER 119

SIZE OF GOVERNMENT

President Hoover warned October 31, 1932, against the Democrat Party's collectivist "New Deal" plans:

> No man who has not occupied my position in Washington can fully realize the constant battle which must be carried on against ... tyranny of government expanded into business activities.

President Reagan stated January 20, 1981:

In this present crisis, government is not the solution to our problem; government is the problem ... We've been tempted to believe ... that government by an elite group is superior to government for, by, and of the people ...

We are a nation that has a government – not the other way around. And this makes us special among the nations of the Earth.

Our government has no power except that granted it by the people. It is time to check and reverse the growth of government, which shows signs of having grown beyond the consent of the governed ...

Reagan added:

Our present troubles ... are proportionate to the intervention and intrusion in our lives that result from unnecessary and excessive growth of government ...

It is my intention to curb the size and influence of the Federal establishment and to demand recognition of the distinction between the powers granted to the Federal Government and those reserved to the states or to the people.

President William Henry Harrison warned:

It is not by the extent of its patronage alone that the executive department has become dangerous, but by the use which it appears may be made of the appointing power to bring under its control the whole revenues of the country ...

There was wanting no other addition to the powers of our chief magistrate to stamp monarchical character on our government but the control of the public finances ...

The first Roman Emperor (Julius Caesar), in his attempt to seize the sacred treasure (in the temple of Saturn), silenced the opposition of the officer to whose charge it had been committed by a significant allusion to his sword ...

I know the importance ... to ... divorce ... the Treasury from the banking institutions ... It was certainly a great error in the framers of the Constitution not to have made ... the head of the Treasury Department entirely independent of the executive ...

A decent and manly examination of the acts of the government should be not only tolerated, but encouraged.

President Trump agreed, exposing the workings of the deep-state "establishment" in his Inaugural Address, January 20, 2017:

> For too long, a small group in our nation's Capital has reaped the rewards of government while the people have borne the cost. Washington flourished – but the people did not share in its wealth. Politicians prospered – but the jobs left, and the factories closed.
>
> The establishment protected itself, but not the citizens ... That all changes – starting right here, and right now ... The United States of America, is your country. What truly matters is not which party controls our government, but whether our government is controlled by the people.

∽

CHAPTER 120

AMERICA IS A UNIQUE EXPERIMENT

John Jay was a Continental Congress President and later nominated by George Washington as the First Chief Justice of the Supreme Court. He wrote in 1777:

> The Americans are the first people whom Heaven has favored with an opportunity of ... choosing the forms of government under which they should live. All other constitutions have derived their existence from violence or accidental circumstances ...
>
> Your lives, your liberties, your property, will be at the disposal only of your Creator and yourselves.

James Wilson, a signer of both the Declaration and the Constitution, was also nominated by George Washington to the Supreme Court. He stated in 1787:

After a period of 6,000 years since creation, the United States exhibit to the world the first instance of a nation ... assembling voluntarily ... and deciding ... that system of government under which they and their posterity should live.

Senator Daniel Webster stated in 1802:

Miracles do not cluster, and what has happened once in 6,000 years, may not happen again. Hold on to the Constitution, for if the American Constitution should fail, there will be anarchy throughout the world.

Why would Webster say "there will be anarchy throughout the world" if the Constitution failed?

Because from the beginning of history, men and women have suffered under dictators, dreaming of the chance to rule themselves without a king. Americans have had this chance. If they blow it, what hope is left for suffering humanity to hope for?

Yale President Ezra Stiles wrote in 1788:

All the forms of civil polity have been tried by mankind, except one: and that seems to have been reserved in Providence to be realized in America.

At the time of the Revolutionary War, nearly every other country on Earth was ruled by a king.

Dr. Pat Robertson wrote in *America's Dates with Destiny,* 1986:

On September 17, 1787, the day our Constitution was signed, the absolute monarch Ch'ien Lung, emperor of the Manchu (or Ch'ing) Dynasty, reigned supreme over the people of China ... Revolts were put down by ruthless military force.

In Japan the shogun (warriors) of the corrupt Tokugawa chamberlain Tanuma Okitsugu exercised corrupt and totalitarian authority over the Japanese.

In India, Warren Hastings, the British Governor of Bengal, had successfully defeated the influence of the fragmented Mogul dynasties that ruled India since 1600.

Catherine II was the enlightened despot of all the Russias. Joseph II was the emperor of Austria, Bohemia and Hungary. For almost half a century, Frederick the Great had ruled Prussia.

Louis XVI sat uneasily on his throne in France just years away from revolution, a bloody experiment in democracy, and the new tyranny of Napoleon Bonaparte.

A kind of a constitutional government had been created in the Netherlands in 1579 by the Protestant Union of Utrecht, but that constitution was really a loose federation of the northern provinces for a defense against Catholic Spain ...

What was happening in America had no real precedent, even as far back as the city-states of Greece. The only real precedent was established thousands of years before by the tribes of Israel in the covenant with God and with each other.

President Theodore Roosevelt stated in 1903:

In no other place and at no other time has the experiment of government of the people, by the people, for the people, been tried on so vast a scale as here in our own country.

President Calvin Coolidge stated in 1924:

The history of government on this earth has been almost entirely ... rule of force held in the hands of a few. Under our Constitution, America committed itself to power in the hands of the people.

America is a republic, where the people are the king ruling themselves through representatives. When people protest the flag, they are saying they no longer want to be king. They reject this system where they participate in ruling themselves.

Reagan opened the Ashbrook Center in Ashland, Ohio, May 9, 1983:

From their own harsh experience with intrusive,

SOCIALISM: THE TRUE HISTORY

overbearing government, the Founding Fathers made a great breakthrough in political understanding:

They understood that it is the excesses of government, the will to power of one man over another, that has been a principle source of injustice and human suffering through the ages ...

The Founding Fathers understood that only by making the government the servant, not the master, only by positing (placing) sovereignty in the people and not the state can we hope to protect freedom and see the political commonwealth prosper.

In 1776 the source of government excess was the crown's abuse of power and its attempt to suffocate the colonists with its overbearing demands. In our own day, the danger of too much state power has taken a subtler but no less dangerous form.

John Adams wrote in his notes on *A Dissertation on Canon & Feudal Law*, 1765:

I always consider the settlement of America ... as the opening of a grand scene and design in Providence for ... the emancipation of the slavish part of mankind all over the earth.

John Jay noted in 1777:

This glorious revolution ... distinguished by so many marks of the Divine favor and interposition ... and I may say miraculous, that when future ages shall read its history they will be tempted to consider a great part of it as fabulous ...

The many remarkable ... events by which our wants have been supplied and our enemies repelled ... are such strong and striking proofs of the interposition of Heaven, that our having been hitherto delivered from the threatened bondage of Britain ought, like the emancipation of the Jews from Egyptian servitude.

Franklin Roosevelt stated in 1939:

Rulers ... increase their power over the common men. The seamen they sent to find gold found instead the way of escape for the common man from those rulers ...

What they found over the Western horizon was not the silk and jewels of Cathay ... but mankind's second chance – a chance to create a new world after he had almost spoiled an old one ...

The Almighty seems purposefully to have withheld that second chance until the time when men would most need and appreciate liberty.

Reagan stated in 1961:

In this country of ours took place the greatest revolution that has ever taken place in the world's history – Every other revolution simply exchanged one set of rulers for another ...

Here for the first time in all the thousands of years of man's relation to man ... the founding fathers established the idea that you and I had within ourselves the God-given right and ability to determine our own destiny.

He stated on October 27, 1964:

This idea that government is beholden to the people, that it has no other source of power except the sovereign people, is still the newest and the most unique idea in all the long history of man's relation to man.

British Edwardian writer G.K. Chesterton stated in "What is America?":

America is the only nation in the world that is founded on creed. That creed is set forth ... in the Declaration of Independence ... that all men are equal in their claim to justice, that governments exist to give them that justice ...

It certainly does condemn ... atheism, since it clearly names the Creator as the ultimate authority from whom these equal rights are derived.

Calvin Coolidge stated July 5, 1926:

The principles ... which went into the Declaration of Independence ... are found in ...

the sermons ... of the early colonial clergy ...

They preached equality because they believed in the fatherhood of God and the brotherhood of man.

They justified freedom by the text that we are all created in the Divine image.

President Millard Fillmore, December 6, 1852:

Our grateful thanks are due to an all-merciful Providence ... Our own free institutions were not the offspring of our Revolution. They existed before. They were planted in the free charters of self-government under which the English colonies grew up ...

(Other) nations have had no such training for self-government, and every effort to establish it by bloody revolutions has been, and must without that preparation continue to be, a failure.

Liberty unregulated by law degenerates into anarchy, which soon becomes the most horrid of all despotisms ...

We owe these blessings, under Heaven, to the happy Constitution and government which were bequeathed to us by our fathers, and which it is our sacred duty to transmit in all their integrity to our children.

∽

CHAPTER 121
LAST STAND ON EARTH

Reagan stated on October 27, 1964:

Not too long ago, two friends of mine were talking to a Cuban refugee, a businessman who had escaped from Castro, and in the midst of his story one of my friends turned to the other and said, "We don't know how lucky we are."

And the Cuban stopped and said, "How lucky you are? I had someplace to escape to." And in that sentence he told us the entire story. If we lose freedom here, there's no place to escape to. This is the last stand on earth.

Franklin Roosevelt warned at the Dedication of Great Smoky Mountains National Park, September 2, 1940:

> There is another enemy at home ... that ... mocks at ideals, sneers at sacrifice and pretends that the American people can live by bread alone.

> If the spirit of God is not in us, and if we will not prepare to give all that we have and all that we are to preserve Christian civilization in our land, we shall go to destruction.

Henry Cabot Lodge, who was the first to have the title Senate Majority Leader, warned in 1919:

> The United States is the world's best hope ... Beware how you trifle with your marvelous inheritance ... for if we stumble and fall, freedom and civilization everywhere will go down in ruin.

Winston Churchill stated at Westminster College in Fulton, Missouri, March 5, 1946:

> It is a solemn moment for the American Democracy. For with primacy in power is also joined an awe-inspiring accountability to the future ... (To) fritter it away will bring upon us all the long reproaches of the after-time.

Reagan stated on October 27, 1964:

> We're at war with the most dangerous enemy that has ever faced mankind ... If we lose ... this way of freedom of ours, history will record with the greatest astonishment that those who had the most to lose did the least to prevent its happening ...

> We were told ... we must accept a greater government activity in the affairs of the people ... Our natural, unalienable rights are now considered to be a dispensation of government ...

> Those who would trade our freedom for the soup kitchen of the welfare state have told us they have a utopian solution of peace without victory ...

SOCIALISM: THE TRUE HISTORY

Should Moses have told the children of Israel to live in slavery under the pharaohs? Should Christ have refused the cross?

Should the patriots at Concord Bridge have thrown down their guns and refused to fire the shot heard "round the world"?

The martyrs of history were not fools, and our honored dead who gave their lives to stop the advance of the Nazis didn't die in vain.

Solzhenitsyn viewed news reports of a power shortage followed by riots, then commented:

There are telltale symptoms by which history gives warning to a ... perishing society ...

Your culture is left without electric power for a few hours only, and all of a sudden, crowds of American citizens start looting and creating havoc. The smooth surface film must be very thin, then, the social system quite unstable and unhealthy.

But the fight for our planet, physical and spiritual, a fight of cosmic proportions, is not a vague matter of the future; it has already started. The forces of evil have begun their decisive offensive.

You can feel their pressure, yet your screens and publications are full of prescribed smiles and raised glasses.

Churchill said in his Iron Curtain Speech, March 5, 1946:

From what I have seen of our Russian ... allies during the war, I am convinced that there is nothing they admire so much as strength, and there is nothing for which they have less respect than for weakness, especially military weakness.

Solzhenitsyn warned:

You know the words from the Bible: "Build not on sand, but on rock" ... Lenin's teachings are that anyone is considered to be a fool who doesn't take what's lying in front of him. If you can take it, take it. If you can attack, – attack!

But if there's a wall, then go back ... Communist leaders respect only firmness and have contempt and laugh at persons who continually give in to them.

On June 30, 1975, Solzhenitsyn warned:

I ... call upon America to be more careful with its trust ... They are trying to weaken you; they are trying to disarm your strong and magnificent country in the face of this fearful threat – one that has never been seen before in the history of the world ... I call upon you: ordinary working men of America ... do not let yourselves become weak.

Reagan stated on October 27, 1964:

We, the people, tell the government what to do. It doesn't tell us. We the people are the driver; the government is the car.

Almost all the world's constitutions are documents in which governments tell the people what their privileges are. Our constitution is a document in which we the people tell the government what it is allowed to do ...

He added:

Man is not free unless government is limited. There is a clear cause and effect that is as neat and predictable as the law of physics, as government expands, liberty retracts.

Truman stated in his Inaugural Address 1949:

We believe that all men are created equal, because they are created in the image of God.

During WWII, Herbert Hoover signed a statement with the widows of Presidents Theodore Roosevelt, Coolidge, Taft, Harrison, and Cleveland, which stated:

Menaced by collectivist trends, we must seek revival of our strength in the spiritual foundations which are the bedrock of our republic.

Democracy is the outgrowth of the religious conviction of the sacredness of every human life. On the religious side, its highest embodiment is the Bible; on the political side, the Constitution.

Truman wrote to John L. Sullivan, 1949:

> America is dedicated to the conviction that all people are entitled by the gift of God to equal rights and freedoms.

Truman told the Federal Council of Churches, March 6, 1946:

> We have just come through a decade in which the forces of evil in various parts of the world have been lined up in a bitter fight to banish from the face of the earth both of these ideals – religion and democracy ...

> The right of every human being ... to worship God in his own way, the right to fix his own relationship to his fellow men and to his Creator ... have been saved for mankind. Let us determine to carry on in a spirit of tolerance ... in the spirit of God and religious unity.

∾

CHAPTER 122
INDIVIDUAL VERSUS GLOBALIST

Water seeks its own level. It will always leak through a crack or find its way downhill. No matter what the form of government, a selfish person will try to manipulate it for their own benefit.

Historically, more people have been killed by power in the hands of government than by power in the hands of business. After all, businesses need customers.

There is one caveat, namely, individual capitalism differs from vulture or globalist capitalism. Individual capitalism empowers citizens with opportunities to improve their lives, as well as be generous.

Vulture and globalist capitalists selfishly want to eliminate competition, sway elections, and support socialist leaders in exchange for exemption from regulations or monopoly contracts.

Senator Ted Cruz discussed with Fox News' Maria Bartiromo, January 20, 2020, "A Handful of Silicon

Valley Billionaires Have the Ability to Censor, Deceive, and Manipulate Votes."

Liberal investors have found out if they buy stock in major corporations, they can attend shareholder meetings and propose leftist resolutions promoting issues such as LGBTQ, BLM, and abortion, requiring employees to attend diversity training and shaming.

A final disturbing development are globalist capitalists who believe the world is overpopulated and seek to use their financial influence to reduce population. In a 2015 TED talk, Bill Gates stated:

> First we've got population. The world today has 6.8 billion people ... Now if we do a really great job on new vaccines, healthcare, reproductive health services, we could lower that by perhaps 10 or 15 percent.

∽

CHAPTER 123
GREED VERSUS THE GOSPEL

No matter how well-intentioned a particular form of government is, whether socialist or capitalist, selfish human nature will try to find a way to twist it for personal ambition. Solzhenitsyn stated in an interview with Joseph Pearce (*St. Austin Review*, February 2003):

> Untouched by the breath of God, unrestricted by human conscience, both capitalism and socialism are repulsive.

George Washington wrote in the draft notes of his Inaugural Address, April 1789:

> The best institution may be abused by human depravity; and that they may even, in some instances be made subservient to the vilest purposes.

> Should ... those incited by the lust of power ... overleap the known barriers of this Constitution and violate the unalienable rights of humanity: it will only serve to show, that no compact among men, however provident in its construction and sacred in its ratification, can be pronounced everlasting ...

SOCIALISM: THE TRUE HISTORY

that no wall of words, that no mound of parchment can be so formed as to stand against the sweeping torrent of boundless ambition on the one side, aided by the sapping current of corrupted morals on the other.

General Douglas MacArthur addressed the 42nd Infantry, July 14, 1935:

The springs of human conflict cannot be eradicated through institutions, but only through the reform of the individual human being ... We all dream of the day when human conduct will be governed by the Decalogue and the Sermon on the Mount.

He stated September 2, 1945:

If we will not devise some greater and equitable system ... Armageddon will be at our door.

The problem basically is theological and involves a spiritual recrudescence, an improvement of human character that will synchronize with our almost matchless advances ... of the past two thousand years. It must be of the spirit if we are to save the flesh.

Mankind needs a systemic change. Not woke socialism, but the Gospel. Jesus came to change each person's heart – one must be born again. When one realizes God loves them, it helps them to love others. In a sense, He invites us to download a new behavioral software program. Instead of the human default setting of selfishness, it is an upgrade to "Do unto others as they would them do unto you" and "love your enemies."

Two threads that can be traced through history: Greed versus the Gospel.

Those motivated by GREED:

• took land from Indians; • sold people into slavery; • participated or turned a blind eye to sex-trafficking, drug dealing, etc.; • voted for candidates who promised hand-outs, yet also supported killing the unborn.

Those motivated by the GOSPEL:

- gave their money to sheltered the homeless;
- gave food & clothes to the poor; • dug wells in native villages; • opened orphanages and medical clinics; • founded hospitals; • taught farming; • provided literacy classes; • provided disaster relief.

William Henry Seward, who served as Secretary of State under President Lincoln, stated in 1836:

I know not how long a republican government can flourish among a great people who have not the Bible; the experiment has never been tried; but this I do know: that the existing government of this country never could have had existence but for the Bible ...

If at every decade of years a copy of the Bible could be found in every family in the land its republican institutions would be perpetuated.

I do not believe human society ... ever has attained, or ever can attain, a high state of intelligence, virtue, security, liberty, or happiness without the Holy Scriptures; even the whole hope of human progress is suspended on the ever-growing influence of the Bible.

CHAPTER 124
THE LOVE OF GOD

Reagan told Religious Broadcasters, January 31, 1983:

Aleksandr Herzen, the Russian writer, warned, "To shrink from saying a word in defense of the oppressed is as bad as any crime." Well, I pledge to you that America will stand up, speak out, and defend the values we share. To those who would crush religious freedom, our message is plain:

You may jail your believers. You may close their churches, confiscate their Bibles, and harass their rabbis and priests, but you will never destroy the love of God and freedom that burns in their hearts. They will triumph over you.

In 1983, Solzhenitsyn received the Templeton Prize for Progress in Religion, stating:

We can only reach with determination for the warm hand of God, which we have so rashly and self-confidently pushed away.

Reagan warned October 27, 1964:

You and I have a rendezvous with destiny. We'll preserve for our children, this, the last, best place of hope for man on Earth or we'll sentence them to take the last step into a thousand years of darkness.

Socialism is an attempt to change society from the outside in, but the only thing that can bring true systemic change is a transformation from the inside out – a change in each human heart from hate to love.

This is why Jesus' Gospel is so powerful. When each person realizes that God loves, forgives and cares for them, they are moved to love, forgive and care for others.

Rev. Martin Luther King, Jr., wrote August 30, 1952:

Far from being the pious injunction of a utopian dreamer, this command is an absolute necessity for the survival of our civilization. Love is the key to the solution of the world's problem, yes even love for enemies. (Matthew 5:43-44)

Reagan commented January 31, 1983:

Malcolm Muggeridge, the brilliant English commentator, has written,

"The most important happening in the world today is the resurgence of Christianity in the Soviet Union, demonstrating that the whole effort sustained over sixty years to brainwash the Russian people into accepting materialism has been a fiasco."

Think of it: the most awesome military machine in history, but it is not match for that one single man, hero, strong yet tender, Prince of Peace.

His name alone, Jesus, can lift our hearts, soothe our sorrows, heal our wounds, and drive away our fears ... With His message and with your conviction and commitment, we can still move mountains.

∽